'This work should take pride of place on the bookshelves of boardrooms throughout Western economies. Building on their previous and authoritative publications, especially *Corporate Collapse and Indecent Disclosure*, the authors develop a compelling argument that systemic flaws in accounting and reporting regimes (as well as fraud and poor corporate governance practices) contribute to business failures and jeopardise market integrity and confidence. In particular, the treatment of the "true and fair" conundrum, the exposure of the use and misuse of labyrinthine corporate groups and the call for a re-examination of fundamental notions of corporate personality and limited liability deserve close consideration by all who depend on the proper operation of the market system – and that is practically everyone.'

The Hon Neville Owen (*HIH Royal Commissioner, 2001–03), UK*

'A thought-provoking study of recent global corporate scandals which condemns the current corporate form itself and offers pragmatic solutions. A welcome addition to the literature questioning the role of the 19th century corporation in the 21st century.'

Jane Gleeson-White, *author of*
'Double Entry: How the merchants of Venice shaped the modern world'

THE UNACCOUNTABLE & UNGOVERNABLE CORPORATION

The corporation is a major vehicle of business activity worldwide. It incurs social costs and generates benefits that continually change – hence, whether it still provides a net benefit to society is contestable. Evidence-based observations of the last decade of corporate sagas and the role of accounting and auditing suggest that a serious rethink is needed about how commerce is pursued and, in particular, whether the current corporate form has passed its use-by date.

The authors of this new book – including internationally renowned accounting scholars – argue that the two major governance tools of accounting and auditing require major makeovers. Beginning by analysing the global sweep of deregulation that corporations have experienced since 2000, the authors go on to discuss the various scandals and crises that characterized the subsequent period, culminating in yet more calls for further deregulation. Having thoroughly assessed the status quo, they provide a series of urgent recommendations for reforms designed to bring the corporation back to the real world and restore its purpose.

This book will be of great interest to students and academics across accounting, business, law and finance, especially more advanced students at undergraduate and postgraduate level.

Frank Clarke is Honorary Professor of Accounting at The University of Sydney, Australia, and Emeritus Professor at the University of Newcastle, Australia.

Graeme Dean is Emeritus Professor of Accounting at The University of Sydney, Australia.

Matthew Egan is Lecturer in Accounting at The University of Sydney, Australia.

THE UNACCOUNTABLE & UNGOVERNABLE CORPORATION

Companies' use-by dates close in

Frank Clarke and Graeme Dean,
with Matthew Egan

Routledge
Taylor & Francis Group

LONDON AND NEW YORK

First published 2014
by Routledge
2 Park Square, Milton Park, Abingdon, Oxon OX14 4RN

and by Routledge
711 Third Avenue, New York, NY 10017

Routledge is an imprint of the Taylor & Francis Group, an informa business

© 2014 Frank Clarke, Graeme Dean and Matthew Egan

The right of Frank Clarke, Graeme Dean and Matthew Egan to be identified as the authors of this work has been asserted by them in accordance with sections 77 and 78 of the Copyright, Designs and Patents Act 1988.

British Library Cataloguing in Publication Data
A catalogue record for this book is available from the British Library

Library of Congress Cataloging in Publication Data
Clarke, Frank L.
   The unaccountable & ungovernable corporation: companies' use-by dates close in / Frank Clarke, Graeme Dean and Matthew Egan.
      pages cm
   Includes index.
   1. Corporations. 2. Corporations–Accounting. 3. Corporations–Auditing.
4. Corporate governance. I. Dean, G. W. II. Egan, Matthew. III. Title.
   HD2731.C53 2014
   338.7'4–dc23
               2013031879

ISBN: 978-0-415-71912-4 (hbk)
ISBN: 978-0-415-71914-8 (pbk)
ISBN: 978-1-315-86757-1 (ebk)

Typeset in Bembo
by Taylor & Francis Books

CONTENTS

ILLUSTRATIONS

Figure

Tables

Boxes

ACKNOWLEDGMENTS

We are indebted to our Sydney School of Accounting colleagues, especially the late Ray Chambers, who stressed the need for research to be drawn from observations of commerce and accounting's role within it; and for accounting to be useful or, as we note, serviceable for the uses ordinarily made of it. This latest work draws on the observations of corporate practices and the role of accounting and auditing in disclosing them. It draws on reports of failed companies, business biographies, reports of takeovers, of employees left without their entitlements when their company was placed into administration after unexpectedly failing, and inquiries and reports into the effects of price and price level changes. Observations up to the middle of the last decade had been catalogued in two earlier books, *Corporate Collapse: Accounting, Regulatory and Ethical Failure* and *Indecent Disclosure: Gilding the Corporate Lily*. These are augmented here by subsequent observations up to the present. Our families have continued to endure our working on this project and such earlier ones. For that we are most appreciative. As always the critical copy-editing skills of Carl-Harrison Ford are much appreciated, as are the typing skills of Nichole Orth. We also thank Neal Arthur and Martin Lawrence for their suggestions upon reading earlier draft chapters. Finally, we thank Routledge Commissioning Editor Terry Clague and his assistant Sinead Waldron for their interest in this project, and Routledge for their commitment to it.

Frank Clarke
Graeme Dean
Matthew Egan

ABBREVIATIONS

AASB	Australian Accounting Standards Board
AAT	Administrative Appeals Tribunal (Australia)
ABCP	asset-backed commercial paper
ACSI	Australian Council of Superannuation Investors
ACTU	Australian Council of Trade Unions
AFR	*Australian Financial Review*
AGM	annual general meeting
AIFRS	Australian International Financial Reporting Standards
APESB	Accounting Professional and Ethical Standards Board
APRA	Australian Prudential Regulation Authority
ASAu	Australian auditing standards
ASIC	Australian Securities and Investments Commission
ASX	Australian Stock Exchange
BCBS	Basel Committee on Banking Supervision
BCCI	Bank of Commerce and Credit International
BIS	Bank for International Settlements
BRW	*Business Review Weekly*
CAMAC	Companies and Markets Advisory Committee
CDO	collateralized debt obligation
CDS	collateralized debt swap
CEO	chief executive officer
CFO	chief financial officer
CGU	cash generating unit
CLERP	Company Law Economic Reform Program
CoCoA	Continuously Contemporary Accounting
CPI	consumer price index
DOA	US Department of Agriculture

DSM	dominant senior management
EBITA	earnings before the deduction of interest, tax and amortization expenses
ESS	Eligible Employment Schemes
EU	European Union
Euribor	European interbank offered rate
FAS	Financial Accounting Standard (FASB)
FASB	Financial Accounting Standards Board (USA)
FBI	Federal Bureau of Investigation
FCA	Federal Court of Australia
FCAG	Financial Crisis Advisory Group
FDIC	Federal Deposit Insurance Corporation (USA)
FINMA	Financial Market Supervisory Authority (Switzerland)
FRC	Financial Reporting Council (UK)
FSA	Financial Services Authority (UK); replaced April 2013 by the Financial Conduct Authority and the Prudential Regulation Authority
FSB	Financial Stability Board (from April 2009 until present; formerly the FSF)
FSF	Financial Stability Forum (from 1999 until April 2009, when reconfigured as the FSB)
FSLIC	Federal Savings and Loans Insurance Corporation
G20	Group of Twenty developed countries
GAAP	generally accepted accounting principles
GFC	global financial crisis
GPP	general purchasing power
GSE	government-sponsored enterprises
GSIFI	global systematically important financial institutions
HBOS	Holding Company of the Bank of Scotland
HIHRC	HIH Royal Commission (Australia)
IAASB	International Auditing and Assurance Standards Board
IAS	International Accounting Standard
IASB	International Accounting Standards Board
IASC	International Accounting Standards Committee
IFRS	International Financial Reporting Standards
IMF	International Monetary Fund
IOSCO	International Organization of Securities Commissions
ISA	international standards in auditing
JCPAA	Joint Committee on Public Accounts and Audit (Australia)
JCCFS	Joint Committee on Corporations and Financial Services (Australia)
KMP	key management personnel
Libor	London interbank offered rate
LPFC	limited-purpose finance companies
MAM	material accounting misstatement

NAB	National Australia Bank
NBFI	non-banking financial intermediary
NCSC	National Companies and Securities Commission (Australia)
NED	non-executive director
NPV	net present value
NSW	New South Wales
NYSE	New York Stock Exchange
PCAOB	Public Company Accounting Oversight Board (USA)
PE	private equity
PN	Practice Note
PwC	PricewaterhouseCoopers
RBA	Reserve Bank of Australia
RBS	Royal Bank of Scotland
SEC	Securities and Exchange Commission (USA)
SFAS	Statement of Financial Accounting Standards (FASB)
SFO	Serious Fraud Office (UK)
SIBOR	Singapore interbank offered rate
SIV	special investment vehicle
SMH	*Sydney Morning Herald*
SPE	special purpose entity
TARP	Troubled Asset Relief Program
TFV	true and fair view
VIE	variable interest entity

PROLOGUE

Increasingly, the modern corporation is unaccountable, ungovernable. What follows is based on the observations of commercial practices and the performance of accounting and auditing over several decades. This account draws on reports of failed companies, business biographies, reports of takeover dilemmas, of employees left without payments of their entitlements when their company was placed into administration, and of inquiries and reports into the effects of price and price level changes. Our observations are in line with social commentator Nicholas Taleb (2012, p. 15), who observes that 'experience is devoid of cherry picking which we find in [academic] studies'. No cherry picking here. Our observations up to the middle of the last decade were catalogued in two earlier books, *Corporate Collapse: Accounting, Regulatory and Ethical Failure* (Clarke, Dean and Oliver, 1997; rev. edn, 2003) and *Indecent Disclosure: Gilding the Corporate Lily* (Clarke and Dean, 2007). The current work draws on observations in respect of modern corporations' behaviour from then to the present. It is underpinned by more than 30 of our opinion pieces or letters to the editor which were published from 2002 in Australian dailies, the *Australian Financial Review, The Age*, the *Newcastle Herald* and the *Sydney Morning Herald*.

Here, we pursue an argument that the modern corporation, especially in its present holding/subsidiary form, may well be nearing its use-by date. The modern corporation may be a conglomerate, or have a more narrow operational focus, it may be national or international in scope, but its 'limited liability within limited liability' characteristic is pervasive. Two of the major governance tools − accounting and auditing − are demonstrated to need serious makeovers; in particular, group accounting needs a radical reform, and auditing needs to be more of a quality control device than it is at present. We argue here that corporate executives' remuneration appears unreasonably high and disconnected with reported corporate performance; that the nature of business regulation generally needs revamping with a view to its being more targeted; that recent regulatory actions entailing negotiated cash settlements do little in the longer term to protect anybody; that regulatory imposed undertakings are ineffective in improving the system as the precedents are not recorded; that whistleblowing legislative reforms are too limited; and that, overall, the Occupy Wall Street movement is possibly more right than wrong. Each contention evidences growing public dissatisfaction with corporate misbehaviour. Importantly, each of those characteristics of business has become increasingly present since the dotcom crash in 2000. Most importantly, all were evident well before the global financial crisis (GFC) really hit in 2007–08 … and they persist.

The matters commented upon directly reflected their Australian manifestation. However, frequent reference is made to similar instances elsewhere, especially in the USA and the UK. None was new to the business scene. The unfulfilled quest for corporate financial disclosure to portray reliably a company's financial position and financial performance has been a problem in the English-speaking world (and elsewhere) for over 100 years. Equally an issue long before the GFC was how to regulate corporate affairs effectively: it led to the creation in the early 1930s of the Securities and Exchange Commission in the USA, and later similar agencies in other countries, including the Financial Services Authority (FSA) in the UK (which in April 2013 was split into two new authorities: the Financial Conduct Authority and the Prudential Regulation Authority).

So too has the differential between executives' and ordinary workers' remunerations been a matter of concern, and the value of company auditors has also been questioned continuously as companies have failed 'unexpectedly' for a century or more. It is the unexpected nature of those failures – 'unexpected' because audited accounts have failed to show the drift towards failure – that leads to the questioning. Finally, as corporate globalization has become the norm, so too has the propensity to arrange business affairs in groups of related companies, frequently exploiting the operation of the corporate veil. The shadow banking use of special purpose entities (SPEs), special investment vehicles (SIVs) and variable interest entities (VIEs) to fund and hold residential mortgage-backed securities, known as collateralized debt obligations (CDOs), in the lead-up to the GFC exemplified this. On reflection, the corporate world as well as its obvious beneficial activities also has much to answer for. The GFC tended merely to highlight longstanding corporate business issues, such as borrowing short and lending long – and using reckless leverage to boost flagging returns. The risk attending such investment and financing strategies seems to have been neglected by many. It certainly is not revealed sufficiently by applying the International Financial Reporting Standards (IFRS) to the entities involved.

Some 150 years ago John Henry Newman wrote in *The Idea of a University* that the function of a university was to expose false doctrines and profess the truth in respect of applied disciplines. To that end the 30-odd opinion pieces and letters published in Australian dailies over the last decade were intended to meet Newman's directive. Synthesized and grouped into six categories, these considerations of commercial practice and accounting form the centrepiece of our broader account of many contestable features of the corporation.

The motivation for this book stems from our realization that, collectively, those opinion pieces were indicative of the tipping point for the manner in which corporate affairs are currently organized. The matters addressed continue to resonate. Time has arrived for a serious questioning of whether current corporate arrangements are capable of regulation; indeed, whether the modern corporation in its corporate group form can deliver an orderly commerce.

The period of our analysis concludes just after the end of 2012. It evidences the impact of deregulatory, then regulatory, oscillations – as in earlier periods. This process began with deregulatory pushes presaging the dotcom mania and related crash in April/May 2000 and the freeing up of the derivatives market. It was generally a period of takeover activities like the notorious AOL-Time Warner acquisition, abruptly halted by Enron, WorldCom and Global Crossing collapsing in the USA, and financial difficulties elsewhere such as France's Vivendi, Italy's Parmalat, as well as HIH, One.Tel, Ansett, Harris Scarfe, FAI Insurance, Westpoint, Great Southern, Baycorp, Babcock & Brown and Allco in Australia. Accounting restatements were a common feature of the post-crash settings. Some of the collapses motivated government regulations (crisis theory-like), such as Sarbanes-Oxley (2002) and Dodd-Frank (2010) in the USA, CLERP 9 (2004) in Australia, and numerous company codes and legislative changes in the UK.

On the financial side the introduction in the USA of the 1994 Riegle-Neal Interstate Banking and Branching Efficiency Act augmented by the Financial Services Modernization Act of 1999, also known as the Gramm-Leach-Bliley Act, opened the way for banks to mix investment and ordinary banking activities. Each piece of legislation was consistent with an underlying deregulatory push coinciding with a five-year or thereabouts period in the following decade of virtually free credit, arising from the 'Greenspan put'. To this was added the use of 'innovatory, grotesquely obfuscatory, financial products', CDOs and the like.[1] The GFC put a brake on that growth and was followed by four years of the eurozone debt crisis. Regulations like the US 2010 Dodd-Frank Act (including the Volcker rule), UK legislation to inject its FSA with a renewed consumer protection focus and Australia's CLERP initiatives were illustrative of the regulatory responses.

The period under review ended as it started, with calls for deregulation to stimulate the financial sector and the economy. The latest backflip entailed the softening of the Basel III requirements – specifically the easing of liquidity rules and the delayed start-up of them from 2015 until 2019.

Countervailing the pro-business forces and following the numerous crises, governments introduced corporate governance pushes, more regulation of the traditional kind, and increased inept corporate accounting and auditing regulation. All of this was accompanied by the growing militancy of the Occupiers against corporate misbehaviour – and against Wall Street and all it stands for.

Enron's failure in late 2001 in the USA and HIH's demise in Australia prompted a predictable rush of government regulatory action to bring corporations into line. *Predictable* because this had been the pattern of responses to similar events in many countries during the previous century. This occurred despite 'audited' accounting and more general governance irregularities in the USA by other large companies such as WorldCom, Waste Management, Global Crossing, Tyco, Adelphi and Xerox. In the

UK the early 1990s failures of the Maxwell Communications Group and Asil Nadir's retail giant Polly Peck gave the governance movement a boost. In Australia, calls for increased regulation followed similar failures. Curiously, few financial observers or commentators seemed to contemplate whether the corporate form is demonstrating that it is incapable of being governed or at least controlled in the environment of modern international commerce.

The same doubt about the appropriateness of the modern corporate form should have been fuelled by the dubious morality of the actions of myriad companies.

There have been increasing incidents of doubtful advertising over the years by those purveying dangerous products – tobacco, asbestos, liquor and the like. Those responsible for gross pollution of the environment have not only fought penalties, but have also had to be harassed continually until they try to make good the damage done – this is particularly evident in the clean-up actions of oil and other mining companies. There have been perennial public concerns over corporate funding of candidates' and parties' electoral campaigns and all that that suggests, and concerns expressed about the actions of those who dreamt up the so-called innovative financial engineering products purportedly to mitigate systemic risk. However, those products proved to be a substantial contributor to increasing risk; they were a major cause of the GFC and a near wholesale financial meltdown of companies. Inquiries have revealed several financial sector executives worldwide were unfazed in promoting their toxic financial inventions to banks, and to superannuation and pension funds. Banks put lenders' monies at risk buying and promoting such inventions, and continued paying huge salaries to executives and favoured employees; then the general public again suffered through government bailouts being financed by taxpayers' monies.

Of course, this 'corporate immorality' had been evidenced long before in many countries. Consider, for example, the 1950s Minamata mercury poisoning scandal by the Japanese company Chisso, and later US corporate scandals such as Union Carbide's Bopal explosion and the purported cover-up, or the 1970s Ford Pinto car scandal with its exploding fuel tank. Of course, who can forget the 1970s corporate bribes and related corruption brouhaha involving many leading multinational companies – the Lockheed bribes being a major instance? The legal quagmire of criminal corporate responsibility for those corporate actions created much concern (e.g. Fisse and Braithwaite's *Corporations, Crime and Accountability*, 1993).

Those corporate capers both in the non-finance and finance sectors have persisted.

Regarding the non-finance sector, corporate bribes or the euphemistically termed 'business facilitation payments' have continued long after Lockheed's troubles. In late 2012 Rolls-Royce (under prompting from the UK Serious Fraud Office (SFO) following whistleblower information) started its investigations into transactions to secure business for its civil aircraft engines in China and Indonesia. The issue, which emerged after allegations by an ex-employee whistleblower, followed bribery claims several years earlier in India. Germany also had its corporate ethics concerns – the actions of high-ranking executives in several large companies, like Daimler-Benz and Siemens, led both companies in the late 2000s to accept fines to settle US bribery allegations. Japan did not escape corporate scandal either. In late April 2012 former Olympus President Michael Woodford blew the whistle on a massive fraud at the camera maker. A few years earlier 'purchases' by Olympus of several companies at excessive prices (it would later be revealed) had been an attempt to hide a $US1.7 billion fraud. Accountants, auditors and Japanese executives became embroiled in the aftermath of what has been said to be a product of the Japanese assets bubble of the 1980s. It has also been reported that BHP Billiton was being investigated in 2013 by US and Australian authorities about bribery allegations in Cambodia, China and Western Australia late in the last decade.[2]

Recent evidence suggests corporate hanky-panky and alleged illegalities by the USA's GlaxoSmithKline, specifically in relation to its reporting to the public of the supposed medicinal benefits of its products. GSK has hit the headlines again regarding bribery suggestions in China. New evidence has also emerged about the German pharmaceutical company Grünenthal's public apology in 2012, which was consistent with its involvement in the late 1950s Thalidomide scandal.

The finance sector has been bedevilled by supposedly illegal – certainly immoral – activities in the aftermath of the GFC. As this book goes to press, civil and even a criminal action or two have been successfully prosecuted. Consider the actions of employees of Barclays Bank and reportedly up to 20 other leading financial institutions – including RBS, UBS, Lloyds Banking Group and Deutsche Bank – allegedly involved in the London interbank offered rate (Libor) manipulations. Indeed, one of the then two main UK corporate regulators, the FSA, has reported that Barclays Bank has agreed to pay a £290 million fine. Further, in December 2012 UBS agreed to a $1.5 billion (aggregate) settlement with three supervisory agencies – the US Justice Department, the UK FSA and the Swiss Financial Market Supervisory Authority (FINMA). Barclays' and UBS's offences are presumably only the tip of an iceberg. In mid-2013 it is reported that an early review of the new UK Financial Conduct Authority involves investigating allegations that major financial institutions have manipulated benchmark foreign exchange rates. Also, the Financial Stability Board (FSB) has set up a global committee to review how all benchmark rates are set.

The unethical nature and lack of accountability for such behaviours underpinned the July 2012 appointment by the UK Chancellor of the Exchequer George Osborne of a Parliamentary Commission on Banking Standards. The Commission was reported to be the first of its kind since the Marconi scandal of 1913.[3] Its brief was to investigate what had occurred and propose new public policy.

A major drugs matter was said to be part of HSBC bank's activities in the last decade, resulting in the US Justice Department issuing a fine of $1.92 billion, but incongruously (to many) it failed to make any criminal prosecutions against HSBC personnel for their alleged drug laundering behaviour. Initial evidence suggests poor control practices at HSBC may have facilitated the laundering of drug monies, and assisting institutions to overcome bans on money flows between certain countries. Two decades earlier the Bank of Commerce and Credit International was described as the 'world's most corrupt financial empire' (Beatty and Gwynne, 1993) for its money laundering and related activities across many jurisdictions.

Charles Ferguson's 2011 Academy Award-winning documentary and best-selling book of the same title, *Inside Job*, were on the money when lamenting that there had been 'few criminal prosecutions and no criminal convictions of financial institutions or their senior executives' related to their behaviour (Ferguson, 2012, p. 196). A 2013 PBS *Frontline* account, 'The Untouchables', reinforces the concerns raised by Ferguson about regulatory inaction. It critically noted that, in contrast to the Savings and Loans debacle where many leading executives in the finance sector were prosecuted and gaoled, following the GFC the Justice Department and the Federal Bureau of Investigation (FBI) failed to prosecute successfully a single high-level executive from Wall Street. Only lower-level loan originators and a few rogue bond traders were targeted and prosecuted. Curiously, in that programme an interview of two high-ranking officers of the FBI and Justice Department revealed that prosecutions were not undertaken for fear of a systemic run on the markets. Again, short-term rather than long-term objectives were given priority – but, even more significantly, one must question whether this is a legitimate factor for prosecutors to take into account.

As well as the HSBC payment to the Justice Department being a 'get out of gaol free' payment for its employees, there was further support in 2012 for Charles Ferguson's lament, namely the Standard Chartered Bank's suggested use of illegal international financial transactions with Iran. Those transactions, if proven, would threaten continuation of its US banking licence. Corporate immorality appears to be winning a race to the bottom.

Corporate immorality is not restricted to large international business. Australia also has its own corporate rogues' gallery. For instance, albeit at the lower end of the financial scale, when Australia launched its carbon pricing scheme much unscrupulous corporate behaviour was revealed. Indicative of opportunistic attitudes in commerce was a national bakery chain that admitted sending an email advising its franchises to gouge prices and blame the new carbon tax for the price increases. Yet another is not-so-small developer Leighton Holdings' alleged involvement in corrupt practices in Iraq's 'oil for food' programme – and it has been reported in a recent newspaper investigation that in the 2000s 'Bribery, corruption and cover ups were rife and known to company executives and directors, according to internal company files'.[4] However, it seems for any of those involved they need not worry too much. In earlier decades few were charged over AWB's illegal actions enabling it to contravene United Nations sanctions regarding sales of Australian wheat to Saddam Hussein's Iraq – proven by the 2006–07 Justice Cole Royal Commission. Embarrassingly for the Australian government, eight officers of two subsidiaries of the Reserve Bank of Australia (RBA) – Note Printing of Australia (wholly owned) and Securency (half owned) – are on trial for their possible part in the encouraging of some Asian central banks to purchase the rights to use the RBA's innovative anti-forgery currency note process. Significantly, this highlights complications of corporate governance, risk management and reporting when groups of companies are involved – irrespective of whether a wholly owned or a part-owned subsidiary is involved. The directors of the RBA (the holding company in this case) have become embroiled in the matter as there are mounting allegations that they were aware of the bribery approaches being used by the note-printing subsidiaries and should have notified police earlier.[5]

The panoply of such behaviour and responses suggests that the net social benefit of the corporation is rightfully being contested. It is argued here that the modern corporation's transaction costs of doing business through subsidiaries or off-balance sheet entities with their 'limited liability within limited liability' arrangements have clearly increased. One such cost is that the modern corporation appears incapable of effective regulation, through either internal or external governance mechanisms. Doubling-up regulation of the same externally imposed 'rules and sanctions' variety that existed before Enron and HIH has been pursued throughout the first decade of the new century as each wave of misbehaviour has hit. It was as if the problem was merely getting those who managed companies to behave. It wasn't. And they haven't.

Whereas the events addressed in the opinion pieces reproduced in this book broadly captured the main commercial and regulatory actions of the period, they could well have fitted nicely into all the decades of the twentieth century. For not only has the general mode of corporate misbehaviour been repeated, but so also has the manner in which remedies have been sought.

Corporate crashes in financial sectors in the early decades of the nineteenth century influenced the legislative creation (through general incorporation by mere registration) of the corporation in Britain. Through general incorporation the government sought to increase large-scale UK investment, such as in the canal and railway companies. As a quid pro quo, compulsory accounting and auditing requirements were introduced in companies legislation as two major corporate governance checks on the use of the corporation in commerce. Towards the end of that century corporations were already morphing into larger, more complex group structures. This often involved the use of trusts and other non-corporate or corporate off-balance sheet entities. Economic booms and related corporate crashes were prominent. The law and accounting sought to redress anomalies that appeared in the aftermath of the many economic busts over the last few decades of the nineteenth century. Fast forward over a century and we find that such unexpected collapses continue to underpin the numerous ineffective regulatory developments, especially in accounting and auditing. Now, other off-balance sheet entities are to the fore, including shadow banking (non-banking financial intermediaries, NBFIs) entities such as SIVs, VIEs and SPEs.

The evidence adduced in our earlier books and below shows that with all the rhetoric regarding improvements in public protection from corporate misbehaviour, with propaganda that tends to lull an unsuspecting public into a sense of false security, we are most likely worse off now than at the beginning of that period. Auditors continue pursuing their mission to report opinions on whether a company's financials show a true and fair view of its wealth and progress – a 'mission impossible' due to their being shackled by the need to comply with the accounting standards. Some company executives continue with remuneration demands in much the same objectionably selfish manner as Ferdinand Pecora's Commission reported to President Franklin D. Roosevelt in the 1930s. As then, present-day executive remuneration continues to be a seemingly insoluble regulatory issue worldwide. Many companies' actions, then as now, are viewed by many as ethically questionable; some undeniably are morally bankrupt. Now, nearly every citizen worldwide has a stake in, is impacted by, what companies do. Whereas few of the general public (outside the USA) invested in shares up to the 1930s, virtually everyone in the developed countries and many in developing countries now either participates in or is affected by stock market gyrations via an equity interest in superannuation/pension-type investments.

We suspect that many of the themes coursing through this book contradict popularly held commercial beliefs. However, we are not out to win friends. We are out to have a more informed, less chaotic (and in that sense a more orderly) commercial environment.

Virtually nothing has really progressed in our lifetime in the investor (consumer) protection field. Things have regressed. Almost all aspects of corporate activity have become more complex, and companies' behaviour is more counterintuitive, less transparent. As a consequence corporations' behaviour is seen by many fair-minded citizens as being anti-social and contrary to the public interest – more slippery, more a public hazard, than it was in the past. Suggesting, as is the wont of many, that there should be more regulation of the same type as is currently in force is contested here. A different tack is needed. Evidence abounds that the monolithic holding company-subsidiary group structure of the modern corporation is well past its use-by date. Undoubtedly, it was a useful innovation in commercial affairs in the late eighteenth and the early part of the nineteenth centuries, but its usefulness in the twenty-first century clearly needs serious evaluation. While not proposing that the corporation per se be scrapped, we hold that several substantial modifications to both its form and to the mode of communications about it are necessary for capitalism to progress and to survive in an orderly manner.

Notes

1 Deregulatory examples in other countries include Australia's scaling back of the six-pillars bank policy and the UK's introduction of the Second Banking Directive (see Farrar *et al.*, 2009).
2 Nick Mackenzie and Richard Baker, 'Police Passed the Buck on BHP Allegations', *AFR*, 17 June 2013, p. 17.
3 Jennifer Thompson, 'Libor Panel Concludes its Grilling', *AFR*, 8 March 2013, p. 18.
4 Neil Mackenzie and Richard Baker, 'Building Giant at Centre of Bribery Scandal', *SMH*, 3 October 2013, pp. 1, 8. This claim is contested by Leighton.
5 Daniel Flitton, 'Investigative Process Shown to be Flawed', *SMH*, 13 August 2012 (accessed 28 September 2012). See also: Geoff Winestock, 'Stevens Admits Failure on Securency', *AFR*, 9 October 2012, pp. 1, 4.

1

CORPORATIONS

Soulless, heartless creations?

The belief that the modern corporation has just about reached its use-by date, that it is perhaps no longer the best way from all parties' perspectives to conduct 'new age global business', underpins a bracket of published opinions and ideas from more than a decade. It also underpins several major reforms outlined below.

When the British Chancellor of the Exchequer William Gladstone shepherded the modern corporation legislation through the UK Parliament in 1844, the commercial and the business settings in which it was fashioned were very different from their present manifestations. The largely *laissez-faire* business environment has moved on. Yet little has changed in respect of the primary commercial structures in which it is organized. Regulation of corporate structures continues to be more than one step behind effective and efficient investor protection. The time for this game of regulatory catch-up has long passed.

Modern corporations

The 1844 UK Joint Stock Companies Act was primarily enacted to legalize a means by which large sums of capital could be raised to fund infrastructure (particularly at the time of new transportation via the canals and railways) and factory capital formation for furthering the Industrial Revolution. It also introduced into the UK corporate lexicon the notion of *shareholder supremacy*. It did this principally by two means.

First, the notion of readily tradable *shares* was promoted as the way in which anybody with access to money could own a part of a company's capital for as long as they liked. In a sense calling their contributions 'shares' encouraged the idea of a share in the ownership of the company similar to that which a capital provider had in a joint stock partnership – up to 1844 the dominant business entity in the British system since the 1720 South Sea Bubble Act. With that the 'residual' that partners had in a partnership most likely seemed a natural right attaching to shares in the new business structure.

Second, that such companies had to appoint one of their number as an auditor strengthened shareholders' importance over other providers of capital (for example, lenders) and other essential resources (for example, the labour and skills of employees) who were guaranteed a financial return – lenders a contracted rate of interest on the amounts lent, and employees a contracted wage for their labour. In view of the fact that shareholders were to receive a dividend from any surplus (profit), it no doubt seemed as if they bore the major risk in the event of a loss – that their interests were akin to those of a property owner. Notably (in the British system), a company shareholder was a property owner with, from the 1856 legislation, the unique privilege of limiting personal potential liability for losses to the amount of the individual paid-up and unpaid equity capital.

All that appears to give a solid backing to what might otherwise be only a populist view, namely that shareholders bore the bulk of corporate risk. That perception prevails. So much so that the pervading view is that corporate managers are to run their companies primarily for the shareholders' benefit. Corporate governance regimes are thus geared to protect primarily shareholders' interests. Legislation provides that the directors are to act in the interests of the corporation, in many jurisdictions equating to the 'interests of shareholders in general meeting'.

Few seem to note that from the turn of the twentieth century the public interest has been, as a consequence, a matter of concern. In the USA, questionable behaviour was noted in Matthew Josephson's (1934) *The Robber Barons: The Great American Capitalists 1861–1901*, which covered the financial shenanigans of people like Andrew Carnegie, Cornelius Vanderbilt, J.P. Morgan, Andrew Mellon and Jay Gould, who were perceived to engage in business activities damaging to the general public, though undoubtedly generally rewarding to themselves. It is mostly agreed that Carnegie, Vanderbilt, Mellon and Gould, who made their fortunes exploiting steel, rail, aluminium and transport, pushed the development of US industry in a manner that would not be tolerated by workers today. J.P. Morgan held tight his control of the nation's purse strings, so much so that his power was necessary and sufficient to end the US currency crisis of 1907 (Bruner and Carr, 2007).

That had a profound impact on the passing of the anti-monopoly legislation. By the end of the nineteenth century it was a major movement and the push against some of the actions by major corporations had strengthened into a major force for regulatory change. Such legislation and concerns more generally about the trust movement in the USA and the UK were set against the backdrop that by 1910 there were approximately half a million companies worldwide, three-quarters of which were registered in the USA and the UK.[1]

Fast forward nearly a century to the post-Enron period and corporate misbehaviour energized the push to increase corporate governance. Later, following the GFC, corporations in the USA have equally bad reputations; they are perceived as being as selfish as the robber barons a century earlier. A particularly sour taste has emerged in reaction to the reported moves by IAG to sue the US government for the way Troubled Asset Relief Program (TARP) funds were used to bail out companies like IAG, which, curiously, indirectly benefited many major financial institution counterparties.[2]

Consider also the acerbic former US Labor Secretary Robert Reich's (2012, p. 20) *Beyond Outrage*: *What has Gone Wrong with our Economy and our Democracy, and How to Fix it*, which notes:

> Corporations aren't spending hundreds of millions of dollars on lobbyists and political campaigns because they love America, these expenditures are considered investments and the individuals that make them expect a good return.

Investigations, as discussed in the Prologue, show that such bad behaviour continues with a vengeance.

Clearly, corporations haven't changed their spots. The evidence continues to indicate that *ex post* sanctions are an ineffective form of regulation. A contemporary example is the dozen or so large financial institutions prosecuted for their actions in the Libor rate and currency benchmark affairs.

Events leading to the 1929 stock market crash influenced Franklin D. Roosevelt to enact the Securities Acts of 1933 and 1934 and the contemporaneous Glass-Steagall and Public Utility Holding Company Acts. Earlier, the Scottish bank failures in the 1860s and 1870s (most notably the Overend & Gurney Co. in 1866 and the City of Glasgow Bank in 1878) were the catalyst for UK audit legislation at the turn of the century. Likewise in the 1920s, the behaviour of the Royal Mail Steam Packet Company fiddling its post-World War I accounts for over a decade presaged the passing of increased accounting disclosure provisions by necessitating disclosure of a profit and loss account under the 1929 UK Companies Act. Only a balance sheet had been prescribed in the 1900 Companies Act following the recommendations of the 1895 Davey Commission of Inquiry.

A counter-argument in the many nineteenth- and twentieth-century commissions of inquiry into the effectiveness of UK companies legislation was the premise underpinning their recommendations: namely that the majority of company directors are honest. This is difficult to dispute and likely is also true at present, but this observation misses the point. Specifically, what are the deficiencies in a system within and outside the corporation that permit obvious abuses in the name of the corporation?

The point is, as commerce expanded nationally and internationally, corporate structures generally became more complex. The costs of controlling the actions of the corporation have increased as corporate misbehaviour has moved in lock step with the added complexity, notwithstanding further regulation through legislation. Such legislative responses have been shown elsewhere to be mere patches or bandaid solutions. The corporation effectively has become unaccountable, ungovernable.

Concurrently, the public interest has re-emerged and overtaken 'shareholder only' interests in the corporation. Primarily because of inoperable regulation, there exists a feeling that accounting and audit fail to protect investors and others by disclosing an entity's financial position and its periodic performance. Thus, most companies' financials fail to disclose a true and fair view of their wealth and progress. Auditors have an impossible mission by virtue of the present mandated accounting rules. Corporate executives' pay packages are grossly out of kilter with ordinary workers' compensation; executives want (and generally receive) bonuses for doing the job they are paid to do, irrespective of whether they do it or not. We argue for and illustrate in chapter 6 a form of group accounting that would dispense with conventional consolidated financial statements. Yet it would better provide the information claimed to be the output of them. We show there that the commercial public would be better off without holding companies and the current dominance of group structures that we now endure.

Hence, the accounting we recommend is a 'second best/once removed' solution. *Second best*, that is, to the *first and best*, namely scrapping the holding company/ subsidiary structure. *Once removed* insofar that a *best* solution − scrapping the modern corporation per se − might be most unlikely to be accepted.

A second way by which shareholder supremacy has been gradually entrenched was Berle and Means' 1932 development in *The Modern Corporation and Private Property* of the idea underpinning what is known in today's jargon as 'agency theory' − that for the modern corporation the 'separation of ownership and control' necessitated shareholders (as owners) to have agents, professional managers, run their company. There, shareholder supremacy is the conventional wisdom. Ronald Coase's contiguous observation that a corporation comprises a nexus of contracts does little to upset the supremacy of any contract that a shareholder has with the fictitious corporate persona. Yet it is the separation of ownership from the control element of agency theory that is exploited by executives who use it to legitimize their encouraging of shareholders to pay bonuses if they do their job. However, by far the most influential statement, inasmuch as it has reinforced a public perception of the function of companies, belongs to Milton Friedman. He claimed in 'The Social Responsibility of Business is to Increase its Profits' (*New York Times Magazine*, 1970) that the 'one and only ... social responsibility of business' was to increase its profits and, furthermore, since shareholders *owned* a corporation, they understandably presumed that they had a right to expect the managers of their company to act in their interests. There, the reasoning was similar to that underpinning the argument half a century earlier in the US *Dodge v. Ford Motor Co.* 170 N.W. (668 Mich. 1919) case, to the effect that 'corporations are carried on primarily for the profit of the stockholders. The powers of the directors are to be employed for that end' (Greenfield, 2006, p. 41). Such a focus encourages short-termism.

So it is that, despite over a century of corporate misdemeanours and defaults and a gradual shift to embrace the public interest perspective (albeit through the broadening of the shareholder supremacy framework), there is generally little questioning of whether the modern corporation is the best way in which to marshal business affairs. In fact, shareholders do not own their company, its assets and liabilities; they merely own shares in it. A notable exception to the popular belief is found in Joel Bakan's

The Corporation: The Pathological Pursuit of Profit and Power (2004). Generally, when companies fail or otherwise go financially awry, the questioning is not whether they are effective commercial vehicles so much as what additional regulations are to be imposed on their management.

Indeed, the recent corporate governance push (see chapter 3) seems to accept without question a hierarchy in which shareholders are the owners of their companies. So too does the back-foot stance taken by the 'stakeholder' movement, which usually is wrongfully promoted in terms that others than 'shareholder owners' have an interest in how companies are managed. Questioning shareholders' ownership credentials might prove a more fruitful tack for them to adopt. The general manner in which corporations' defaults are addressed remains by increasing conventionally styled regulation. So, disappointingly, much of that increased regulation is merely a doubling-up exercise – more of the same. With that in mind, provoked by the payouts to the disgraced James Hardie executives (of which we have more to say in chapter 5) and the excessive payouts to other executives, the *AFR* opinion piece in Box 1.1 appeared.

Box 1.1 No heart and soul in the pitiless corporate body

It may be wrong to expect companies to carry a social conscience. As the anguish continues over former James Hardie executives Peter Macdonald and Peter Shafron collecting between them about $10 million in exit payments, it's time to rethink the futility of expecting companies to exercise human characteristics that they cannot possess.

Of course such calls for greater corporate responsibility are not new. They have been made for nearly a century both here and overseas. All the talk of corporate responsibility and social awareness is mumbo jumbo. Recourse to notions such as corporate citizenship is to invoke the wraiths and hobgoblins of modern commerce.

When push comes to shove, fatuous appeals to a company's better nature are futile. It doesn't have a nature, better or worse. As a creation merely of the law, a company has neither a conscience nor a soul. As such it has been an object of concern for many social scientists for decades.

Nonetheless, such futile exercises serve to illustrate the shaky foundations that underpin so much of the corporate governance brouhaha of the recent past. Clearly companies have not measured up to public expectations, notwithstanding that they have satisfied the perceived canons of good governance. It is sobering to note that James Hardie received four and a half (of five) stars in a recent governance tick-a-box rating exercise. James Hardie also received 'gold' in the 2004 Annual Report Awards, notwithstanding the criteria being supportive of the triple bottom line notion, which is supposed to capture social awareness. To many, those outcomes must be less believable than the creatures of *Jurassic Park*. But they illustrate how litanies of governance rules and their terms of engagement are never found to be enough.

Clearly, controlling corporations is not the problem. It is controlling the individuals who run them. We might be better off with less talk of corporate governance and more of corporate-person governance. Virtually all of the governance rules are made to control individuals, not the structures, per se. Yet it is the corporate structures, particularly 'group' structures as in the James Hardie case, in which they legally operate that provide the framework in which they can do their thing. The paranoia induced by the alleged pressure on, and influence in, government policy making in the US surrounding the operations of the Carlyle Group, Kellogg Brown & Root, and the likes of Halliburton, is indicative of how the corporate umbrella shelters individuals' alleged questionable commercial operations. Individuals are exceedingly difficult to control. One way, is to limit access to their toys and to ensure continuous, contemporary, verified accounting of those toys.

We might wonder why this situation persists. Is it that public expectations are unreasonable? Is it that they're reasonable, but history is yet to catch up with them that optimum criteria are just around the corner? Or are the reformers barking up the wrong tree trying to dress up the traditional corporate governance structures in a style at odds with the contemporary commercial environment?

Arguably, the expectations of the public are reasonable in today's commercial environment. But that environment differs substantially from the setting in which the 1841 Gladstone Committee fashioned the basic corporate vehicle (as we know it) and shepherded it through the British parliament as the 1844 Companies Act. Protection of the interests of shareholders and creditors was the primary focus. The current wider stakeholder-based set of interests was far from contemplation.

Unquestionably, the idea that companies have a responsibility greater than merely that owed to their shareholders is the prevailing public perception. That idea underpins virtually everything that has been said in the criticism of James Hardie in the current imbroglio. It was a similar case in the 1998 Patrick/Maritime Union of Australia waterfront saga. Confusion between a parent company's enforceable legal obligations and the unenforceable social obligations attributed to it in line with current expectations creates an impasse, despite all the governance measures in place.

For the past 160 years there have been almost non-stop changes in corporate regulation as the corporate form grappled with changing, often new, commercial settings and associated crises – takeovers at the turn of the 19th century, the spurt of industrialization, the hyperinflation in the post World War I period, the 1929 crash and Roosevelt's regulatory aftermath, the Great Depression, post World War II reconstruction and more recently the pressures of extensive globalization.

Regulatory mechanisms have been cast and re-cast, massaged and reshaped, embellished with bells and whistles. However, the corporate structure is basically the same now as it was in 1844, albeit most frequently set in a group structure and its implied limited liability within limited liability (i.e., subsidiary companies within a corporate structure). There is little reason to suspect that the current governance regimes will see companies meeting public expectations. Everything points to new fissures appearing just as the successive gaps are closed.

Arguably it's time to contemplate that the prevailing corporate structures will most likely never be compatible with current public expectations and to do something about it.

(AFR, 1 November 2004, p. 71)[3]

What to do about it was the issue considered. Such a question was long overdue. We suggest, ideally, scrapping the corporate form as we currently know it. Scrapping the *group* (holding company and subsidiaries) arrangement is our preference. However, such a radical change is an unlikely candidate in the post-GFC recovery-oriented business world. So, instead, some adjustment to the corporate features of the corporation and a new form of group accounting is proposed.

That 2004 opinion hinted that perhaps part of the current governance problem lay in attributing to the corporation human characteristics that clearly it does not possess. Eight years later we can add a global financial crisis and a eurozone debt crisis and another catalogue of likely corporate misdemeanours and felonies to the events that make the contemporary corporate environment substantially different from that faced by the Gladstone Committee in its deliberations in the early 1840s. All of that highlights whether companies (as we know them) are the best structures in which to undertake modern business.

The point is, corporations are purely fictitious, created by the state to serve the populace. They have no soul, no heart to bleed, or, as Bakan (2004, p. 134) lamented, corporations are 'purely self-interested, incapable of concern for others, amoral, and without conscience'.

Today, there seems to be a greater public questioning of the appropriateness of the corporate form. A movement for 'sustainability reporting' has strengthened the original push for additional corporate environmental disclosure. The recent international drive for integrated reporting of six capital measures continues this push (www.theiirc. org). Apparently other stakeholders are commanding increasing influence over the corporation, which, in turn, is expected to add to motivations for the corporation to take a longer-term perspective in its own best interests. Importantly, opposition to corporate globalization has fuelled vigorous demonstrations, and the occupation movement worldwide (from the questionable 'holy ground' of Wall Street in New York to that of the less ecclesiastically contestable St Paul's courtyard in London) has vented opposition to its perception of corporate misbehaviour.

However, opposition to corporate misbehaviour has a long history. It has likely connections with the current discontent. Thom Hartmann, for example, in *Unequal Protection: How Corporations became 'People' – and You Can Fight Back* (2010), links the British East India Company's monopolistic behaviour leading to the 1773 Boston Tea Party, with the present Occupy Wall Street movement. The Boston Tea Party anticipated in many ways the contemporary protests against transnational corporations. Hartmann, notes with approbation that '[t]he people assembled in Boston at that moment faced the same issue that citizens who oppose combined corporate and co-opted government power all over the world confront today' (2010, p. 79).

Of course, the British East India Company was incorporated in 1600 by Royal Charter, but, as Percival Griffiths noted in *Licence to Trade: A History of the English Chartered Companies* (1974), the fundamental rights, obligations and economic power of Royal Charter companies were much the same as, and in fact presaged, those Gladstone later husbanded in 1844 with the enacting of the first Companies Act in the British Parliament, with its general incorporation by mere registration. Importantly, the persona imposed by incorporation – the notion of a company being legally a separate legal entity – has been an enduring feature.

Arguments questioning the usefulness of the corporate form are becoming more frequent, not only by mass movements like Occupy Wall Street. They are also consistent with themes followed by a number of pre- and post-GFC commentators – by, for example, Ted Nace in *Gangs of America: The Rise of Corporate Power and the Disabling of Democracy* (2003), John Truman Wolfe in *Crisis by Design: The Untold Story of the Global Financial Coup and What You Can Do About It* (2011), and Reich in the aforementioned *Beyond Outrage* (2012). For Hartmann (2010), his main thrust is that in the unequal protection that corporations enjoy in the USA the trouble started when they were improperly attributed the same rights as a *human* under the First and Fourteenth Amendments to the US Constitution. Remove their incorrectly attributed human status and the problem could be kneecapped in the USA, he proposes.

Misused corporate persona

The idea of a corporate persona has long been exploited. The bankruptcy actions of undercapitalized (so-called $2 companies) and phoenix companies in many countries have resulted in a vast array of corporate abuses. In more recent times, this is especially the case in the USA, where the greatest corporate power currently resides despite the GFC and antecedent crises like the Savings and Loans fiasco. Having a written Bill of Rights has brought notions of the corporate persona into question in the USA in a manner not experienced in Britain.

In particular, purportedly a law clerk's interpretative *headnote* suggested erroneously that the US Supreme Court declared a corporation's persona was the same as that possessed by human persons. Hartmann explains how the misreporting of the *Santa Clara County v. Southern Pacific Railroad* case in 1886 in the US Supreme Court underpins the prevailing belief in the USA that companies are people within the meaning of the Fourteenth Amendment. The point being, Hartmann (2010, p. 23) explains: 'corporations given the powerful cudgel of human rights secured by the bill of Rights, their ability to amass wealth and power could lead to death and war, and the impoverishment of actual human beings on a massive scale'.

The case note written by the court reporter Bancroft Davis implied that the judgment had included that corporations were identical to human persons, and indeed had the same rights as them. His headnote read: 'The court does not wish to hear argument on the question whether the provision in the Fourteenth Amendment to the Constitution which forbids a State to deny to any person within its jurisdiction the equal protection of the laws, applies to these corporations. We are all of the opinion that it does.' Curiously, although a headnote has no legal standing and is not part of the law the case presents, the doctrine has been upheld and reaffirmed many times in case law. The headnote is not included as such in any of its governing corporation legislations. All of this begets the questions: What are the obligations of that legal persona? How are they enforced?

Granting legal persona has been a serious miscalculation. Many aspects of corporates' actions (particularly since the reporting of the *Santa Clara* decision) are as if they had humans' rights. This, in essence, is what Occupy Wall Street and others who rail against private equity and currently oppose corporate globalization object to.

In 2010 Jeffery Clements's *Corporations Are Not People* explained how a US Supreme Court case that year, *Citizens United v. Federal Election Commission*, strengthened the Bancroft Davis idea that corporations are people under the Fourteenth Amendment and that therefore they have *free speech* under the First Amendment. That strengthens corporations' capacity to use their wealth to control governments – particularly in the USA to say what they like, even perhaps to disclose in their financials what they choose. It is claimed that corporate money is the lion's share of the estimated $US5.8 billion spent on the 2012 presidential election.[4] The argument runs that, because of company money, government is controlled by wealth – that it is not, in Abraham Lincoln's words, 'government of the people, by the people, for the people', but government by those with the greatest wealth at hand.

Although few could deny the contribution that corporations have made to increasing living standards over the past century or so, equally few could deny that corporations have offended many of the social norms generally considered essential in a well-ordered society. Importantly, there is no good reason to suppose that society could not have advanced as well as it has economically without the dominance of the current corporate form – namely, the behemoths with their holding company, subsidiary company (sometimes pyramidal) forms and intertwined financing arrangements.

It is worth noting that, in the main, the corporate governance movement has emerged in response to public dissatisfaction with corporate misbehaviour. The basic idea underpinning the governance movement since the early 1990s appears to have been that the corporate structure is useful but for a few 'bad apples' – that what is needed is a set of internal rules to weed out and punish those bad apples. This was consistent with a 'light' regulatory touch of the primarily free market-trained corporate regulators. After a concentrated effort over more than 20 years, it is contestable whether much has been achieved, other than *wish lists* of 'measures' – of what companies ought to have in place and of what has to be ticked off as implied compliance. Chapter 2 spells out how annual financial disclosure, perhaps the longest-standing governance activity, has failed miserably. Since it was first imposed on corporations in

1844, we have had to endure inept accounting regulation that fails to produce financial statements disclosing a company's wealth and financial progress. Thus, in 2012, following the Australian Federal Court's 19 June approval of the Centro PricewaterhouseCoopers (PwC) settlement, it was apt for us to note in the *Australian Financial Review*: 'We assure the public that accounting is so chock full of unnecessary complexities, inconsistencies and commercial contradictions that this [PwC's alleged audit failure in not detecting a misclassification of several billion dollars of debts] was (at a technical level) child's play.'[5]

In chapter 4 we also explain how compulsory audit vies with financial disclosure as being the first governance cab off the rank. Both are in a shambles. Corporate regulators, like the Securities and Exchange Commission (SEC) in the USA, the FSA in the UK and the Australian Securities and Investments Commission (ASIC), appear more hell bent on taking scalps than consumer protection by preventing corporate executives from behaving badly. Public outcry isn't enough. The persistent US financial analyst Harry Markopolos recounted the sorry Bernie Madoff fraud in his co-authored *No One Would Listen: A True Financial Thriller* (2011), explaining that an 'inept SEC' was front and centre for nearly a decade as he tried to garner action by it on Madoff's fraudulent activities before the GFC derailed the Ponzi scheme. The SEC, and their FSA and ASIC counterparts, have proven by such systemic failures to be unable to shield effectively investors and the general public from corporate wrongdoing. Some governments set up special commercial financial protection agencies (amongst them the Consumer Financial Bureau in the USA and the Consumer Protection and Markets Authority in the UK) to protect investors' financial interests. In Australia there are rumblings about pursuing something similar.

Despite overwhelming suggestions that a lack of regulation underpinned the GFC, more to the point is our observation that there is a greater volume of direct corporate regulation now than ever before. The problem is whether it is regulation of the right kind. Prevention is always better than cure. Governments worldwide have abrogated their responsibilities by embracing the governance movement. Companies are now considered prima facie to be 'behaving well' if they can tick off a full list of the governance structures they have in place. As with humans, regulation of companies is fast becoming an internal rather than an external operation. This is scarcely surprising, given the prominence of free-market thinking within regulatory agencies. Also, many companies that have become poor investment risks have boasted extremely full good housekeeping lists. Somewhat as a consequence, most of the corporate regulation now in place is more directed at apprehending wrongdoers, issuing enforceable undertakings and pursuing settlements than preventing the activities of which those wrongdoers are accused. Similarly, awards for corporate social responsibility are often based more on the quantity and comprehensiveness of voluntary 'sustainability' reporting than the detail or impact of any underlying sustainability initiatives.

Ex post financial settlements (increasingly, at least in Australia, to settle a class action) and enforceable undertakings with the regulatory authorities are now considered cost-effective ways for governments and other parties to proceed to regulate corporations. However, with regard to the former, especially those in the USA, one must question whether any worthwhile benefits accrue to the public from the penchant for negotiating the agreed 'no fault' financial settlements that effectively put an end to legal action by the regulators and investors. Settlements seem to be contagious. Lately Australia's ASIC has been eager to pursue them. A notable instance was the reported 2012 Centro/PwC $AU200 million civil action settlement. Auditor PwC's share was said to be a 'no fault' $AU69 million. All settled, but without blame. It was almost as if nobody offended. One might well ask, why part with good money when blameless? It should not surprise that this kind of regulation has done little to prevent repetition of similar behaviour. Alleged wrongdoers, it seems, can muzzle discussion and buy their way out of trouble. The Centro settlement shows that Australia too has perhaps learned how to launch a questionable compensation mechanism – 'questionable' insofar that in the USA the SEC's settlements frequently appear to avoid a further pursuit of criminal offences. No offence is established. What occurred, how, when and 'if so' then 'by whom' are never established. Mostly the details remain merely 'alleged'. Lessons and precedents are effectively denied.

Additionally, settlements usually punish stakeholders by the payment reducing the accused company's assets and occasionally forcing it into bankruptcy. The Centro settlement was a civil matter, but 'no fault' is the outcome. Although settlements of the Centro variety open the way for investor compensation, it is doubtful whether they really inform those compensated whether there was (as in Centro's case) an 'accounting and audit failure' from which lessons could be learned. Perhaps Australia's ASIC might pursue PwC on the auditing issue, for $AU69 million is a large sum to pay when one is confident of there being 'no fault'. The absence of hard data for observers to deduce lessons is a general issue emerging from the spate of 'no fault' settlements.

Governance regimes: ticking boxes, preventing nothing

Governance regimes became particularly fashionable following the Enron crash and its aftermath in the USA: Ken Lay became the poster boy for *bad directing*, and Arthur Andersen received top billing for alleged defective auditing. *Independence* was the primary buzz word, the independence of directors and of auditors the major issue. Governance took an about-turn in the aftermath of the likes of Enron. It became overloaded.

When Enron crashed in late 2001 the clarion call was for more government action, more regulation, some heads on poles. Sarbanes–Oxley (2002) fulfilled the former; Kenneth Lay, Andrew Fastow and the auditing firm Arthur Andersen the latter. In this respect there was little difference in approach eight years later when Lehman Brothers failed, king-hit in the GFC, and, surprisingly to some, Lehman Brothers was allowed to file for bankruptcy, apparently being viewed by all and sundry as not 'too big to fail'. We show in chapter 3 that more regulation had also been proffered as the solution in the UK in the 1990s following, *inter alia*, the collapse of Robert Maxwell's empire of 400 public and 400 private intertwined companies and the tanking of Asil Nadir's equally complex Polly Peck retail monolith. While certainly these combines were demonstrably not too big to fail, they may have been too big to regulate effectively.

We should note that then, as now, it was not seriously debated whether the corporate group form remained a suitable vehicle for modern commerce – in the UK, the USA or elsewhere. Nor was it really debated whether more regulation similar to that already existing would fix the problem. More tinkering, more cosmetic changes, continue to be the accepted wisdom of the regulators. In the UK the FSA was established as the one-stop regulatory prescription, it failed and was replaced. Sarbanes-Oxley, and then the GFC-related Dodd-Frank legislation, are the latest 'solutions' in the USA. The FSA and Sarbanes-Oxley failed to meet expectations as soon as the GFC hit, not with the criticism that either was really ineffective, but with (as we noted above) yet another round of regulation, of much the same variety – more boxes to be ticked.

Basel II.5 or III prudential standards require that there should be additional capital, leverage and liquidity constraints for the 28 global systematically important financial institutions (GSIFI). Even more recently, US and UK prudential regulators have unveiled cross-border rules that seek to force shareholders and creditors of their 12 large financial institutions (part of the 28 GSIFI) necessarily to take losses when incurred.[6] This was not the case in the aftermath of the GFC. They also require holding companies of those GSIFI to have greater capital requirements as a buffer, but as a trade-off, perhaps, their operating subsidiaries are allowed to continue operating, even if their holding companies suffer extensive financial losses. Such a measure highlights the significance of the holding company/subsidiary company separate legal entity discussion in chapter 6.

Bad news days

Clearly, many are far less than satisfied with the financial games played with apparent impunity by big public companies. Saving up bad news for when there is going to be flak in any event, when it is convenient to release all the bad news for public consumption, is hardly meeting the much-touted continuous disclosure requirements imposed by securities markets worldwide. The continuous disclosure mantra is a feel-good factor that has been used for decades and has been relied on by regulators seemingly everywhere since the dotcom bust. Two Australian instances provide evidence to question the effectiveness of such a disclosure regime. Impairment write-downs in 2012 totalling billions of dollars by the multinational Rio Tinto in respect of its 2010 Mozambican coal acquisition and its 2007 Alcan acquisition (with its aluminium assets) reinforce the expectational process inherent in that impairment calculus. Over the six years since the Alcan purchase and two since the Mozambican coal acquisition, one wonders what the 'real' (as opposed to the reported 'after impairment') performance of Rio Tinto was each year.[7]

Another Australian instance is revealed in the early 2013 PPB administrators' report to creditors into the failed Hastie engineering group. It further illustrates the potential dilemma lurking in the reported financials of listed companies. Overstated goodwill valuations were claimed to be in the books as well as inadequate impairment calculations (with asset values and reported results being at best contestable) in several years prior to its 2011 collapse.[8] When impairments were made it was suggested they were made in the wrong years. Significantly, the reported products of these impairment calculations were embedded in many of Hastie's contractual arrangements – such as appeared in prospectus data and in annual executive remuneration hurdle criteria. There is more on this latter point in chapter 5.

Consider the *AFR* opinion in Box 1.2, discussing continuous disclosure.

Box 1.2 Taking a bath can be financially indecent

ASIC must investigate past financial misstatements implied by 'big bath' write-downs.

Recent disclosure that companies have written down assets by $44 billion (Paul Garvey and Khia Mercer, 'Write-downs punch $44 billion hole in profits', the *Australian Financial Review*, August 31) should have the Australian Securities and Investments Commission scurrying to request explanations from directors as to whether the diminutions occurred solely in the year ended June 30.

References in the *AFR*'s September 9 banner headline reporting of companies 'clearing the decks' invite suspicion that some companies are engaging in a 'catch-up' of losses accrued over previous reporting periods.

Those inferences are encouraged by comments implying companies are taking a 'big bath', engaged in 'bare-faced spin' ('Stripping out the bad news is bare-faced spin', John Kehoe, *AFR*, September 9) – that the market downturn is being exploited by companies to 'clean up their balance sheets by pushing all possible bad news on asset impairment and bad debts out the door at a time when investors may be more forgiving given general weak results across the board'. Indecent disclosure of a most virulent kind!

ASIC should be concerned. For to the extent that there is a catch-up going on, it has missed or condoned previous misstatements. Catching up means that previous years' financials have been misreported. If so, those responsible ought to be called to account. Directors have declared that the financial accounts fed to ASIC show a true and fair view of their company's financial performance for the year just passed and its financial position at its end. Catch-ups are not on the agenda.

To the extent that what is in the accounts affects share prices, virtually all working Australians are hit through their superannuation funds; those personally active in the market (arguably relying on trends and current data) are directly misled, and most analyses of companies' financial structures are consequently most likely misleading. That is, profits and losses are wrong, rates of return, earnings per share and interest-cover calculations are incorrect, and red flags regarding solvency are shredded. Companies' gearing is miscalculated at a time when leverage has been such an important issue, asset backing and indications of collateral for borrowing are incorrect, and whether borrowing covenants have been observed, for instance, is at risk of being misread.

There are also possible trickle-down next-year effects.

Catching up in 2009 doesn't set things right. So, not only are those who prepare the financials and the directors responsible for them not entitled to take a 'big bath' in 2009, by doing so they are threatened with the difficulty of explaining the extent of and the reasons for their misleading disclosure in previous years.

Auditors also should be concerned. They have either to plead being duped and misled by company officers – which may question their competencies – or fess up to being a party to 'boardroom' antics.

Whereas in the present climate the estimated $44 billion write-down is nonetheless a staggeringly large number that may put things on the right track now, it places both directors and auditors in invidious positions.

And ASIC, as a regulator with public obligations, cannot allow this to pass without action. It must inquire further and report the outcome of its deliberations.

(AFR, 22 September 2009, p. 63)

Both *clearing the decks* and the idea of *catching up* contradict the notion that the function of accounting is to inform the public about an entity's current wealth and performance since the last reckoning. For the catch-up envisaged in those *AFR* headlines (and in similar headlines in other countries that allow the annual reporting of clearly erroneous asset and income numbers) had a much longer gestation period in mind. It amounted to an allegation that, in many instances, public companies were delaying, saving up bad news, sometimes for years, until things were so dire that disclosing a bit more financial grunge would cause little additional grief.

That opinion piece supported the observation of financial journalist John Kehoe's criticism of entering catch-ups in financial statements being a legitimate strategy of getting anguish over (the accumulated bad news out) in one fell swoop. It was noted that directors knowingly engaging in such a tactic were admitting that either a previous declaration by them was known to be incorrect or that they were so inept that they didn't know about it. Whatever the reason, directors place themselves between a rock and a hard place.

Further, the opinion piece also pursued the line that these days virtually every worker has (at least) an indirect interest in companies' wealth and progress by virtue of their superannuation (compulsory in Australia, resulting in close to $AU1.3 trillion as at June 2012) and, for example, the approximately $US3 trillion of 401(k) funds in the USA. There were two main concerns. First, the continuing individual public perception noted was that 'few Australians played the stock market'. Notwithstanding that, few through their superannuation (pension) holdings were indeed unaffected by the manner in which companies behaved. Second, a prevailing notion exists that institutional shareholders were able to look after their members' financial interests, presumably because they were somehow 'in the know'. That claim persists, not-withstanding that it was rumoured few were doing so. In any event, exactly how institutions voted on critical issues is rarely revealed other than in occasional financial press reports. One upside of the GFC is the increased transparency it has provoked regarding institutional behaviour on some corporate issues. In Australia and the UK, institutions seem to have influenced the outcome of voting on executive pay pack-ages (see chapter 5), but superannuation fund members do not appear to know in advance, do not direct, and are not consulted beforehand or informed afterwards on how they want their funds to vote.

Presumably, continuous disclosure is directed at avoiding this, but taking a bath in bad times is not new. Indeed, nor are claims by those suggesting virtue in making things appear (declaring their financial positions to be) worse than they are, so that one can look like 'a champion manager' when revealing a considerably healthier position later on. 'Chainsaw' Al Dunlap is said to have used such a tactic before Sunbeam tanked under his command in the 1990s. Not exactly the big-bath out-come, but equally entailing financial deception.[9] Stakeholders fed such misleading information are equally duped by financial understatements as they are by over-statements. The US Government Accounting Office 2002, 2003 and 2004 reports revealed the extent of restatements (up and down) in the immediate post-Enron years (see Clarke and Dean, 2007, pp. 41–43). Both deliberate misstatements are grossly (and equally) dishonest; one is no more virtuous than the other. Of course, conven-tional notions of conservative (sometimes labelled equally incorrectly as prudent) accounting foolishly and certainly illegally encourage understatement of the worth of a company's assets. Letting the bad news out gradually is certainly a frequent tactic. Doing so appears to have been suspected of, for example, Australian developer Leighton Holdings as it reportedly became embroiled in an alleged Iraq oil bribery scandal in 2012.

Private equity

Failure of the governance measures to rein in corporate misbehaviour (more on this in chapter 3) perhaps has contributed to many an acquisition and ultimate decimation by private equity (PE) firms. PE was a well-known phenomenon prior to the GFC. It had big names amongst its ranks – for example, the Carlyle Group, Halliburton, Goldman Sachs, BlackRock, KKR, TPG Capital and Apollo. Recently PE had gone public with, for instance, American Capital Ltd, Ares Management LLC, BlackRock Group L.P. and Kohlberg & Company. PE firms generally finance their acquisitions by having their 'target' borrow heavily, with large payments to be made in the future. This has made the questionable corporate structure even more vulnerable to failure. PE had earned its reputation for asset stripping, loading up the acquired company with debt, downsizing an acquisition's workforce, selling off 'loose' assets and ultimately selling a weakened corporate shell.

In 2011 the *AFR*'s back-page financial commentator, Chanticleer, implied that with the cashed-up PE firms having been sidelined during the roughest days of the

GFC the corporate world should expect a wave of leveraged buyouts at which the PE firms were the past masters. That prompted the *AFR* letter to the editor in Box 1.3.

Box 1.3 Public pain private gain

Chanticleer's 'Private equity takes another swing' (June 29) was well targeted.

Hopefully, it encourages a closer look at private equity activity. Overseas evidence suggests that the more PE struggles in Australia, perhaps the better.

Josh Kosman's 2009 *The Buyout of America*, for example, catalogues PE's unflattering contribution to the United States' precarious economic situation.

He notes First Boston Consulting Group in 2008 predicting half of the 3,188 American companies (employing 3.7 million) that PE bought between 2001–8 debt-defaulting, becoming insolvent between 2011 and 2015 and, bumping up the unemployed by (approximately) 1.85 million – close to the number of 'GFC attributed' US jobs lost in 2008.

With acquisition tactics entailing meagre cash outlays, heavy debt (for which the acquired company usually is liable), poor after-acquisition service, cost cutting and employee retrenchment, Kosman predicts PE will cause the next great financial crisis. He details uninspiring PE performances in the US, the United Kingdom and continental Europe.

However, the impacts of possible European defaults may be dwarfed if the lure of extravagant returns from PE activity captures greater interest of the retirement funds.

Securitization of debt by PE and major investment banks is similar to CDO securitization in the GFC. And debt bubbles created by PE debt financing and subsequent deleveraging may be little different from the subprime housing loans bubble. If commentators like Kosman are correct, it seems that in the end only the PE firms will be on the winners' podium!

(AFR, 6 July 2011, p. 52)

For those with money, PE is potentially a profitable investment, but for those who had nurtured a business and for its employees it is a financial hazard.

In his introduction to *The Buyout of America* (2009), Kosman showed that the reality of PE even 'for those with money' is not always rosy. Economic downturns and upticks in interest rates are critical. Kosman's analysis is certainly a sad story for those without money in most economic scenarios. He detailed how four times more companies' debt defaulted from the beginning of 2008 to November of that year than had tanked in 2007, and that 62% had 'recently been involved in transactions with private-equity firms' (Kosman, 2009, p. 8). Kosman, there, was pursuing his reporting of the Boston Consulting Group's 2008 prediction that 'almost 50 percent of PE-owned companies would probably default on their debt by the end of 2011'. That estimate looks rather pessimistic at this time of writing, but nonetheless its theme is consistent with Kosman's other reporting of bank predictions that '10 to 15 percent of PE-owned companies will default annually from 2012 through 2014 … putting 1.875 million Americans out of work' (Kosman, 2009, pp. 50–51) – a loss of US employment comparable to that created by the GFC.

At issue is whether the predicted collapse of PE-owned companies will promote the next global credit crisis.

Governance overload?

Inability of the governance regimes to eliminate corporate misbehaviour has been a theme coursing through this chapter. It may be that not only are the codes inept, but also possibly too many have emerged. This theme underpinned the 2004 *AFR* opinion piece in Box 1.4, when obviously there were fewer such governance codes than now.

Box 1.4 NAB's nemesis: over-governance

The wood has got in the way of the trees … [former leader of the Australian Liberal Party] John Hewson recently observed that rather than a lack of information at National Australia Bank [NAB] there was substantial information but little willingness to accept responsibility (*AFR* Opinion, April 2).

Another explanation for NAB's problems is that they are the outcome of over-governance rather than under-governance.

A dominant feature of the current claims and counter-claims made by NAB directors and others is the lack of clarity regarding where both intermediate and ultimate responsibility resided.

Whatever else can be gleaned from the current brouhaha over which directors should go and which should stay, the NAB affair ought to evoke fresh thoughts over the direction corporate governance is taking.

NAB's labyrinth of committees – the board per se, its audit committee, risk management, internal control and the like – appear[s] to have created a silo-like mentality in which, as Hewson suggests, information was collected on virtually everything.

But proprietary rights attaching to who knew what and who 'owned' the information ensured a form of information asymmetry, fracturing the flow of information to those with the power to make decisions. Arguably, NAB illustrates how many of the governance problems relate more to over-governance than to under-governance.

Of course that view runs counter to the current CLERP 9 proposals and the ASX [Australian Stock Exchange] Corporate Governance Council's guidelines.

Like the so-called Sarbanes–Oxley masterpiece in the US and the UK's Combined Code, the Australian push is to layer governance mechanism upon governance mechanism to cover every possible kind of malfeasance and misfeasance.

Coverage of the NAB meltdown illustrates how the focus in most of the governance proposals is on individuals' personalities, tending to cloud the real issues regarding governance structures.

That is fair enough, in so far as once accused of improper practice one has to defend one's reputation. But the cult of the individual has taken over, as the NAB affair now so vividly illustrates.

If governance proposals were more directed at the overall system of governance, rather than at providing the means of looking over every corporate officer's shoulder, perhaps information would reach those who are not only empowered to make the decisions but are responsible for them.

We suspect that the layering of corporate governance mechanisms acts against that. Perhaps the NAB affair points to the need to rethink corporate governance reform. It may be that the current swath of governance proposals is attempting the impossible, fixing the system with additional layers of rules of the kind that have failed in the past. It could be that the modern corporate structure, complex and global, is ungovernable using the conventional means. Rather than attack complexity with more complexity, perhaps a better outcome would be to invoke simplicity. Rather than more rules and more board subcommittees creating information silos (and producing more barriers between the board and the information they need to make the decisions) there needs to be less filtering and less sanitizing.

The best part of a century ago the educational philosopher Alfred North Whitehead explained that if something is said often enough, everyone begins to believe it. That seems to describe the present corporate governance push declarations that more compulsory procedures and more rules must be followed and that more mechanisms have to be in place to purge companies of their management ills. It is noteworthy that the PwC report on NAB points to a focus on process, documentation and procedures manuals.

The same observation appeared in the HIH Royal Commission report. What evidence is there that separating the functions of audit committees, internal control overseers, risk management committees, probity committees, remuneration committees, audit appointment committees and the like has achieved anything worthwhile? There isn't any. Contrary to the avowed intention, it could be that the path corporate governance reform is taking is making complex modern corporations ungovernable.

Perversely, the NAB affair might be a valuable catalyst for some new thinking on corporate governance.

(AFR, 4 April 2004, p. 60)

The above practice was prompted by the fact that Australia was in the process of revving up its governance regime. HIH's failure had evoked a political push. This, no doubt, was encouraged by the Sarbanes-Oxley legislation in the USA two years earlier. The connection between HIH and Enron (and earlier the notorious activities of Australia's Bond Corporation), which were all audited by the international Arthur Andersen partnership, invited the political urge to beef up Australian governance rules, especially those pertaining to independence of directors and auditors.

We suggested that NAB's management problems were perhaps the consequence of too many rules, too many committees, a poor understanding of the nuances of foreign exchange dealing, and the tortuous route information had to travel to reach directors. PwC had pointed to NAB's obsession 'with process'. In a way this was forgivable, for such is the dominant characteristic of corporate governance regimes – in the UK's Combined Code, Sarbanes-Oxley in the USA and the ASX's *Principles and Recommendations*. HIH Royal Commissioner Justice Neville Owen was extremely critical of corporate governance being perceived as a set of processes. To him corporate governance entailed directors and management creating a framework that would result in an ideal commercial environment where the interests of stakeholders were protected (see especially the Report by HIHRC, 2003, pp. 103–6).[10]

Of particular note is that none of the regimes protected UK and US investors against substantial losses due primarily to managers' misbehaviour or otherwise poor decision making when the worst of the 2007–09 financial meltdown occurred. Processes and rules regarding auditor and director independence, compulsory audit committees, and in the USA rules separating audit and non-audit services, prescribing auditor rotation, imposing ex-auditor employment moratoria and the like, offered scant protection.

However, it may be that argument that there are too many governance rules, that NAB suffered from governance overload, inadvertently implied that the current corporate structure was redeemable. It ought not to have done so, as we seek to demonstrate in this monograph.

Against that backdrop it is not surprising that the great American jurist Judge Louis Brandeis (see Hartmann, 2010, p. 209) wrote in 1933 in his dissenting judgment in the *Liggett v. Lee* case, which drew on the *Santa Clara* decision:

> The prevalence of the corporation in America hassled men of this generation to act, at times, as if doing business in the corporate form were inherent in the citizen, and has led them to accept the evils attendant upon the free and unrestricted use of the corporate mechanism as if these evils were the inescapable prize of civilized life, and hence, to be borne with resignation … Although the value of this instrumentality in commerce and industry was fully recognized, incorporation for business was commonly denied long after it had been freely granted for religious purposes. It was denied because of fear. Fear of encroachment upon the liberties and opportunities of the individual. Fear of the subjection of labor to capital. Fear of monopoly. Fear that the absorption of capital by corporations and their perpetual life might bring evils similar to those which attended mortmain [immortality]. There was a sense of some insidious menace inherent in large aggregations of capital, particularly when held by corporations.

Both the US and the UK governments post-GFC have enacted more of the same regulations, notwithstanding that the GFC evidences that they cannot protect

investors. Especially in boom periods, corporate Australia, as with its overseas counterparts, is out of control. Surely that invites serious thought regarding the modern
corporation and, more importantly, how effectively it is structured as well as how to
account for its wealth and financial progress? Indeed, what are the best ways through
which to prosecute modern commerce?

Notes

1 Details of company formations are provided in Hannah, 2013.
2 A detailed analysis of TARP appears in a 2010 APRA working paper by Grant and Ellis
(2010).
3 Unless otherwise stated, all opinion pieces (shaded material) and extracts thereof
reproduced in the monograph are written by Frank Clarke and Graeme Dean.
4 The Center for Responsive Politics predicted that in the 18-month run-up to the 2012
election the cost of fundraising and spending on the election would be $5.8 billion,
including 'outside monies' of $508 million, up from $286 million in the 2008 campaign. See
www.opensecrets.org/news/2012/08/2012-election-will-be-costliest-yet.html (accessed
29 July 2013).
5 'Standards Hobble Auditors', *AFR*, 21 June 2012; the full opinion is reproduced in
chapter 4.
6 US and UK plans for banks 'too big to fail' are noted in Brooke Masters, 'US and UK
Reveal Plans for Banks Too Big to Fail', *AFR*, Companies and Markets, 11 December
2012, p. 18.
7 Jamie Freed, 'Rio Reviews Troubled African Mine', *AFR*, 22 January 2013, pp. 1, 6.
8 Adele Ferguson, 'Wake-up Call on Director Disclosures', *SMH*, Business Day, 22
January 2013, pp. 1, 4.
9 M. Agostini and G. Favero, *Accounting Fraud, Business Failure and Creative Auditing: A
Micro-analysis of the Strange Case of Sunbeam Corp*, Universita Ca'Foscari Venezia,
Working Paper Series n. 12/2012 September 2012.
10 In chapter 4 we note that similar major frauds persist, one of the latest being the $US1.5
billion scam against UBS. For details, see: 'Kweku Adoboli Guilty of Fraud Over $2.2
bn UBS Loss', *The Australian*, 21 November 2012; reproduced from the *Wall Street
Journal*.

2

ETHOS ABANDONED – HERITAGE LOST

Recovering true and fair

Accountability underpins the privilege of incorporation under government legislation. Reporting the financial wealth and progress in regular accounting statements of corporations is the universal requirement. In the British system, 'true and fair view' is the longstanding ethical and quality criterion defining modern accounting. Nonetheless, Alfred North Whitehead's notion of 'misplaced concreteness' endures: if one says something long enough, it will eventually be accorded a misplaced attribute of 'truth'.

Certainly such a misplaced concreteness is alive and well in the Australian commercial environment. There is a contestable view that the 'true and fair view clause' (TFV) in the financial reporting and disclosure provisions of the Australian Commonwealth Corporations Act, while retaining its position in the legislation, has been downgraded to a second order priority.[1] Some influential observers have even suggested it is an anachronism (e.g. McGregor, 1992).

Yet true and fair remains an outstanding quality criterion, unique to the British system of corporate governance. The arguments we pursue apply equally to the comparable US and IFRS phrase 'presents fairly' (see Zeff, 2007).

Commentators have claimed since the early 1990s both in the UK and Australia that 'true and fair' no longer has that role – that it is no longer a quality criterion that must be satisfied by entities in preparing and reporting financial data about their financial affairs. The downgrade in Australia has been contested by, amongst others, Melbourne commercial lawyer Mark Leibler (2002), Sydney School of Accounting Professors Walker (2002), Clarke and Dean (2002, 2007), Clarke *et al.* (1997, 2003), and respected Australian practitioners like Stuart Grant and Michael Coleman. However, it remains a convenient convention for many practitioners in the profession and regulators to claim that compliance with the accounting standards of the day will satisfy the legislative requirements.

In the comparable (albeit not identical) UK jurisdiction we note that this prominence of the TFV clause is supported by the UK Financial Reporting Council's

(FRC) 21 July 2011 Practice Note (PN 338). It confirmed that the TFV criterion 'remains of fundamental importance in UK GAAP [generally accepted accounting principles] and IFRS'; and it augmented the 19 May 2008 FRC PN 222 statement (following the QC Martin Moore's commissioned opinion) that 'true and fair' is what is meant by the (current wording) 'presents fairly' now used to accord with European Union (EU) directives. *True and fair remains the cornerstone of British financial reporting and auditing.* These practice notes reconfirmed the authority of the similar ideas in the 24 June 2005 FRC PN 85 and the 9 August 2005 FRC PN 119.

Once the 4th Directive had to be complied with by UK accountants and auditors in keeping with their EU membership obligations, the 'true and fair' clause had to be removed from the UK Companies Act and the 'presents fairly' wording inserted. However, it is important that this did not break the century and a half tradition in British financial disclosure, as the legal opinions just noted confirm. This interpretation creates a problem for there are differences in the versions of the IFRS used by different EU member states producing different financial outcomes, yet it is implied by each state that its corporates' compliance with its version of the IFRS 'presents fairly'. Clearly, to the extent that reported outcomes differ, if one version presents fairly then the others cannot. We suspect that none does, and since Australia has its own version – the Australian International Financial Reporting Standards (AIFRS), which differs again – if any European version does present fairly in the UK sense of showing a true and fair view, then the complying Australian accounts cannot.

Further, bearing in mind that the USA is yet to sign up for IFRS compliance, its primarily historical-cost-based company accounts differed substantially from their counterparts in the UK and Australia, 'fairly present' – God only knows what! Note also that the actual practices of some companies (granted not many) in several countries employ the override. Most notable, for example, were the directors and auditors of Société Générale, who in the 2007 financial year opted to report affairs as being true and fair; this followed neither the international accounting standards nor International Accounting Standard (IAS) 10 (Events After Balance Date) and IAS 39 (Financial Instruments: Recognition and Measurement). Société Générale backdated foreign exchange market (forex) losses that some argued had 'occurred' in 2008 into the 2007 financial accounts. The two auditors, Deloitte & Touche and Ernst & Young, and the French regulators approved of this use of the true and fair view override as possible under International Accounting Standards Board (IASB) rules. Several pre-IFRS UK instances of the override (1998–2000) are also cited in Livne and McNichols (2009).

In Australia, it should have been no surprise, then, when the Centro decision by the Hon. Justice John Middleton in *Australian Securities and Investments Commission v Healy [2011] FCA 717* put the issue before the community again. Critical to the company's reporting of unexpected financial difficulties was the unsupportable proposition that compliance with the accounting standards necessarily satisfied the requirements of the companies legislation.

Of importance is the relationship between the amounts reported to be due and reasonably described as *current liabilities* and those reported to be *long-term liabilities*. Obviously, whether liabilities are due within the immediate future or do not have to be paid for years has immediate liquidity and solvency implications. The inferences conventionally drawn from such descriptions and evaluations usually derived from them formed a theme coursing through the case. This is because of the relationships between the various categories of the monetary worths and amounts of assets and liabilities that distinguish one company's *financial* position from that of another. They also indicate the possible financial opportunities and constraints each separately faces, relative to those others.

Importantly, the notion of financial position implies that the financial statements are to provide insights into singular facts, aggregate commingled facts, and the inferences that might be drawn from them. In that context financial performance, being linked (articulated) to financial position, can only reasonably mean the financial outcome of the commercial activities and events causing a company's financial position to change since the previous reckoning – an all-inclusive notion. Juxtaposition of the financial position with the state of affairs in the Australian Corporations Act 2001 Part 2M.3 Division 1 (ss 296, 297, 299) in respect of the contents of the directors' report evokes an impression that the latter is injected by way of extending the prior concepts of financial position and performance, and by specifying general information about operations and activities.[2]

Several *financial opinion* pieces over many years were prompted by an understanding of such a background. Clearly it is central to our primary theme that accountants cannot tell it as it is and auditors cannot assure that what is said in the accounts can be relied upon, unless and until the true and fair matter is resolved.

In particular, the Centro litigation spurred several opinion pieces. Justice Middleton's 2012 judgment accepting a settlement emerging from an Australian class action by Centro's companies' aggrieved investors against its auditors and directors set the cat amongst the pigeons as far as the true and fair issue was concerned. Centro directors, CFO and CEO were found in a June 2012 prosecution by ASIC to have breached their duties by accepting, or otherwise missing, the misclassification of $1.3 billion 'current' liabilities as 'long term'. Clearly this liabilities misclassification would upset working capital, solvency and liquidity assessments. The $200 million class action against the company had been brought by two Centro shareholder groups in May 2008. In its defence Centro issued a cross-claim against its auditor, PwC. At the time of the settlement the financial press reported Centro's insurer would bear $38 million of the settlement, Centro Retail Australia $85 million, Centro Properties Group $10 million, and PwC $67 million.

Moreover, the decision confirmed that directors were responsible for the financials. Directors could not delegate that responsibility and they had to be financially literate to undertake it. More so, that such a misclassification was 'misleading' could only make sense insofar as it implied that the truth and fairness quality criterion specified in the Australian companies law had not been met.

Box 2.1 reproduces a June 2011 opinion.

Box 2.1 Fresh focus on 'true and fair'

The Federal Court decision in the Centro case on whether financial statements showed a 'true and fair view' has set the cat among the pigeons.

Whereas this turned on whether liabilities were reasonably classified long-term rather than short-term and whether the directors could be excused for relying on the auditors because of the purportedly technical nature of accounting, the implications may be wider than the Australian Securities and Investments Commission likes.

The decision notes that it is the directors who are responsible for the accounts. Auditors verify them.

But the outcome emphasizes the primacy of 'true and fair' as the quality criterion by which the contents of published financial statements are to be evaluated.

At issue is how does ASIC stand now regarding financial statements of corporations that conform with accounting conventions and the mandatory standards but nonetheless do not show a true and fair view of a company's financial position and performance.

Some day someone is likely to challenge a witness on whether the data in a company's financials that ASIC has 'let through' are serviceable for determining its wealth and financial progress, whether its derived solvency or debt-to-equity ratios, asset backing, interest cover and the like can sensibly be calculated – in short, whether the data yield the financial indicators which they are habitually used to determine.

And the honest, under-oath answer will have to be 'No'. That means it is neither true nor fair in any meaningful sense, for the products of many of the current standards fail miserably.

They contain fictions such as the deferred tax asset and liability figures, the goodwill 'globs' like those which appeared in the HIH Insurance accounts.

For decades some of our colleagues have railed against accounting's illusory nature in producing data that lack serviceability for those evaluative, analytical and decision-making purposes.

The argument is that misleading (creative) accounting is as much the consequence of compliance with the standards as deviations from them.

ASIC has nailed Centro directors and produced a needed victory. But we wonder whether it is homing in on the individual, seeking 'heads on poles', rather than trying to ensure the accounting system is effective.

The implications for many listed companies of the parlous state of accounting should be obvious – it is time the regulators also ensure that, irrespective of compliance with the current standards, the accounts of all listed companies are 'true and fair'.

(AFR, 2 June 2011, p. 63)

To our way of thinking the Centro case highlights that the financials must show a true and fair view, that auditors applying their honesty, their accumulated wisdom and other professional accountanting skills must give an opinion on whether they 'do' or 'do not', and that mere compliance with the accounting standards will not necessarily achieve that end. Mostly, compliance with the standards has been demonstrated in our other works not to show a true and fair view of either financial position or of financial performance. Creative accounting, we argue, is caused more by compliance with, rather than deviation from, the accounting standards. However, we know of no ASIC prosecutions for not showing a true and fair view on the grounds alone of either the directors of a company issuing financials compliant with the standards or of auditors approving them. Yet showing a true and fair view overrides standards compliance – by dint of its last position in the sequence of legislative requirements in Australia and the legal counsels' opinions in Britain – is the ultimate accounting qualitative criterion in the British system.

The class action led to a 14 May 2012 article in the *AFR* by Agnes King and letter to the editor by Antony Robb on 23 May. Our 22 June *AFR* opinion 'Standards Hobble Auditors' followed, an extract from which states:

> Agnes King is right enough in her assessment of *gatekeepers failing* in the Centro-PwC affair (*AFR,* 14 May). Antony Robb's letter ('Incomplete IAC standards in Centro', *AFR*, 23 May) supports King's claim, contesting the view of some that there was not a systemic accounting failure at Centro. King was also right in that accountants do not like bad publicity. But we question whether PwC will remain the poster-boy of 'auditors behaving badly' for long. Importantly, following the Cambridge Credit collapse in the 1970s, the introduction of class actions in corporate matters has made a mark. So the importance of this brouhaha is that the action demonstrates an effective method by which disgruntled corporate investors can chase compensation from inept corporate directors and auditors. Here, it seems there was a rather elementary costly error underpinning PwC's current troubles. But we can assure the public that accounting is so chock-full of unnecessary complexities, inconsistencies and commercial contradictions lending many to question in future class actions, that this affair was (at a technical level) near to child's play.

This theme had underscored several of our earlier opinion pieces that had considered ASIC's role in reviewing accounts. These were written with a view to informing the public that the true and fair override must be in directors' minds as they sign off the annual financials. In what follows regarding the Centro decision it is worth noting that ASIC somewhat agreed, by implication, with our override position of the true and fair view and indeed our understanding of financial position. There we explain that such a view should convince every financially literate person that the balance sheets of most listed companies are creative (to say the least), but, as noted above, by 2011 no such conclusions had come from Australia's regulator.

In many respects ASIC could be very pleased with the particulars of the Centro judgment, though it appeared happier with having collected scalps. ASIC thereby implied that it was comfortable with the idea that the true and fair override is well and truly alive, and has to be satisfied as the ultimate disclosure quality criterion. However, there were other implications for ASIC. Objection to passing off liabilities due for payment in the immediate future as being due in the distant future strongly implies that the nature and amount of liabilities – that is, when they are due, whether secured or unsecured, and the conditions attaching to payment – are critical elements of a firm's financial position. It implies that financial position is the relationship indicated by the nature, composition and current money's worth of its assets and the nature and money amount of its liabilities. It makes no sense to object to a financial (a monetary) misclassification unless the classification has such a financial implication.

That had been pointed out earlier in an opinion, 'A Moment of Truth for Accounts', and an even earlier opinion, 'Uninformed Prone to Shocks' (see Box 2.2). The former noted that the:

> rub for ASIC is that such is almost certain regarding the financials of most companies subject to its regulation. Yet virtually no company's accounts are subjected to either a director's abjuration or an audit qualification alleging that without amendment, adjustment and additional information, they fail to show a true and fair view of their financial performance and financial position. And published analyses of companies' performances – rates of return, earnings, interest covers and similar indicators, and their financial structures – debt to equity ratios, current ratios, working capital, asset backings, nature and worth of asset classes, nature and amount of liability classes, and the like, continue to be calculated (mostly) with the published income statement and balance sheet data.
>
> Response to the commission's present move ought to have the public on side, but protection of the investing public would be enhanced further were ASIC to stop the broader disclosure nonsense now.
>
> *(AFR, 15 October 2009, p. 63)*

Not that this is surprising. The matter has a long history, having been discussed a few years earlier during the apogee of the GFC when the financial mayhem for investment banks and other international financial institutions was also adding to the confusion regarding mandated financial disclosure. In a perverse way the GFC was fortuitous. An upside was the increasing publicity that inadequate disclosure received. Not that inadequate disclosure was ever a well-kept secret. It certainly has not been so in the English-speaking world since the late 1920s Royal Mail affair. Unexpected failures or companies experiencing unexpected financial difficulties are always accompanied by concerns that disclosure practices are inadequate for informing the public of the deleterious drifts in companies' wealths. The GFC batch – including New Century, Countrywide, Washington Mutual, Bear Stearns, Lehman Brothers, AIG, Fannie Mae and Freddie Mac in the USA – caused panic and outcry. Similarly, the financial crises of the UK's Northern Rock, Bradford & Bingley, Royal Bank of Scotland and Anglo Irish Bank (now Irish Bank Resolution Corp), France's BNP Paribas, Iceland's Glitnir, Germany's Sachsen Landesbank and Australia's Westpoint, Baycorp, Fincorp, Great Southern, Babcock & Brown, Allco, Centro and MFS highlighted the necessity for true and fair financial information, especially in overheated financial settings.

A 2008 opinion (Box 2.2) had considered the 'true and fair' issue highlighting the dilemma for the uniformed.

Box 2.2 Uninformed prone to shocks

Much of the present focus on regulation is seemingly not lost on [Australian] Prime Minister Kevin Rudd, who is now 'becoming more assertive ... to force investors to tell the market more about the complex financial instruments they hold'.

Note here his emphasis is on investors' disclosures – about directors' and others' loan margin calls, short selling and the like. Rudd's London press release, 'Leading the world in investor protection', lauds a global uniform regulatory approach. But the likely effectiveness of what amounts ultimately to more of the same doesn't warrant optimism.

Recent observations by Charles Macek that unnecessary systemic risks operate to the detriment of investors, and US Treasury Secretary Henry Paulson's 'blueprint' for overhauling the US financial regulatory system, deserve comment. They echo the call for 'new' regulations to show government is acting.

The ongoing 'transparency', 'self versus government regulatory' rhetoric invites the misleading inference that the problem lies exclusively in what is 'not disclosed' (in Donald Rumsfeld's terms), what we know we don't know – known unknowns – rather than with what we think we know, but really don't.

Recent financial meltdowns – Bear Stearns in the US, the UK's Northern Rock, Germany's [Sachsen] Landesbank, Australia's Tricom, Allco, Centro and Opes Prime – highlight again the folly of perceptions in overheated settings that asset market prices (especially property and shares) never fall. Our *Indecent Disclosure* captured the claim now being made by Macek and others that, 'This cycle shares characteristics with the past'. Greed and fear are perennial – in an upswing 'we allow standards to drop, we ignore fundamentals, we fail to undertake proper due diligence of the risks as we pursue easy gains'.

When the music stops, in the inevitable downswing, emotion snatches at scapegoats for the loss of confidence in the system nurturing such massive price corrections – seemingly so unexpected! Not surprisingly, Paulson's blueprint clamours for 'new' regulation. But the proposals are mere bandaid solutions – they are again mere sideshows to the substantive problems that have existed for decades.

In the previous round of boom and new-millennium bust, the sideshows concerned director and auditor independence and options-based executive remuneration. In the decade before that perceived 'unethical managers' exploiting the circumstances underpinning a debt binge were the culprits.

While each of the present reform proposals possibly has merit, are they really anything more than 'patches'? They are instances of *déjà vu* – more of the same with a twist – mostly on the fringes of the problem, overlooking (again) the critical role of financial information when it comes to injecting the inevitable 'trust' required in commercial dealings.

Those misplaced responses are unlikely to address well the major concerns aired regarding the financial dilemmas tormenting Allco, Centro, MFS and Opes Prime – problems sourced in the financial complexity of structures exacerbating intertwined related-party transactions allegedly not disclosed properly to the market under the existing consolidated reporting regime.

The present reactive vigilance of the regulators entails a system of continuous disclosure rules, monitoring and governance recommendations. All, however, are incapable of delivering an orderly, well-informed commerce, where the public has a reasonable chance to evaluate risks and benefits.

Soon, someone, somewhere, somehow, some day will be quizzed in a litigious setting over whether conventional consolidated financial disclosures are serviceable for disclosing a company's wealth and progress, for determining its critical financial characteristics.

And when they cannot explain away the nonsense, the focus might properly turn to those who thought up, passed into law, enforced and used for clients practices they certainly would not employ to assess, analyse or evaluate their own wealth and progress, solvency, capital security, borrowing capacity and the like.

(AFR, 9 April 2008, p. 71)

However, investors' greed in no way justifies inadequate, misleading disclosure. A matter of public concern at the time was the extent to which financial disclosure by listed companies was informative for institutional investors such as superannuation and retirement funds, and for public instrumentalities, as they evaluated their investments on behalf of shareholders, investors, members and ratepayers. That is, whether the financials told it as it is – 'it' being a true and fair view of the investments' worth, of the securities' actual current worth or the investees' financial wealth and progress. The financial institutions that, against expectations, either failed or were in severe financial difficulties had clearly given investors little reliable disclosure. Bandaid solutions comprising purportedly 'new' regulatory rules were inevitably proposed, but unless they focused on producing true and fair data they would be useless.

Some had already agreed with that. Witness the US complaint supporting the March 2008 filing for a class action against Bear Stearns. It drew heavily upon allegations that audited conventional disclosure misleads, confounds and deludes; that the disclosure fails to provide reliable data on liabilities and the market worth of assets.

In this regard what occurred in 2012 in a related Australian setting is heartening – namely, the judicial decision in representative proceedings or class action under Part IVA of the Federal Court of Australia Act (Cth) by several local councils against Grange Securities, a unit of Lehman Brothers. The ruling and settlement may prove to have ramifications universally for investors and advisers. The Hon. Justice Steven Rares ruled that the action brought under the 'misleading and deceptive conduct' provisions of a morass of legislative consumer protection provisions (thousands of pages), including the Corporations Act, should be upheld. There was evidence that, in promoting the sale to the local councils of the so-called innovative synthetic and other CDO financial investment products (referred to by the judge in *obiter* as a 'speculative bet'), there had been a lack of transparency by representatives of Grange regarding the riskiness of those assets. A settlement agreed to by all parties was approved by the court.

Significantly, and more generally, the judge suggested that the myriad legislative rules that need to be considered when bringing such actions need to be simplified. He recommended that in order to protect investors better the government bring simplified legislation, such as the former s. 51 (all of two pages) of the Trade Practices Act, before the parliament.[3] We agree.

Similarly, in what may also prove a watershed for future class actions in many jurisdictions, the Hon. Justice James Jagot ruled in a related class action case also brought in the Federal Court of Australia (FCA) by 12 councils against their local government financial services adviser that Standard & Poor's and several financial institutions had misled investors and breached their duty of care when they gave 'grotesquely' complex and risky assets (proportionate CDOs) a AAA rating.[4] Seemingly along similar lines to the FCA case, the US Department of Justice has issued a civil lawsuit against the ratings agency Standard & Poor's, claiming it inappropriately rated a particular CDO as AAA, causing investors to be misinformed about the CDO's risk. We await the outcome of this action with interest.

As the 9 April 2008 opinion (Box 2.2) notes, the Australian securities market then was uninformed. It generally remains so. The unexpected nature of the Centro, Allco, Babcock & Brown failures, coupled to the lack of transparency of the financial risks associated with investment products (like the CDOs), shouldn't really shock; it is inevitable. Based on reported financials, each looked to be a highly respectable investment vehicle with little, if any, evidence disclosed of impending financial difficulties – up to the time of each crash. Their financials were shown later to be either inadequate or misleading in one way or another, not being in any meaningful manner either true or fair. Centro evidenced that pattern of indecent disclosure. How assets and liabilities are valued and classified was clearly a critical matter and provided the opportunity for many market shocks. This theme had clearly appealed to Melbourne's *The Age*, when it published the opinion piece 'Indecent Disclosures Ensure there are Plenty of Market Shocks in Store', only a part of which is reproduced:

The aftermath of Centro's recent market mauling will determine whether it joins Enron, WorldCom, HIH, [and others] as household names ... In the 1970s, there were finance company–cum–property disasters in Australia such as Associated Securities Ltd and the secondary banking property market crisis in Britain. In the US, real estate investment trust sagas were prominent. The next decade produced the savings and loan fiascos in the US.

In the aftermath of these crises of market confidence, there were calls for greater transparency of corporate structures – and improved accounting for them.

These sagas have several common features:

- Rapid growth, often by takeover.
- Basic financial mismanagement, particularly mismatching risk associated with the maturity of financing and related asset acquisitions – refinancing risk (once referred to as the risk associated with 'borrowing short and investing long').
- Investment and financing strategies using complex (opaque) corporate structures.
- The familiar cries of alarm when the structures fall, with the suggestion that greed and the inability of effective checks and balances were the major culprits.
- The calls for improved accountability (and accounting).

The resulting corporate reforms seem designed to rein in the malpractices of a few. But their likely effectiveness in preventing similar collapses and providing an informed market are contestable ... Wealth and performance are likely to be understated as much as they are overstated. It is virtually impossible to know. Auditors face an almost impossible task. Serviceable financial disclosure requires a principle-based approach ... If [Australia's and other countries'] continuous disclosure system fails to provide reliable figures for liabilities and fails to disclose the market worth of a company's assets, it is unquestionably indecent, useless, and the market remains uninformed. Shocks, such as those surrounding Centro, are inevitable.

(The Age, 29 December 2007, p.16)

Evident to us from the particulars at Centro was the need for more transparency, the need for improved mechanisms for ensuring market confidence. This boils down to there being a lack of trust in the continuous disclosure system. ASIC failed on several occasions to have the High Court confirm what is required under this system. There is a regulatory review of the disclosure system as this monograph goes to press, but such concerns have had a long history. Double standards are a perennial problem likely to become worse with the advent of different versions of the IFRS in many adopting countries that began in 2005. Accordingly, the impact of the Australian version (the AIFRS) was assessed in the *AFR* opinion piece in Box 2.3.

Box 2.3 Double standards: a different take on true and fair

There is a sting in the tail of corporate disclosure reform under the International Financial Reporting Standards.

The Parliamentary Joint Committee on Corporations and Financial Services reported recently, and concluded that the Australian versions of the International Financial Reporting Standards meet the requirements of the Corporations Act.

Compliance with the new regime is going to produce data contradicting that which emerged under the Australian Accounting Standards Board standards, which were previously endorsed as resulting in a true and fair view of companies' financial performances and their financial positions.

Implying that compliance with the new AIFRS will show a true and fair view means what was previously signed off by directors (and accepted by the Australian Securities and Investments Commission and the Australian Prudential Regulation Authority as satisfying their regulatory requirements, met the ASX Corporate Governance Council's financial reporting guidelines and was backed by the professional accountancy bodies) was incorrect, presumably neither true nor fair!

Those who acted on what appeared in companies' financials have good reason to feel aggrieved by the implication that their decisions were based upon misleading financial information. The congratulations all round by those who have pushed so grandiloquently for the introduction of the AIFRS will provide cold comfort for those misled in the past.

How will those penalized in the past for deviating from the previous AASB [Australian Accounting Standards Board] standards feel, now that they are forbidden to comply with them? Will they let bygones remain bygones? Imagine the prospect of court deliberations relying on those older, now discredited, AASB standards.

Myriad users of the data in financial statements are now to understand that what they were told was relevant, reliable, comparable and understandable, was not although for the most part all this has arisen in good faith, without any intention by either regulators or practitioners to mislead.

Despite the best of intentions those earlier profits and losses attested to were incorrect. Reported rates of return were wrong. The salient financial characteristics of companies calculated, circulated, commented on, peddled by analysts, brokers and commentators, the nature and composition of assets and liabilities, the worth of assets, gearing ratios, asset backing, assessments of solvency, asset backing and the like, declared financial performances and financial positions were wrong, misleading.

Many commentators contend that using the AIFRS will be commercially positive. Most submissions to the parliamentary inquiry suggested that it would be, despite some critics' uneasiness about AIFRS achieving comparability.

A prevalent view is that this is the way to go because the AIFRS are purported to be principles rather than rules-based. But nowhere has a general qualitative principle been declared. And frequently those who bleat the principles-based claim express an inconsistent desire for interpretations to avoid variations in the way those standards are implemented.

There has been uneasiness over practical issues such as how the AIFRS will apply to many smaller as well as listed companies, the impact of excluding many intangibles, moving to the asset impairment regime and its use of fair-value measurement, and the recourse to compulsory discounting.

But, surprisingly, there has been little concern that what was reported in the past as a consequence of compliance with the (now outlawed) AASB amounted to a form of 'compulsory creative accounting', equally misleading as the feral practices of those intending to mislead.

Our conclusion in *Corporate Collapse: Regulatory, accounting and ethical failure* (Cambridge University Press, 1997), that creative accounting is more the consequence of complying with the standards than deviating from them, is more than justified.

Critical has been the profession's downplaying of the true and fair criterion through promotion of the idea that compliance with the prevailing accounting standards meets the true and fair criterion specified in the Corporations Act.

The current rejection of the previous AASB exposes the compliance fallacy. A company's financials are to reflect the true and fair view of its financial performance and financial position. That is the most supportable overriding principle that accountants, auditors and directors can observe.

Interestingly, in its submission the Group of 100 noted that apparently the AIFRS had to be complied with even if that did not result in a true and fair view, contrary to the intention of the International Accounting Standards Board's aim. The point hits the spot.

If the outcome of the latest reform is that the AIFRS are taken to be other than general guidance to be pursued in the absence of disclosures considered more likely to achieve a true and fair view, little will have been achieved. That would be as untrue and as unfair as it can get.

(AFR, 11 March 2005, p. 83)

There the idea was reinforced that compliance with the current accounting standards is a major cause of misleading accounting. By then the official view was unintentionally confirming just that. By dropping the previous accounting standards and adopting the IFRS on 1 January 2005, officials were inadvertently admitting that many of the previous financials compliant with inconsistent standards were now deemed to have been wrong – misleading, no doubt neither true nor fair. Nobody, it seemed, cared, and certainly not the leading companies comprising the Australian Group of 100: they had championed the 'technical (in compliance with the accounting standards)' interpretation of what showing a true and fair view entailed.

Such was the euphoria surrounding the introduction of the new financial reporting regime. Without a restoration of trust in the system, commercial affairs will continue to be shackled.[5] The 29 December 2007 opinion highlighted a way forward: the reporting system needs to 'provide reliable figures for liabilities and … to disclose the market worth of a company's assets … [without which the system] is unquestionably indecent … and the market remains uninformed'[6].

True and fair: a turbulent history

The repetition (decade after decade) of the unexpected nature of many corporate collapses and the inadequate regulatory and professional responses needed an explanation. Unfortunately, the advent of the AIFRS following CLERP 9 (chapter 3 details its development) was of little help. Over many years it has been stated by members of the profession (both practitioners and academics) that true and fair is an 'anachronism'. By remaining silent on the issue and allowing the criticism of true and fair to pass without official challenge, ASIC (at least by implication) acquiesced to the proposition that compliance with accounting standards will necessarily ensure a true and fair view is satisfied. One wonders why the 'true and fair view' clause was not deleted when the Australian parliament had an opportunity (in the CLERP 9 deliberations, 2002–05) when considering whether Australia's GAAP should be supplemented by IFRS and have the 'force of law'. As noted (note 1), initially it had been proposed to be deleted in Australian Treasurer Peter Costello's 2002/03 draft CLERP 9 legislation. This followed the recommendations in the 2002 Report 391 of the federal parliament's Joint Committee on Public Accounts and Audit (JCPAA) inquiry into independent auditors and related issues, as well as the 2003 HIHRC recommendations. Arguably underscoring all the debate and concerns was a virulent form of the rewriting of the history of true and fair and what it was intended to achieve. For the phrase or its stronger equivalents had survived continuously in the legislation for nearly 150 years before the allegation that it had passed its use-by date was made in the early 1990s. This followed nearly two decades of press and practitioner rumblings. Table 2.1 provides a snapshot of that history and some more recent events.

The context of the 1844 UK Companies Act and the associated early requirement that companies were to provide *full and fair* accounts (see also chapter 4) makes it clear that, amongst other aims, it was drafted to assist in the funding of the growing capital needs of the expanding Industrial Revolution. To do so, the legislators knew they also had to honour the intention of providing the necessary protection for investors (shareholders and creditors) in companies incorporated under its provisions. The report of the 1841 Gladstone Committee of Inquiry into several major insurance and other financial frauds on creditors and shareholders in the late 1830s and early 1840s supports that view. The Committee proposed what was to be the antecedent Bill to the 1844 UK Companies Act containing the full and fair clause. It was by far a stronger criterion than the modern day-true and fair, though, as some have stressed, the overall intention was the same.[7]

TABLE 2.1 Selected dates in the history of the true and fair quality criterion>

Year	Event
1844	UK Companies Act – accounts required to show a *full and fair* balance sheet; focus on *investor* and *creditor* protection
1855	Limited liability introduced into the UK Companies Act
1856	UK Companies Act requires a *full and fair* balance sheet, *just and correct view* of the company's financial affairs – as part of a voluntary Table A
1900+	UK Companies Act requires accounts and audited balance sheet – profit and loss eventually was prescribed in the 1929 UK Companies Act
Mid-1930s	Some Australian states adopt the 1929 UK Act as own legislation
1945	*Fair* substituted for *correct* after 1945 UK Cohen Committee Inquiry and 1948 UK Companies Act
1961	Australian Uniform Companies Act adopts true and fair nomenclature
1970s–80s	125+ years without equivocation (perhaps the longest uninterrupted professional ethos in legislation)
	Accountants' and regulators' uncertainty increases – deviations irk regulators' – accounts must comply with standards *and* show a *true and fair* view
1988	UK QC Arden confirms that true and fair view is operative as a quality criterion
Early 1990s	The explicit override is said to be deleted from Australia's corporate legislation – described in textbooks in early 1990s as an 'anachronism' and contestably suggested by regulators as 'inapplicable'
	Profession presses the *technical interpretation* – that compliance with the standards leads to true and fair view; the *override* actually remains – different wording – explicitly the final disclosure criterion; Notes to Accounts disclosures if standards compliance does not provide a true and fair view
2002	Mark Leibler's submission to JCPAA, and Walker's and Clarke and Dean's suggest true and fair view is alive
June 2005	UK FRC PN 85 and similar August 2005 UK FRC PN 119 dictum – retain true and fair and professional judgment
May 2008	UK QC Martin Moore's opinion and the June 2008 UK FRC PN 222 dictum – true and fair is confirmed to be the cornerstone of British financial reporting
November 2011	UK FRC PN 338 reiterates true and fair's primacy

Most importantly, there appears to have been neither doubt nor any general unease that such a full and fair view of a company's financial state of affairs could easily be obtained by a professional acting honestly. Nor was there any unease with the appointment of one of the shareholders as an auditor, that knowledge of the company's business outranked today's obsession with the independence push. Nor was it contemplated (or so it seems) that either *full and fair* separately or in conjunction with one another had been, or were to be, attributed any special meanings in an accounting context.[8] Much the same can be said of *full and correct* in the nineteenth-century UK Companies Acts, and *true and correct* and then later *true and fair* in the1948 UK Companies Act following the 1945 UK Cohen Committee company law inquiry. *True and fair* in the Australian Companies (now Corporations) Acts has been retained since 1961.

For the most part of a century and a quarter there appears to have been general contentment with the true and fair (or its equivalent) format. We have more to say on fairness in the next chapter (p.60–63), but by the late 1960s through to the mid-1970s, in Australia at least, 'true and fair' produced considerable uneasiness. Likely this arose by virtue of the use of the override as justification for deviations from the accounting conventions of the day. Corporate Affairs Commissioner for New South Wales F.J.O. Ryan was an early antagonist, as his *Abacus* piece (1967) reveals. Calls for change had increased by the early to mid-1970s when, for example, the professional accounting standard prescribing depreciation on land and buildings was not being complied with by many companies. During 1975–77 thousands of corporates' financial accounts reviewed by the New South Wales Corporate Affairs Commission revealed the following annual percentage deviations from one or more prescribed standards: 25%, 55% and 85%. In the next four years another regulatory review found an average annual deviation of 41%. It was claimed by preparers that following the standards, especially the depreciation on land and buildings standard, would result in untrue and unfair accounts. This continued into the early 1990s with other standards being in focus. Despite the rhetoric, there was nonetheless little prosecution to prove the allegations that the override was being abused.

Bearing in mind the differences between the approved accounting practices then and those under the post-2005 AIFRS, the abandonment of the former in favour of the latter suggests that the prior practices were faulty. Unless, of course, we accept the untenable situation – that the financial position, financial performance and state of affairs are different now from what they were then. So, the likelihood is that those who deviated from the standards may, perversely, have been closer to disclosing a reliable view of a company's state of affairs – its financial position – than were those complying. Such a situation would be consistent with our theme regarding the current state of play – namely that creative accounting is more the consequence of compliance with, than deviation from, the accounting standards.

The statutory quality criterion

Despite the wrangling over what 'true and fair view' or 'presents fairly' means, they represent unquestionably the quality criterion to be met by the financial statements – the balance sheet is to show financial position and the income account financial performance. They are to be related to the change in the entity's cash flows over the relevant period through the required statement of cash flows.

Presently, Part 2M.3 of Australia's Corporations Act, 2001, requires company directors to prepare financial statements that comply with the approved accounting standards (ss 296 and 304) and show a true and fair view of its financial performance and financial position (ss 297 and 305). However, these requirements are modified by the caveats in sections 297 or 305 that, where a true and fair view does not emerge from complying with the accounting standards, such additional information as is necessary is to be shown in the *notes to and forming part of the accounts*. Three matters there are worth noting: first, the possibility that standards compliance will not result in a true and fair view is contemplated; second, rather than a second order requirement, showing a true and fair view is in effect the quality criterion to be met; and third, that neither financial performance or financial position, nor the more general state of affairs, are defined in the Act.

Taking the last point first, we might reasonably assume that those drafting the legislation (and similar legislation in other jurisdictions) perceived no difficulty in those terms, expecting them to be used as ordinary words in their ordinary meanings. They are terms one uses almost daily without any great difficulty. The financial position of the largest mining company in the world, BHP Billiton, is no different in specie than that of an individual, though no doubt infinitely more complex. The same can be said for financial performance and state of affairs.

The legislators have not seen fit to define financial position and financial performance. Accordingly, one would think that the following accord with most ordinary (non-accounting) thought:

Financial position: *position*, as noted in the above opinion pieces, is a relative term – where something specified is relative to where others are – for example, where a particular ship is relative to (say) another ship, or to a particular port or to the nearest landfall, etc. A company's financial position is influenced by the financial characteristics of its assets and those of its liabilities relative to the like positions regarding the assets and liabilities of other companies – that is, whether its assets are worth more or less than those of the others; whether its assets are more or less liquid, more or less necessary for manufacture of its products, etc., relative to the comparable positions of those others. Thus, the nature and composition of assets is a critical aspect of financial position. Because it is a dated position, *financial* characteristics of assets mean their current money's worths (if not money, then the amount of money each of them then 'embodies', the money amounts that can readily be converted into in the ordinary course of business) at that date or thereabouts. Likewise, regarding liabilities; also critical is their nature and composition – for example, whether secured (and, if so, relative to what collateral), when due for payment, whether they are necessarily to be refunded in the future (and, if so, when) are critical elements of financial position. At a specified date, the financial measure of liabilities is their face amount then owing.

Importantly, a company's financial position is not a number; it is the relationship of its assets to its liabilities, and is comparable to a similar relationship of other companies. For the nature, composition and monetary amounts of a company's assets and liabilities influence assessments of its solvency, liquidity, its gearing, general financial stability – indeed all the matters, advantages and constraints affecting its capacity to adapt to its economic environment. In sum, the financial position of a firm at a specified date is determined by *the nature, composition and money's worth of its assets, and the nature, composition and amount of its liabilities*.

Financial performance: this refers sensibly to the financial differences between a company's successive net equity calculations, from all sources other than additional capital inputs.

True and fair view: the true and fair view of financial position and performance of a company, as it is at a specific date, meaningfully refers to the *serviceability* of the data in its financials – that is, the effectiveness with which the data in its financial statements can be used in determining the company's financial characteristics. This notion of true and fair uniquely links the nature and composition, and the individual money's worths of a company's assets and the amounts of its liabilities, and the aggregates and sub-aggregates of various classes of them, with the significant financial characteristics habitually used to distinguish different companies. For habitually, a company's financial strengths and constraints are compared to assess its wealth and progress. These include indicators of earnings and notions of earnings (underlying EBITA, etc.), rate of return, solvency, liquidity, leverage, asset backing, interest cover, dividend cover and corporate earnings per share are calculated. The worth of one asset or class of assets is compared with that of another, and the amount owing by one creditor or class of creditors is compared with that of another (or with those due to be paid at a particular time). All that is a matter of financial commonsense, nothing special – other than it is not the way accountants appear to understand financial matters.

As discussed, 2005 saw the much-heralded introduction of the IFRS regime into Australian commerce, and, with its universal scope, commerce everywhere. It was Australia's Group of 100 companies' enthusiastic (at least its publicly reported) acceptance that motivated one of the opinion pieces above. Research for *Indecent Disclosure* more than alerted its authors to the inherent defects of the IFRS – in particular the nonsense perpetrated by the continuation of the 'goodwill' debates involving the financial amount of asset impairment (see Bloom, 2008), the continued recourse to future estimates in balance sheets, and the extra uncertainty created by the international standards setters' five-, then three-level fair value hierarchy. However, most importantly, it was reasonably difficult to swallow by all who had somehow argued for company financial data complying with the accounting standards with which they had to comply up to that point to now be told that those data were clearly defective and were to be replaced with something else. Curiously, investors in countries adopting the IFRS seemed to lap up being told that what they had thought to show financial position and performance pre-2005 clearly now did not; that what auditors had vouched for was clearly defective. For the differences in the newer IFRS and those prepared under the old standards were so marked that they both could not possibly be true and fair, though both could be wrong and unreliable.

They were, and generally remain so.

Technical nonsense

Since at least the early 1990s the accounting profession in Australia, amongst others, has pressed the idea that 'true and fair' has two official meanings. One (the profession's favoured stance) is a *technical* interpretation; the other is a *literal* interpretation that accords more with the layperson's understanding. In the former, whatever emerges from using the accounting standards is perceived as a true and fair view of financial position, financial performance and state of affairs as just defined. In itself, this is a reasonable proposition insofar as it *ought* to be that compliance with the approved accounting standards currently in vogue would provide the necessary relevant, reliable, understandable and comparable financial data showing financial position and financial performance. However, by virtue of the known instances of accounting under the AIFRS failing to produce reliable data, and the legislation's not too strongly veiled warning that they may not, maintaining such a façade of professional integrity is unforgivable and easily demolished. Yet few textbooks note this and few auditors see fit to question additional data. Auditors apparently believe what they see. Auditors habitually appear to accept data provided by management even if these are subjective or expectational (not factual). What seemingly is critical is that doing so accords with the standards.

Imagine that the understandings of financial position, financial performance and state of affairs that we pose were to be accepted by our accounting colleagues. First, it is almost certain that few accounts complying with the present AIFRS would be unchallenged regarding whether they showed financial position, performance or state of affairs. Second, either the auditors would have to qualify the accounts or insist that the audited missing data were set out in the Notes to meet the 'true and fair override' requirement. That issue was shown via an illustration of a publicly listed (though there unnamed) company's set of accounts in *Indecent Disclosure* (Clarke and Dean, 2007, pp. 81–85).

Relying upon the AIFRS compliance to show a true and fair view is perhaps seen as a let-out clause by auditors. ASIC's silence on the issue coupled to the profession's almost somnambulant attitude strongly implies its agreement with, or acquiescence to, the profession's stance. In respect of the profession's stance it would appear that ASIC supports the idea that standards compliance will result in a corporation showing a true and fair view of its financial position. There are many signs to support this claim.

In a 2010 Australian Administrative Appeals Tribunal (AAT) hearing, *Opus Capital Limited v. Australian Securities and Investments Commission*, reference was made to ASIC's *Response to submissions on CP 150*, 'Disclosing financial information other than in accordance with accounting standards', and the related *Regulatory Guide* (especially RG. 000.21–RG.000.37). Opus was successful. The reasoning in the AAT hearing was logically valid, insofar as it followed from evidence given by the applicant Opus Capital Limited regarding its representation of the financial disclosure requirements of the Corporations Act, but it was based on a substantial error of omission. For it is (at best) only a half-truth to imply that the Corporations Act requires financial statements to be prepared only in compliance with the Accounting Standards. This conveniently leaves out what emerges to be the ultimate disclosure requirement – namely, that the financials *show a true and fair view of the financial position and performance* of a corporation.

In a 2004 *BRW* article, 'True and Fair – Harder to Avoid' (of which an extract only is provided here), the significance of the true and fair clause was emphasized by Clarke and Dean as being 'harder to avoid':

> Directors and auditors now have to satisfy themselves that the data in the financials can be used to determine their company's wealth and progress, and is also serviceable for deriving those financial indicators – rate of return; solvency; debt to equity; asset backing; the nature; composition and money's worth of physical assets, and the amount of liabilities; and the like – ordinarily calculated with that data.
>
> We might presume that there is a greater likelihood now that one day directors' judgments on those matters may be scrutinized in court. It will be interesting to hear their arguments about how accounting entries – such as 'deferred tax debits' or 'credits', 'deferred expenditures' or the amount 'paid for an asset in the past' – are legitimately part of the denominator in rate of return, gearing ratios and the like. Our guess is that such arguments will be hard to sustain.
>
> Corporate stakeholders can only welcome the end of an era where much of the data did nothing other than confuse and delude. The day for such scrutiny of accounting data is fast approaching.
>
> *(BRW, 5 August 2004, p. 108)*

Attention there focused on the overriding direction that accounts must be true and fair for auditors to say explicitly that they are, but, of course, those pushing the 'compliance angle' wanted to argue that the US system of *in accord with GAAP* was better than what had served well for nearly a century and a half in the British system. Almost a decade earlier the first edition of *Corporate Collapse* (Clarke *et al.*, 1997, pp. 185 ff.) had demonstrated that some of the data – for example, tax effect accounting balances and other bookkeeping contrived debits or credits (with no external commercial referent) – would not meet the bill. Under the AIFRS, employing tax effect accounting became compulsory. Nothing has altered the situation. It remains a time bomb, yet to explode.

Understanding markets

In the USA the GFC autopsy, amongst other things, produced the suggestion that fair value accounting in its mark-to-market format had caused the financial meltdown. There, dispute arose following complaints by the banks required to mark to market financial assets reported as 'available for sale'. In contrast, those where the said intention was that they would be 'held to maturity' could be reported at their purchase price. That so-called business model-based rule had become a get out of gaol card for banks. *Intention* is impossible to adjudicate; it is impossible for auditors to verify. Understandably, marking to market as security prices tumbled meant that confidence dropped, which in turn forced prices down even further. Banks complained that they were unable to meet their Basel II capital requirements. That situation affected their borrowing capacity, lending capacity and ability to satisfy existing borrowing covenants, notwithstanding their claims that the 'intrinsic values' of their assets were 'in fact much higher than indicated by the market' and its associated 'temporary values'. Several matters are to be noted: first, 'intrinsic' is a nebulous term. Second, what was occurring is merely how markets work. Third, counterparties of one kind or another (lenders, borrowers, investors, buyers or sellers), those suggesting the values of mortgage-backed assets were temporary and that asset prices would rise in the future, could follow their individual assessments, as always happens in markets. Every confident purchaser and every seller believes their individual evaluations of the likely costs and benefits are more reliable than those held by those with opposite opinions. That situation is endemic to markets. It is the mechanism underlying business transactions. The market prices were merely, but importantly, the message to the public of (on average) the current weight of informed opinion. Interestingly, this had been argued before. Berger, King and O'Brien (1989, 1991) looked at operational matters in applying market values in illiquid markets, and even earlier the matter was well rehearsed in the current cost accounting debates of the 1970s (see Tweedie and Whittington, 1984).

An *AFR* opinion that examined financial disclosure telling a company's whole story – *telling it*, that is, *as it is* – was published near the beginning of the GFC (see Box 2.4).

Box 2.4 Accounting for a company's whole story

Corporations need less governance and more meaningful disclosure … Evaluating risk is back on the agenda in the current market maelstrom. Essential to that is that companies' financials 'tell it as it is' – their wealth and progress, how and to whom they are indebted. The Australian Securities and Investments Commission's latest consultation paper proposing voluntary disclosures quite rightly places disclosure up front.

But sceptics immediately pointed to flaws. We agree that this voluntary 'patch' will not prevent the unexpected collapses of intertwined private and public groups such as Westpoint. There remains a failure to recognize fundamental flaws in the disclosure regime, not only for debenture issuers but for other private and listed company groups.

Risk assessments necessitate an understanding of companies' wealth and performance. They require knowledge of whether an entity or enterprise perspective is used by complexly structured borrowing groups. You cannot get that easily from the current disclosure regime. ASIC's war ought to be on those fundamental matters.

The current pursuit of compliance via the raft of misdirected corporate governance and accounting rules hinders rather than helps. There is governance overload. Yet, the financials of virtually every listed company (and their consolidated group) disclose data mostly not serviceable in uses ordinarily made of them – assessing wealth and progress, risk and return, solvency, gearing, testing borrowing covenants. All these require data indicative of actual money or its equivalent.

Consider the wider disclosure regime than that examined in ASIC's latest consultation paper. Following mandated international accounting prescriptions (AIFRS – the Australian equivalents to international financial reporting standards) produces a potpourri of data for assets and liabilities – actual cash, cost, amortized cost, future net present value (NPV) speculations, fair values. There is a failure to report systematically assets and liabilities at their current market prices.

Accountants and auditors striving in that setting to tell it as it is face a virtually impossible task. Auditor-certified financial disclosures are almost certainly misleading, notwithstanding the best of intentions of directors, accountants and auditors. There have been repeated episodes of corporate crises, asset stripping, companies delisting or 'going dark' and private equity deals. Despite this, virtually no serious discussion has addressed whether the traditional corporate group is the most suitable medium for conducting public commerce in an orderly fashion.

Present accounting and governance regimes designed to rein in the malpractices of a few are unlikely to deliver to the honest majority an orderly, well-informed commerce. The general public has little chance of evaluating the financial risks and rewards. It is time to rethink entangled corporate structures, complex financings and inept accounting. Currently, it is impossible to tell from the financials of an individual parent company or its related group how they are travelling. Their wealths and performances are as likely understated as overstated.

What, then, is the alternative? Simply require that companies are run honestly and report honestly. That's a message clear enough from the companies legislation. Scrap most of the governance rules and accounting rules. Replace the AIFRS with a system based on a single quality criterion. To tell it as it is requires evidence-based financials capable of being verified by audit. This should be underpinned by the same sole 'serviceability' principle regulating the quality of goods and services elsewhere – that the data are 'serviceable' and 'fit' for the uses ordinarily made of them. That would produce financial disclosure without accounting artefacts, free of the counterfactual, where indecent disclosure always requires the deliberate intent to mislead, not merely a well-intended compliance with compulsory prescriptions: an uncomplicated system of auditable mark-to-market accounting; with data indicative of actual current money or its equivalent; a new-look accounting for corporate groups; and reinstatement of the true and fair honesty criterion as practitioners' primary guide.

All price and price level changes, all gains and losses would be brought into contemporary account. Tax effect 'deferred debits and credits' would be abandoned, expense capitalization would go. Depreciation would properly be the decreased asset price – neither the product of accountants' 'allocation of cost' nor the AIFRS's convoluted 'impairment' charge. The guesswork in NPV calculations would be gone. Accruals would accord with legal capacity to recover, not anticipated revenue. Money spent would be reported as 'gone', not as an asset's worth. Individual companies' legal separateness would be recognized formally and related companies' data arranged to provide insight into financial implications of the relatedness.

Consolidated financial statements could be replaced with 'group accounting data' rearranged to give the financial insights sought about related companies. Group companies' indebtedness could be arranged to distinguish who is indebted to whom internally and externally, and which in the group are net-lenders and net-borrowers internally and externally. This would be essential solvency information for each company in the group.

(AFR, 28 August 2007, p. 63)

Nonetheless ASIC's aim was then, and remains, unquestionably to ensure the accounting standards were complied with. Its counterpart international regulatory agencies have also adopted this approach.

With the illiquid markets battle intensifying, asset valuation and the mark-to-market issue remained top of the regulatory agenda. In relation to mortgage products and illiquid markets, the temporary valuations mantra was often trotted out to justify not writing down mortgage-related assets: four years on, those same types of mortgage valuations are being lampooned as 'outdated and lazy', albeit this time in the Australian setting,[9] and they are the subject of criticisms by judges in several Australian class actions rulings met earlier.

In April 2009 in the USA the actions of Congress and the Financial Accounting Standards Board (FASB) prompted the following *AFR* piece.

Box 2.5 Toxic plan is nothing but humbug

Rule makers' capacity for double-talk is unlimited. The debate leading to a decision to allow US banks to keep losses from toxic assets out of their income calculations and to give them greater flexibility with the mark-to-market models they use to value their toxic assets beggars belief.

As a world player, Australia is exposed to the illusion of US banks appearing to meet capital adequacy requirements, satisfying borrowing covenants, and increasing their income by as much as 20%. Curiously, the US accounting rule maker's announcement was received favourably by the stockmarkets. Banks will now find it easier to leave non-marketable toxic financial assets on their balance sheets at considerably more than they could fetch in the market. And where there isn't a market, more flexible guidelines are anticipated regarding the models they can use to 'invent' a non-existing price.

More flexibility is also predicted for classifying financial assets – whether to be 'held to maturity' or 'available for sale'. It is the latter that attracts the mark-to-market valuations, but now with greater flexibility regarding the models used to invent a number where the market is 'thin', so-called distressed, or where no market exists.

Thus we are faced with US banks having the capacity to parade balance sheets legally showing financial positions possibly far healthier than the previous misrepresentations underpinning the financial crisis in the first place. How can this do anything other than further mislead the market? True, the mark-to-market requirement has been a popular whipping boy; the alleged cause of the present crisis.

Without mark-to-market, many financial assets would be disclosed to be worth more than they could fetch in the market – that is, far in excess of the amounts they could contribute to discharge the banks' financial obligations.

Who is likely to have confidence anywhere where such nonsense is peddled? Loss of confidence is contagious, pushes the market down further and exacerbates the position. That is how markets function. Marking-to-market did not cause the problem; it merely reported the financial consequences of it.

There was always doubt whether some banks could afford to sell their 'toxics' to Treasury Secretary Tim Geithner's aggregator bank. By selling, some risked failing their borrowing covenants or meeting capital adequacy requirements once losses under the Public-Private Investment Program were brought into account. For many, that dilemma may have gone. Some may even profit from the deal.

But the Geithner plan may be less affordable for Geithner and the private partners. Possibly another grand plan has been scuttled by nonsensical meddling.

Those from the Sydney school have long supported the 'MTM' basis for asset valuation. Our objective is to best tell it as it is, which requires companies to disclose serviceable indications of their financial positions. The US version of mark-to-market had its flaws. But this latest meddling is utter humbug.

(AFR, 14 April 2009, p. 55)

While the actions of regulators generally will be explored in more depth in the next chapter, it is worth recalling the reported words of an informed insider, William McDonough, the esteemed former president and chief executive of the Federal Reserve, New York (1993–2003). He candidly contested the reassurances during 2008 of policy makers and practitioners that all was well with the system: 'Mark my words … this is a market of incendiary toxicity.'[10] Confirming this assessment[11] are numerous examples of major US financial institutions (like Citigroup, Sun Trust Banks in Atlanta, Hudson City Bancorp) which for four years (2008–12) had not written down their toxic GFC-related assets (mainly mortgage loans), arguing that the impairments were 'temporary'. However, not long after 2008 the music surely had well and truly stopped. Finally, it seems that at least in those reported cases institutions are no longer prepared to kick the can down the road. Impairments are now no longer deemed temporary. They perceive that such transparency moves will be good for the companies' share prices, but that begs the question of the market being ill-informed for those last four years – aided by accounting standards that permitted faulty values, deemed temporary by managers, to be retained.

The meddling of politicians in affairs of accounting at the nadir of the GFC exacerbated this toxicity and its implications. The transparency function of accounting, namely for it to indicate clearly the present financial position and financial performance of a company, its wealth and progress, was no doubt set adrift in such meddling. Telling it as it is had underpinned our opinion pieces a decade earlier, as revealed in a November 2002 *AFR* piece (Box 2.6).

Box 2.6 Accounting – telling it as it is [extract]

The IFSA (1997 Blue Book), recent ASX Corporate Governance Council directives, revised editions of [UK] Cadbury's 'best practice', Henry Bosch's [former Australian National Companies and Securities Commission (NCSC) chairman] latest code, CPA Australia's 'Financial reporting framework', the Ramsay Report, the government's corporate governance manifesto (CLERP 9) and the Federal parliament's August 2002 JPCAA Report (on auditor independence) have missed a golden opportunity to put 'truth and fairness' into companies' financial statements. They all fail to redress investors' uncertainty and overall discomfort with the financial reporting system ... Their recommendations and directives pertain only to the infrastructure of companies' governance systems, not to the tangible products of those systems ... not to the serviceability of reported financial information. Irrespective of the business acumen and ethics of company executives, auditors, and audit committees, the critical confidence issue is whether the financial statements disclose the actual financial outcomes of executives' management or mismanagement.

Without that, talk of radical corporate governance reform is empty ...

Surprise has been the confidence-sucking element, not because of any lack of controls but because of the failure of conventional accounting data to disclose the drifts in the companies' periodic wealth and progress ...

Noticeably, none of those pursuing that line says what those underlying principles are. CLERP 9 enumerates more rules, but no principles.

Clearly, no unique principle underpins Australian corporate regulation. But one is surely needed!

Arguably, corporate governance prescriptions would be more to the point were they to invoke a fundamental 'core principle' to ensure that audited accounting data were serviceable for indicating the wealth and progress of companies, were those data to provide the financial red flags signalling a company's actual financial performance and its actual financial position.

Compliance with the sophistries of the current raft of accounting standards doesn't do that, and neither will the adoption of international standards planned for 2005.

It should not so much be a matter whether the financials 'fit the rules' as that in accord with professional judgment they show a 'true and fair view' of a company's wealth and progress. Such a judgment requires the specification of a general quality criterion. In virtually every field other than accounting, serviceability (or fitness for use) is the primary quality criterion. The evidence is that it should be likewise for corporate financial information.

Accounting failure is the core governance problem. And, whether intended or accidental, accounting failure induces corporate governance failure, audit failure, executive failure, regulatory failure and ethical failure. Until accounting is reconstructed to tell it as it is, effective corporate governance is a pipe dream.

(AFR, 7 November 2002, p. 63)

Legislators and regulators have failed to get the principles right. All the huff and puff of the corporate governance debate has turned reform of corporate regulation into theatre, mainly farce. Irrespective of what the accounting standards require, the need is for financial statements to tell it as it is – to show a true and fair view of financial position and performance. Compliance with the AIFRS occurred, as noted, generally on time in 2005, as did compliance with IFRS in many countries. It was, however, accompanied by the continuation of unexpected failures with questionable accounts late in the previous decade, and, with the demise of numerous merchant banks and related shadow banks during the GFC, there was continued use of off-balance sheet vehicles accounted for under conventional consolidation accounting and, contestably, continued misuse of fair value accounting with inventive feral accounting for Repo 105s and 108s, again using the shadow banking sector. With all of those corporate misdemeanours the warnings in many of our opinion pieces were more than justified.

Furthermore, in 2010, ASIC acquiesced to the omission of the 'true and fair' caveat in its argument in the *Opus v. AAT* case. That was inexplicable and unforgivable. We argue here that, on any reasonable reading, the financial disclosure criterion in the Corporation Act lies with showing a true and fair view.

Most disturbing is that the respondent there, ASIC, failed to challenge Opus's representation regarding the Corporations Act's disclosure requirements, when that glaring omission made its financial representations in effect untrue and grossly misleading. ASIC thereby gave implicit support for the idea that a true and fair view would necessarily result were the AIFRS complied with. In such cases where ASIC doesn't pursue the true and fair view of financial position and performance requirements, then it is not satisfying its oversight of compliance with all of the provisions of the Corporations Act.

Somewhat softening concerns with this case and its approach is the reported Australian proceedings on behalf of 43,000 investors owed $1.8 billion being brought in the Western Australian Supreme Court (*Williams v. Great Southern Finance & Ors (S CI, 2011 03616)*, 29 October 2012) by Ferrier Hodgson, the liquidator of Great Southern, an agriculture investment business that collapsed in 2009. The formal writ against the directors and Great Southern alleged that seven of its directors overstated assets and understated liabilities and expenses in financial statements in the reports leading up to the 2006 fiscal year. It is claimed that the statements neither complied with accounting standards nor gave a true and fair view of the company's financial position.[12] At least from the liquidator's perspective in this instance it seems that 'true and fair' is being afforded an equal standing with the accounting standards. As previously noted, however, an ongoing concern in situations like this is that the Act is silent on the notions of *financial position* and (as implied by the grammar and confirmed by tradition) *financial performance*. They certainly need defining in an articulated fashion, underpinned by a decision usefulness focus, and the notion of true and fair needs greater elaboration.

A workable meaning of true and fair (presents fairly)

Both *Corporate Collapse* and *Indecent Disclosure* articulated the case for injecting the notion of *serviceability* (usefulness) into the accounting framework. There, serviceability was suggested as the primary criterion underpinning assessments of whether data in financial statements showed true and fair representations of (or fairly present) financial position and financial performance.

By serviceability, the financial data are meant simply to be fit for the purposes for which they generally are used in the ordinary course of events. *Fit*, in the sense that they can not only be used with confidence to produce a result of a predictable genre, but that the outcome also satisfies all the technical bookkeeping and mathematical rules that such a product is expected to have. *Generally used* refers to the uses made of the data in the ordinary course of financial calculation in business affairs to predictably indicate known financial attributes and characteristics of firms. *Used … in the ordinary course of events* insofar as the uses are the usual ways in which the data are used in the daily business affairs in everyday commerce. Each of those aspects is important. The first necessitates that technical niceties are in order. It specifies that the data have been constructed in accord with the double entry bookkeeping rules. Additionally, that the rules of arithmetic are complied with – that either numbers of like purchasing power dimensions are added, subtracted, multiplied or divided, or that the result of the arithmetical process is adjusted to compensate for any difference. Thus, as the general purchasing power (GPP) dimension of money varies from time to time, it is necessary that, before or after monetary sums are arithmetically manipulated, an adjustment is made to compensate for their different GPP dimensions. For, whereas it is logically correct arithmetically to manipulate numbers with different dimensions, the product is uninterpretable unless the difference is compensated for.

Monetary amounts are sensibly used in the context of the purchasing power they had when received or expended. So, whereas $200 received at t_1 when the index of the changes in the general purchasing power of money was (say) 100 can be added to

$200 received at t_{10} when the same index stood at 400 to produce a legitimate total received of $400, it is meaningless to suggest that the $200 at t_1 had had the same financial significance as those at t_{10}, for the former had four times the general purchasing power of the latter $200. It is financially sensible to refer to financial power only in terms of dollars with equivalent purchasing power. That is, to note that the amount received at t_{10} has the financial significance of $50 received at t_1 or that the $200 received at t_1 had four times that received at t_{10}. Thus, numerators and denominators of financial ratios must also have to be in the same GPP dimensions for the quotients to be useable for evaluative purposes.

Against that background, specifying 'in the ordinary course of business' imposes the matter of reasonable frequency on the use, such that it is not unusual, not abnormal, their use is more or less predictable. It necessitates a level of normality. Envisaged is the common meaning that accountants producing the financial data, auditors attesting to their reliability and company officers issuing them to the public understand them to have in everyday commerce.

Used … in the ordinary course of events automatically excludes improper, impossible uses deliberately enforced or resulting from rank ignorance of what individuals in commerce habitually do with such data. Just as virtually everyone understands that motor mowers are for cutting grass – that they are not designed for shaving inches off concrete kerbing – a reasonably held commercial commonsense might be expected to inform virtually all that companies' financial statements inform about, and are used to assess, their financial state or condition – their wealth and financial progress.

Serviceability is a common enough term used elsewhere to indicate the necessary quality of goods and services in a fair trade. It is the paramount criterion underpinning consumer protection. Indeed, it dominates the consumer protection criteria in nearly every field of human endeavour … except accounting. Of course, it may well be claimed that accounting data are not products or goods in the way other products and goods unquestionably are, but individuals use the accounting data in financial statements in observable ways to discover observable financial characteristics. We know, for example, that the data in financial statements are extracted and used to calculate myriad absolute quanta and numerous ratios for *intra* and *inter* company, temporal and inter-temporal analyses. We know the data are so used because daily the financial pages of newspapers and the financial press report the outcomes of such analyses, television news bulletins usually devote time to them, brokers' broadsheets cover such things, as generally do stock exchange analysis services. There is little dispute either regarding what the various aggregates – totals and sub-totals for various classes and subclasses of assets, equities and liabilities – mean. Nor is there much disagreement regarding meanings of either the commonly cited characteristics – for example, solvency, liquidity, rate of return, return on assets, asset backing, interest cover, dividend cover, working capital – or the financial characteristics of which they are indicative.

Some hope of commerce being more of a fair game accompanies the above-mentioned Australian class action decisions by the Hon. Justice Steven Rares relating to a unit of Lehman Brothers, and the contemporaneous ruling of Mr Justice Jagot against Standard & Poor's and several financial institutions that they misled investors and breached their duty of care in giving complex and risky assets a AAA rating. This is augmented by the US Justice Department's early-2013 action against Standard & Poor's for their misleading AAA ratings with respect to certain CDOs.

There has been little disagreement on such matters in authoritative texts and scholarly dissertations, with few complaints regarding the core understanding of the moving financial relationship between financial positions and financial performances.

Where the data in financial statements measure up to those features, they most likely are as true and fair as one could reasonably expect. There is no good reason to accept less.

Notes

1 By way of background, two of the authors (Clarke and Dean) were invited to make a submission to the Australian Federal Parliament Joint Committee on Corporations and Financial Services (JCCFS) in late 2004. See JCCFS Report and submissions at www.aph.gov.au/Parliamentary_Business/Committees/Senate_Committees?url=corporations_ctte/completed_inquiries/2004-7/aas/report/index.htm (accessed 28 November 2012). The Committee was then considering the draft CLERP 9 legislation. Amongst other things, it was considering whether the true and fair view clause should be retained. In a somewhat 'deep throatish' exercise (as we understand it) two of the senators on the Committee had discovered that the 'true and fair' clause had been 'secretly', or at least without prior discussion, omitted from the draft Act. They sought someone in the administrative section of the Joint Committee to 'leak' the omission to Clarke and Dean, ask them to make a submission and request that they go to Canberra for the Public Hearings (Dean, 2005). There, the history of the clause and its ongoing importance as an overriding quality criterion was emphasized. Other submissions adopting a similar view included those by leading Australian accounting professor Robert Walker and leading commercial lawyer Mark Leibler. Following subsequent hearings into that draft legislation the true and fair view clause was reinstated. It retains its position.

2 The following extract from s. 299 is apposite: '(1) The *directors'* report for a *financial year* must: (a) contain a review of operations during the year of the *entity* reported on and the *results* of those operations; and (b) give details of any significant changes in the *entity's state of affairs* during the year; and (c) state the *entity's* principal activities during the year and any significant changes in the nature of those activities during the year; and (d) give details of any matter or circumstance that has arisen since the end of the year that has significantly affected, or may significantly affect: (i) the *entity's* operations in future *financial years*; or (ii) the *results* of those operations in future *financial years*; or (iii) the *entity's state of affairs* in future *financial years*; and …' (emphasis added).

3 Federal Court of Australia, *Wingecarribee Shire Council v Lehman Brothers Australia Ltd (in liq)* [2012] FCA 1028.

4 Federal Court of Australia, *Bathurst Regional Council v Local Government Financial Services Pty Ltd (No. 5)* [2012] FCA 1200.

5 A similar point in *obiter* is made by the Hon. Justice Steven Rares in *Wingecarribee Shire Council v Lehman Brothers Australia*.

6 For discussion of the need for trust to ensure an informed, equitable and efficient financial system, see Sapienza and Gonzales, 2012; and Chambers, 1993. This position is further supported by the following headline and argument in Jonathan Weil, 'Come On, Fess Up: Now's the Time to Write Red Ink Off the Balance Sheet' (*SMH*, 15–16 September, 2012, pp. 10–11); and Rares's judgment (see note 3).

7 For example, Chambers, 1973; and Chambers and Wolnizer, 1990, 1991. The last two articles are reproduced in Parker, Wolnizer and Nobes, 1996. An article by Nobes 2009, provides some contrasting views about the override.

8 This is well explained in Chambers, 1973.

9 G. Wilkins, 'Auditors Implicated in Lender's Downfall', *SMH*, Business, 15 December 2012, p. 4.

10 Reported to have been said in an interview with William McDonough in the offices of Merrill Lynch, prior to its being subsumed within Bank of America, as cited in Justin O'Brien, 'Where the Buck Stops', *AFR*, Review, 27 July 2012, p. 1.

11 See the headline in the *SMH*, 15–16 September 2012, pp. 10–11.

12 Jonathan Barrett, 'Great Southern Seven Cited', *AFR*, 5 October 2012, p. 7.

3

REGULATION MISPLACED

Corporate regulatory agencies such as Australia's ASIC, the Securities and Exchange Commission, the Department of Justice and the FBI in the USA, and the UK's Financial Services Authority and its Serious Fraud Office (SFO) have been criticized in particular over the last decade. Concerns have broadly been: slowness to act after a major corporate dilemma has been revealed; actions have been deemed to be reactive rather than sufficiently proactive; overemphasizing settlement prior to court decisions has resulted in a lack of precedents; and failing to produce systemic reforms.

A recent PBS *Frontline* report into the GFC and the lack of any criminal prosecutions was pointed in its criticism of regulatory agencies in the USA.[1] The inability of the Justice Department or FBI to mount a criminal action against any Wall Street bankers contrasted with the swift actions resulting in approximately 1,000 finance people being prosecuted after the Savings and Loans fiasco. It also stood in stark contrast to the many post-GFC prosecutions (by the same agencies) against smaller 'loan originators', leading to many being gaoled. The suggestion put by the representatives of the Justice Department and the FBI that prosecuting for fraud in such complex circumstances was not appropriate appeared limp. This was especially so given the publicity and level of expectations associated with President Barack Obama's mid-2009 announcement of the US Fraud and Fraud Recovery Act, which supposedly made such prosecutions simpler to mount.

In Australia ASIC, for example, has been lampooned for not pursuing possible criminal behaviour more strongly, most recently in the Securency scandal. Indeed, where it has pursued such action it has done so seemingly ineptly, losing large corporate litigations, such as against directors Jodee Rich and Mark Silbermann at One.Tel and most recently against 'Twiggy' Forrest, founder of the large Australian miner Fortescue Metals. Further criticism, including from judges, relates to the regulators' desire to engage in out-of-court settlements that entail fines with associated 'no liability' clauses by those being prosecuted (often directors, auditors and companies).

Judges have resented being perceived as rubber stamps of negotiated fines.[2] Other concerns relate to impositions like the SEC's 'no new clients for a specified period' penalty. Also, further concerns in many jurisdictions focus on the addition of more and more layers of regulation. This is contrasted below with the suggestion that a less detailed, but more focused, mode of regulation seeking consumer protection is more likely to produce a better, more informed commercial outcome.

National corporate sector institutional regulatory frameworks take various forms. Often multiple agencies have designated responsibility for different parts of the system. In Australia, for example, four main agencies administer policy: the Reserve Bank of Australia, the Australian Treasury, the Australian Prudential Regulation Authority and the Australian Securities and Investments Commission. Together they comprise the Council of Financial Regulators, which the International Monetary Fund (IMF) recently described as 'a non-statutory, coordinating body chaired by the Governor of the RBA created to contribute to the efficiency and effectiveness of financial regulation by providing a high-level forum for cooperation and collaboration among its members. The CFR operates in normal times and in crisis situations, meeting quarterly and, as necessary, on an ad hoc basis'.[3]

The multiple agency form of administration applies elsewhere, such as in the USA. There, agencies like SEC, the Justice Department and the Commodity Futures Trading Commission operate, with the Federal Reserve overriding monetary controls. In the UK the FRC is said to be more of a one-stop regulatory shop – despite the fact that the Bank of England and the Treasury formally have major oversight roles. This changed on 1 April 2013 after a review. Under the Financial Services Act 2012, a new regulatory framework for financial services abolished the Financial Services Authority and restored to the Bank of England its responsibility for financial stability, melding macro and micro prudential regulations through its Financial Policy Committee, the Prudential Regulation Authority and the Financial Conduct Authority.

It is unclear what constitutes the best regulatory regime. Nor is it clear whether it is contingent on cultural and national features, such as whether lobbying is dominant or not. Gary Rivlin's revealing article, 'How Wall Street Defanged Dodd-Frank' (*The Nation*, 20 May 2013), showed that US countervailing forces against re-regulation in the post-GFC period were extremely well marshalled, with millions of dollars spent to ensure the financial sector retained most of its flexibility and profit potential.

Inept theory

In discussions on regulation generally many commentators revert initially to outlining theories of regulation like the public interest, industry capture and private interest theories (e.g. Stigler, 1971; Zecher and Philips, 1981). Those longstanding theories come out of mainstream economics and provide generalized arguments for describing both the factors motivating regulation and the form it takes. They generally merely put things into boxes.

In abstract terms, each theory envisages key groupings of players – producers, consumers and government – and provides some general but descriptive insight into the regulatory process. However, because of that generality none is able to explain regulation in specific institutional, historical and technical settings. The inability to predict the strength of the lobbyists is a major deficiency in all proposed theories. Furthermore, while some of these descriptive theories anticipate poor regulation from the perspective of the public (particularly regulatory capture and private interest), they do little to provide normative guidance on how to drive system reform that is better focused on the public's needs. To this end a recently completed doctoral thesis at the University of Sydney made the following acerbic observation in an analysis of financial sector regulation:

> the rationale for regulation in the banking sector (see *e.g.* Goodhart, Hartmann, Llewellyn, Rojas-Suárez, and Weisbrod 1998; Llewellyn 1999; Schinasi 2006; Peláez and Peláez 2009; and Grossman 2010) … usually tracks through various well known theories of regulation after invoking some kind of market failure as the central impetus for regulation. For example, with respect to banking, modern appraisals of the need to regulate typically cite information asymmetries as crucial. Unfortunately many of the standard theories – industry-capture theory, public interest theory, economic interest theory and so forth – are limited as they do not explain (or describe) well the existence of current regulatory regimes, in banking and otherwise. Much of the poverty of these theories can be traced to neglect of particular institutional arrangements, forfeiting detail for the promise of generality.
>
> *(Tuite, 2013, p. 159)*

For much of the GFC and the ongoing eurozone debt crisis, there has been a penchant for pursuing the regulatory blame game. Chamley *et al.*'s (2012) autoptic and plausible assessment in the *American Economic Review* detailed a plethora of actors who closed their eyes, resulting in trust taking a holiday, and precipitating the contagion that characterized the GFC:

> The list of culprits for the crash of 2008 … includes regulators, rating companies, politicians, housing policy, Fannie Mae and Freddie Mac, boards of directors, bank managers, the Federal Reserve, derivatives, bad lenders, bad borrowers, accounting, a housing bubble, repeal of the Glass–Steagall Act, illiquidity, fraud, opacity, and leverage. The crime's victims were initially localized, but quickly spread to most asset markets, product markets, and financial institutions, harming millions upon millions of innocent people.
>
> The spectre of large financial intermediaries undergoing actual- or near-death experiences flipped expectations. Suddenly, everyone expected bad times and took steps to ensure that outcome. Fear became well worth fearing. Politicians stoked the fire, suggesting that depression was right around the corner. And as if guided by an invisible hand, employers started laying off workers in

droves. By the end of 2008, the firing free-for-all was putting 700,000 people on the street each month. *Trust in financial companies took a holiday*. Those who knew the system best, the bankers, were the first to panic. They understood what everyone else soon learned – that no one, not even the heads of the banks, really knew what particular banks, including their own, owed and owned and that, when push came to shove, no bank could *trust* any other bank.

(Chamley et al., 2012, p. 113, emphasis added)

Importantly, revisiting what was highlighted in chapter 2, Chamley *et al.*'s overview identifies the need for transparency and trust in any properly functioning financial system. A market-based system needs to operate as a fair game for all interested parties. The fairness concept is a will-o'-the-wisp,[4] but it pervades commerce. It underpins public finance theory, with references such as a 'fair tax' base. Also, a fair game is integral to modern secular finance theory. Universally it is part of all stock exchanges' primary objective, namely to ensure a 'fair and orderly' market in securities trades and it pervades contractual dealings generally (albeit augmented by bonding and monitoring arrangements) and wage negotiations in particular (see chapter 5). Also, in chapter 2 it was shown to be critical when discussing the legislative true and fair view requirement for corporates' financial information disclosures. The fairness notion, when expressed positively, is often perceived as problematic. Yet contracting parties generally know when it is absent in their dealings.

Repetitive periods of economic boom and bust are characterized by oscillating pushes for less and for more regulation. The late 1980s to mid-1990s and the late 1990s to the mid- to late 2000s are especially illustrative. Gillian Tett's (2009) analysis of those periods in *Fool's Gold* shows that the securitization products, credit derivatives such as CDOs (and variants like CDOs squared) of asset-backed securities and the now infamous collateralized debt swaps (CDSs) were initially developed and trialled nationally on a small scale by financial institutions in the late 1980s and early 1990s. They were claimed to have the microeconomic benefits of removing 'risky assets' from their balance sheets and providing a means to increase their reported profits. It was not initially appreciated how the systemic risk inherent in these new forms of financial intermediation was amplified by the unfettered interconnected activities of the shadow banking sector. In July 2010 a US Federal Reserve Staff Report revealed the extent and significance of that interconnectedness (Pozsar *et al.*, 2010, revised 2012). Recent FSB analysis of 25 countries and the eurozone area suggest the shadow banking sector has grown from around $US14 trillion in 2002 to around $67 trillion at the end of 2011 – that is, to about half the $130 trillion for the entire banking sector and 'significantly larger than the $US43tn held by insurers and pension funds'.[5]

There were many catalysts for securitization. They included attempts to circumvent Basel I's and II's stringent lending rules, namely the increased capital reserve requirements with their concomitant increased borrowing costs, attempts to redress declining profits from traditional commercial lending, magnified by losses due to the dotcom (internet technology) crash. Tett's analysis cites J.P. Morgan Chase's experiences to confirm this. To facilitate the chances of successfully promoting such derivatives' products and reduce the regulatory costs faced, financial institutions sought deregulation with the Federal Reserve and Bank of England, stressing the purported macroeconomic benefit of risk mitigation of the then new, albeit untrialled, products. They were claimed to mitigate economic cycles and allow greater risk sharing across companies and countries. Their promotion melded well in an increasingly globalized market culture. Further, it was claimed that they enhanced market liquidity and ensured financing, in particular that house mortgages would be more readily available to the lower-income class – something the US Congress had requested.

Initially the purportedly simple products were taken up on a small scale. They were relatively simple for finance specialists, though hindsight has shown that they were still perceived as complex by the non-finance specialist. The new investment assets entailed securitized tranches of 'conforming loans' that had satisfied the finance sector's credit risk standards. They were also marketed on an individual basis. Mass marketing soon followed, and the take-up increased substantially. There were critics of securitization. Products were said to be opaque, complex, and many purchasers were said to be too unsophisticated, too easily fooled by the marketing patina, a gloss that failed to disclose adequately those products' underlying high risks. This was exacerbated as the complexity of the products increased in the early to mid-2000s. Risk increased as sub-prime loans replaced the conforming loans as the base for the securitization. With CDSs becoming the main product in the early to mid-2000s, systemic risk increased. Securitization, it would emerge, had falsely fuelled expectations of dispersed risk. With the interconnectedness of the finance sector (and globalization generally), the opposite occurred in late 2007 and 2008. Effectively, the major financial institutions worldwide with their own interests paramount had used excessive leverage to increase their loan book of credit derivatives. The increased leverage risk seems to have been overlooked, or at least downplayed by the re-engineers, regulators and consumers. As noted in chapter 2 (notes 3 and 4), some judges are now viewing the promotion and sale of these products as having been undertaken in a misleading manner.

Charles Ferguson's 2011 documentary, *Inside Job*, and the 2012 book of the same name (especially pp. 240 ff.) provide compelling evidence to suggest politicians and academic economists became bedfellows in the deregulatory push, facilitating the mass securitization of those initial 'relatively simple' mortgage-backed securities into purportedly AAA-rated tranches as part of the more complex synthetic CDOs, so-called CDOs squared, and then the even more toxic CDSs.[6]

Former Federal Reserve Chairman Alan Greenspan is reported to have said that the major financial institutions, regulators and ratings agencies were sufficiently staffed and resourced to understand fully the nuances of these innovative products. This view coincided with a much freer (lower-cost) credit described in contemporary criticisms of this approach, such as Fleckenstein's *Greenspan's Bubbles* (2008), as the Greenspan 'put'.

Critiques like those of Fleckenstein went unheeded. As Tett's account shows, these new financial products (both the initial relatively simple and the later more complex and riskier derivatives) were minimally tested by their promoters, and only reviewed in a fashion by various regulators, ratings agencies and auditors. They were tested in the sense that they were found to be capable of being sold and financed. However, they were not subjected to sufficient rigorous independent pre-testing of new developments, as occurs in other areas – as with new model cars or medical innovations. Even if it were possible to devise appropriate testing, it appears that the prudential regulatory agencies were unable to meet that task as, contrary to Greenspan's reported view, they did not have available sufficient resources (mainly staff with the required skills).

Digressing briefly, consider for a moment the gatekeeping role of the major ratings agencies, Moody's, Standard & Poor's and Fitch, in facilitating this securitization-based asset bubble.[7] Ratings agencies have existed in the USA since the mid- to late 1800s, with the triopoly emerging by the 1930s. Their valuations of those synthetic assets were critical, and their related 'issuer pays' fee model became the subject of much concern. It is reported that the aggregate credit rating revenues of the triopoly were $4.9 billion by the end of 2005, having grown at a compounded annual growth rate of 17% during 1998–2005 (Langohr and Langohr, 2009, p. 419). According to Coffee (2008, pp. 71–72) in a congressional testimony:

> Today, the rating agency receives one fee to consult with a client, explain its model, and indicate the likely outcome of the rating process; then, it receives a second fee to actually deliver the rating (if the client wishes to go forward once it has learned the likely outcome). The result is that the client can decide not to seek the rating if it learns that it would be less favorable than it desires; the result is a loss of transparency to the market.

Ratings agencies' functions were reviewed post-GFC and additional restrictions on their activities initially occurred as part of the Dodd-Frank Wall Street Reform and Consumer Protection Act of 2010 (see especially ss 931–39H).

In earlier boom and bust periods auditors were often described as the high priests of the financial world, with their attestation of the reported asset and liability values. Gillian Tett (2009, p. 118) appositely bestows the high priest tag this time on the ratings agencies. Waxing lyrical, she observes: 'Like priests in the medieval church, ratings agencies' representatives spoke the equivalent of Latin, which [while] few in their investor congregation understood ... [they] were comforted by ... the priests' ... guidance and blessings [which] after all made the system work: the AAA [ratings] anointment enabled SIVs to raise funds, banks to extend loans, and investors to purchase the complex instruments that paid great returns, all without worrying too much'. SIVs' roles and those 'AAA anointments' during the GFC are now pivotal in class action suits by aggrieved investors who felt the opinions were flawed, leading to investors being misinformed (see notes 3 and 4 in chapter 2).

The financial pressures of the GFC saw the deleterious impacts of those highly speculative untried financial products and resulted in most of Greenspan's (and many others') claims being rebutted. Individual institutions tanked in what one commentator referred to as 'the greatest heist of the century' (Ferguson, 2012). It facilitated what is likely to be known as the greatest meltdown since the 1930s Depression. Many were bailed out by governments under the TARP and similar governmental arrangements. Some were taken over. At the macro level, countries such as Iceland and Ireland were bankrupted; others like Greece, Cyprus, Spain, Portugal and Italy have haemorrhaged financially for several years, and regulatory-imposed expenditure cut backs (the contestable austerity measures) have resulted in unemployment levels rising substantially, with associated social unrest. The problems continue for those governments, and fears persist that what occurred in the Great Depression – a long period of economic downturn worldwide – might be repeated. Five years after the onset of the GFC those fears endure.

Financial engineering wins

The post-GFC period has revealed how toxic those financial engineering products actually were. It was briefly noted above that, instead of looking closely at the nature of the inherent risks of the products, and at how they had been developed and marketed, diversions appeared. Any deficiencies in those products, it was said, would be corrected by natural selection. Re-regulation was not the answer for many in the financial sector. It was seen by many as simply too hard because of the political lobbying wall that confronted effective financial reforms.

Scapegoats were immediately sought: 'Fair value accounting' prescriptions via the mandated Financial Accounting Standard (FAS) 157 and IAS 9 requirements and the regulatory prescriptions of the USA and other countries to increase home availability were attacked. FAS 157, Fair Value Measurements, for instance, required in an inactive market setting that fair values be determined on a three-level hierarchy (five levels had initially been proposed) for asset valuation purposes:

- *level 1 assets* – for which a market and prices are available;
- *level 2 assets* – where the existence of a market for like assets allowed some discretion for owners regarding which prices they chose; and
- *level 3 assets* – where markets are inactive, and owners could mark-to-model, or 'mark-to-myth' as Buffett (quoted in Davies, 2010, p. 114) observed.

Further, regarding the abovementioned US Congress-backed drive to increase home availability for the poor through the mid-2000s, the regulatory actions of Fannie Mae and Freddie Mac (purportedly influenced by politicians from Capitol Hill) immediately spring to mind. Inevitably there were pleas for fewer of those sorts of interventions – rather, pleas to let the market sort things out. This resonated for a while, but the re-regulatory push was never far away, again to be resisted vehemently by the free marketers.

Following the submissions to and tabling of the January 2011 report of the US Congressional inquiry into the causes of the GFC, subsequent analyses coupled to a strange mix of political forces forged implementations of the US Dodd-Frank Wall

Street Reform and Consumer Protection Act. It was initially passed in July 2010 with approximately 60 major proposed reforms. Re-regulation was now the catch-cry, seeking a return more akin to the regulatory regime that followed the Great Depression. Dodd-Frank certainly put consumer protection in focus. In principle, it entailed financial regulatory rules seeking greater transparency and controls, especially over financial derivatives – like CDSs and forex swaps. Also, there were concerns that the shadow banking sector needed to be brought under the regulatory umbrella – the so-called Volcker rule springs to mind – but this drive faces renewed counter-punching from the finance sector, with it being suggested that US Treasury Secretary Tim Geithner was a major advocate.[8]

Deregulatory moves in the finance sector had occurred in the previous decade. These included a resistance in the late 1990s to any attempts to restrain the liberalization of derivatives' use by, supposedly, the then Treasury Secretary Robert Rubin, Federal Reserve Chairman Alan Greenspan and leading economist Larry Summers. Their deregulatory push had shepherded legislation that forbade 'any' regulation of derivatives, now or in the future, according to Ferguson (2012, p. 249). However, returning to the 2000s, there were also moves to re-regulate the system, entailing the return of the separation of commercial and banking investment arms of financial institutions. This separation had been enforced since the 1930s through the Glass-Steagall Act until its repeal under President Bill Clinton's 1999 Financial Services Modernization Act, also known as the Gramm-Leach-Bliley Act.

What is missing from much of the oscillating debates above is any in-depth discussion of what corporate regulation seeks to achieve. Surely, given that the corporation is a social construct (chapter 1), its continued role as a part of society (through legislation) requires continued review as to whether maintaining its special status as a 'legal' (not 'human') person should persist. It is essential that investors are confident that such a legally created person will not engage in anti-social behaviour, and that there is confidence that there is *trust*, in a commercial system within which the corporation plays a major part. Regulations then should provide protection for investors in the broader sense and for other corporate participants, employees, customers and the state. Within this general regulatory framework, accounting's function needs reassessing. As we propose, it needs to communicate effectively to investors and the other participants financial information that is generally relevant for their normal uses, such as by allowing relative assessments of risk, solvency, liquidity, profitability.

The heads-on-poles syndrome

In *Indecent Disclosure* (Clarke and Dean, 2007, p. 33) it was suggested that for many decades in several countries (the latest then following the early 2000s market failures such as Enron and WorldCom in the USA, Maxwell's insurance empire and Polly Peck in the UK, and HIH and One.Tel in Australia) there had been a misplaced emphasis by regulators seeking a swift review, seeking individuals to blame, and enforcing independence rather than honesty in commercial affairs.

Getting heads on poles appears to be the way to gain brownie points by the modern regulator. In that respect, commonsense has been out-gamed, for financial commonsense would have one believe that the primary objective of financial regulation is to prevent wrongdoing. As already pointed out, a successful prosecution evidenced that consumer protection had failed either because the defaulter was smarter at the game than the regulators or because the regulators had not kept their eye on the ball. Neither is particularly flattering for the regulator. Some of the problem may well lie with governments insofar as the funding made available is insufficient to recruit many of the top, the smartest, individuals to the regulators' ranks. It may also be the result of agency officials preferring to recruit many second-rate functionaries rather than a few of the best. Or that the regulatory objective is not well appreciated.

Whatever the cause, the prevention objective is lost on most of the agencies. Perhaps they are seduced by the contestable belief in market efficiency favouring a totally self-regulatory approach. Most regulatory agencies claim that they are strapped for resources. In *Take on the Street: What Wall Street and Corporate America Don't Want You to Know* (2002), onetime chief accountant at the SEC Arthur Levitt outlines political interference by the US Congress to starve the SEC for funds if it did not toe the line on government policies – that is, unless it did not sacrifice its supposed 'independence'. Lobbyists were far too strong. Following the Enron affair and when swamped with the corporate accounting irregularities over the next five years, the SEC had fewer staff on tap than before Enron, despite the surge in its workload. Not surprisingly, agencies like the SEC fall back on the market efficiency argument.

Harry Markopolos in evidence before the US Congressional hearing into Bernie Madoff's greatest fraud in US history expressed his strong conviction that the SEC did not have the necessary skills to have unearthed Madoff's Ponzi scheme, even if they had listened to his pleas for action over the previous 10 years. Several books attest to events that occurred (see Arvedlund, 2009; Markopolos et al., 2011). In Australia, similar calls for greater resourcing of regulatory agencies are common. Greg Medcraft as chair of Australia's ASIC was keen to herald in 2012 how effective his staff had been under adverse budgetary conditions, but contemporaneously he suggested that investors needed online testing before being permitted to invest. He thereby strongly implied the ineptitude of ASIC in protecting the public.[9]

Post-GFC, both the UK and the US governments have strongly indicated that their corporate regulators have failed to protect investors and others by recommending new agencies that they claim would offer such protection. This view has been backed by evidence in damning reports into the activities of both the UK's Serious Fraud Office by the attorney-general (November 2012) and the Securities and Exchange Commission by the 2010–11 US Senate inquiry and report into the origins of the GFC.

Regulatory episodes noted above suggest that regulatory concerns persist. The regulatory focus generally has sought to tinker with or to patch over the system's defects. Such patching (increasing existing rules and sanctions, generally) has been the dominant mode of regulatory reform. This has been to the detriment of a fundamental rethink of how the system might be changed to become more service-able in protecting relevant commercial parties. The Bank of England's Andrew Haldane agrees (Haldane and Madouros, 2012).[10] Drawing on several recent articles mainly pertaining to risk and uncertainty, he suggests that, in complex situations like the world of commerce, the persistence with a strategy of more regulation may not necessarily be better than less regulation in achieving desired outcomes. He particu-larly questioned the efficacy of ongoing attempts to refine the Basel capital ratio now in its third iteration (an example of more of the same type of regulations). Haldane's proposition will be shown below to apply equally to the tinkering or refinements (more corporate governance, regulations) to control the ubiquitous modern corporation.

The case particulars of the opinion pieces in this chapter relate primarily to reg-ulatory responses to concerns expressed in the decade after the dotcom, Enron and HIH-type episodes. The catalysts for the pieces are many, some new, some old. Underlying each, however, have been the ever-increasing complexity and inter-connectedness of commerce partly due to increasing globalization, and the com-plexity of present-day corporate structures and their related intertwined financing and operations (see chapters 1 and 6), coupled to the increased use of the relatively unfettered shadow banking sector.

Categorized as regulation entailing 'rules and sanctions', the recent regulatory *modus operandi* is consistent with concerns associated with the evidence adduced earlier in *Indecent Disclosure* (Clarke and Dean, 2007, p. 28). There, successive reg-ulatory reforms for over a century were shown to have proven ineffective. Consistent with a tick-box mentality, an ever-increasing rules and sanctions approach has proven inappropriate in mitigating the types of behaviour evident pre- and post-GFC.

Most significantly, corporate regulators like the SEC, FSA and ASIC continue to employ patching variants designed for corporations of a different variety and operat-ing in different commercial environments. Particulars immediately below augment ideas outlined in chapter 2 on specific accounting regulation, namely the true and fair view quality control criterion.

The public generally has very poor perceptions of the actions of the financial sector and related financial regulation. The UK Attorney-General Department's inquiry into the Serious Fraud Office provides evidence to support this claim. Also, corre-spondents to financial dailies portray succinctly the public's worst perceptions of inadequately controlled activities. Consider the following 2012 *AFR* correspondent: 'The relentless bad behaviour by banking titans must be addressed through an over-due, radical disclosure. Offending banks should publicly disclose their nefarious roles running a mismatched book, packaging worthless mortgages into CDOs [given AAA ratings by official ratings agencies], rigging Libor or facilitating money laundering in every communication for 10 years' (*AFR*, 2 August 2012). Throughout the preced-ing month there had been concerns expressed about banks' poor corporate citizen-ship. Financial press headlines in articles and letters appeared, like the following: 'Where are the Watchdogs when Predators Prowl', 'ASIC Palms Off Regulatory Responsibility', 'Backflip on "Too Big to Fail" Banks' and 'Where the Buck Stops'.[11]

The Prologue notes that those perceptions have been reinforced by fines imposed and settlements agreed to by major regulators on major financial institutions in the Libor and European interbank offered rate (Euribor) manipulations.

The Australian Prudential Regulation Authority (APRA) was also in the Australian Treasury's firing line: 'APRA No Good in a Crisis: Treasury'.[12] At issue was APRA's limited avenues for reining in any rogue activities of local branches of foreign financial institutions if it felt they were putting Australia's financial system at risk. In later criticisms the attention switched to APRA's inability to monitor the non-(shadow) banking sector. Many of its overseas regulatory counterparts were equally lambasted on this matter. They are under the spotlight for not *keeping watch* effectively. However, as chapter 6 notes, in contrast, during the latter part of the first decade of the 2000s APRA was on the front foot in seeking to unravel group operations.

Regulatory reforms under the microscope

Given this, one can take a bead on the actions generally of regulatory agencies. A common regulatory response to the public perceptions of anti-social corporate behaviour is for the government to which the agency answers to create an image of swift action, to enact a form of 'regulatory theatre', seeking high-profile prosecutions. Such responses, however, reinforce the cult of the individual and do little to rectify systemic defects. The evidence reveals this feature had been prevalent in earlier decades (see Clarke *et al.*, 1997, pp. 9–16).

In the late 1980s to early 1990s US prosecutors went after the leading junk bond buccaneers, Ivan Boersky and Michael Milken, for their roles in the junk bond financing of the Savings and Loans entities.[13] A decade on, other perceived corporate villains, like Enron's Kenneth Lay and Jeffrey Skilling, were targeted, as was Conrad Black for his involvement in the Hollinger International saga. In the UK a good example is the 20-year affair ending in 2012 with Polly Peck's founder and CEO Asil Nadir being prosecuted by the SFO and sentenced to 10 years' gaol on charges of theft from Polly Peck International. In all cases the system deficiencies, such as complex corporate group structures, inadequate controls over intra-group financing, as well as uninformative group accounting, remain essentially unaddressed.

This has elements of *déjà vu*. Australia had experienced in the early 1970s attempts to prosecute Australian high-finance flyers like Kenneth Nestel of the largest securities trader, Minsec Securities Ltd, and Alexander and Thomas Barton of Brins Australia Ltd fame. The financial papers were full of headlines regarding them at the time. This followed the 1960s prosecutions at H.G. Palmer, Reid Murray and Latec Investments. Each time, individuals were carpeted and sometimes imprisoned for short periods, but, notwithstanding the regulator's bathing in the glory of having embarrassed a corporate bigwig, the system remained basically unaltered: investors remained poorly protected. One might reasonably argue that the strength, indeed the effectiveness, of a regulatory system lies more in its preventing default rather than in achieving prosecutions. Unfortunately, policing, capturing and ineffective prosecuting (like no-fault settlements), rather than providing ongoing protection by preventing wrongdoing, continues to be the regulators' preferred way.

Regarding the regulatory frameworks in the USA, UK and Australia, much has happened over the last two decades following numerous corporate crises, but reforms are more procedural, cosmetic rather than effective. As noted, the UK prudential regulatory powers of the Bank of England were transferred in 1997 to the newly created Financial Services Authority, which together with the Treasury provided a tripartite model to regulate the financial sector as a whole. This was similar to Australia's Reserve Bank, ASIC and APRA tripartite regulatory model, which had operated since the late 1990s. However, in the USA the regulatory system, which was said to be more fractured, is ever present, with action by enforcement agencies like the SEC, the Justice Department, the Commodity Futures Trading Commission as well as the post-GFC Federal Reserve's monetary controls, QE1, 2 and 3. However, there were also major deregulatory developments over the period, such as the 1999 Gramm–Leach–Bliley and the 2000 Commodity Futures Trading Acts.

Australia's Company Law Economic Reform Program (CLERP) initiative is instructive. It was announced by the treasurer in March 1997 with the declared objective 'to ensure that regulation is consistent with promoting a strong and vibrant economy and provides a framework which assists business in adapting for change'. Accordingly, issues of deregulation and reducing business costs were prominent. Fundamental reforms to securities regulation were forecast to 'facilitate a more efficient and competitive business environment'. Key factors necessitating such reforms were identified as: globalization and market behaviour; liberalization of world capital markets; and information and technological developments in the information industry and in the financial system. Corporate law, it was said, 'hadn't kept pace'. An 'economic approach' to corporate regulation was said to be the way for a future that would feature 'information transparency' and 'cost effectiveness'. Against that background, it was to be expected that the nature of accounting standards and the mechanisms by which they would be established would receive attention. There were to be reform programme papers (initially only six were expected) open for public comment, and from which subsequent legislative proposals would be developed. Indeed, nine CLERP sets of legislative amendments have resulted in the nearly 15 years since.

CLERP 9 was the major financial regulatory reform. It began life as an Australian Treasury discussion paper in March 2002 against a backdrop of extensive corporate accounting and auditing capers and market failures in Australia and elsewhere. Under a clarion call for re-regulation, albeit tempered by a Liberal federal government sponsoring a free-market approach to commercial affairs, it represented a review of Australia's financial reporting and disclosure laws. Also influencing the reform deliberations were the outcomes of the government-sponsored Royal Commission into the HIH affair (HIHRC, 2003), the federal parliament's Joint Committee of Public Accounts and Audit's *Review of Independent Auditing by Registered Company Auditors* (JCPAA, 2002) and the Ramsay Committee's report (Ramsay, 2001) on auditor independence, as well as the passage in July 2002 of the US Sarbanes–Oxley corporate governance requirements. The main matters addressed in the CLERP 9 were:

- audit reform (auditor rotation, moratorium on ex-auditor employment by ex-clients, auditor independence, a likely ban on non-audit services);
- a disclosure framework (continuous disclosure regime, conflicts of interest issues in respect of financial products, the disclosure of information relating to debenture issues, a 'sophisticated' investor test to be applied to *test the adequacy* of financial disclosures); and
- advocacy of greater participation by shareholders (in companies' AGMs and matters of director remuneration, etc.).

With the enactment of CLERP 9, claims were made that the legislative responses were 'lighter' than their Sarbanes–Oxley counterparts. They were claimed to be principles- rather than black letter law-based. There is evidence for the former, but little for the latter claim.

Examination of corporate failures over several decades (especially immediately pre-GFC) exposes the longstanding penchant across multiple jurisdictions for the abovementioned regulatory theatre and the regulatory/deregulatory oscillations:

> The Depression in the 1930s coincided with or created the forces leading to several national stockmarket downturns and finance sector manipulations revealed in examinations, like Ferdinand Pecora's US Senate and Banking Inquiry … the New Deal's SEC emerged as the US corporate cop. 'Big Business' would be subjected to greater controls as its purposes were reconsidered within a regime of greater social scrutiny. After a brief regulatory surge in the first half of the 1930s, the business professionals (accountants and lawyers especially) responded by taking over the running. Self-regulation would re-emerge as dominant in what has been described as an extended co-regulatory environment. The initial regulatory response and counter deregulatory initiatives are understandable if one considers the differing theories of regulation … [T]he early 1970s and 1980s accounts by Posner, Zecher and Phillips, and Cranston, provide sound summaries of the public interest and private sector pushes for regulation and deregulation. That framework aptly explains how (for example, in more recent times) the US *SOX* legislation is being criticized for being overly burdensome on companies, how the Australian corporate regulator ASIC is being attacked for its performance – as indeed is the financial services regulator APRA. 'Where were the regulators?' is a commonly asked question today – as it was in the 1930s. Perhaps the regulators continue to employ remedies designed for corporations of a different variety, operating in a different commercial environment. Or perhaps it is not unreasonable to suggest that regulators then and now are employing trade-off tactics to secure convictions of prized scalps – the immunity from prosecution of Crown witnesses …

The SEC has entered into several financial settlements as a means of 'moving on'. It is not suggested here that there should not be deals entailing fines – but the imposition of them seems to be supported on the questionable grounds that they will be a deterrent ... a legitimate concern of such deals is whether the shareholders really benefit from such tactics. They initially lose through the wrongdoing on the part of suspect actions of some executives, then lose again as the company is fined for the wrongdoing *per se*.[14]

The second five years of that decade were a repeat of the first. Persistence explains well the cyclical features of regulatory strategies over time. The numerous banking scandals disclosed in official inquiries seeking causes of the GFC led banking oversight agencies to propose numerous reforms, but unfortunately what they proposed was more of the same in the sense of the 'rules and sanctions' model, with a patch or only a cosmetic twist.

Now that the US Senate has reached a compromise agreement post-GFC on the shape of its regulatory reform and UK Chancellor George Osborne has outlined a revamped financial industry regulation model in the UK, it is a good time for Australia to reconsider the effectiveness of its regulatory regime, not just its formal structure. APRA did not perform too well under pressure in the HIH affair. Consumer protection for the local government and eleemosynaries buying financial products from a unit of Lehmans was questionable. ASIC's record as a proactive regulator has of late been less than stellar, and as a reactive prosecutor of its perceived wrongdoers less than impressive.

In both the USA and the UK bank regulation is to be handed over substantially to respective central banks – to the Bank of England in the UK and to the Federal Reserve in the USA. In both countries there is to be an agency with oversight for consumer protection – the Financial Consumer Protection Agency in the USA and the Consumer Protection from Unfair Trading Regulations in the UK. Initially President Obama mooted a potential scrapping (or de-fanging) of its Securities and Exchange Commission. Possibly this was punishment for its inactions in the Enron and WorldCom affairs, and a woeful effort in respect of Harry Markopolos's decade-long whistleblower revelations of Bernie Madoff's activities. However, Democrat and Republican political wheeling and dealing saved it. In contrast, the UK has scuttled its Financial Services Authority for its poor oversight performance pre-GFC in respect of Northern Rock, HBOS,[15] and Bradford & Bingley, and its general failure to keep the UK out of the financial soup.

Australia remained relatively unscathed by the GFC, and ASIC has been given additional responsibilities regarding the national stock exchange, ASX. Turning to another governance mechanism, auditing, disturbingly, the UK FSA's 2013 White Paper (*Enhancing the Auditor's Contribution to Prudential Regulation*) was highly critical in its view that the auditors of banks have been too accommodating, not sufficiently querulous regarding compliance with the assumptions underpinning management's asset valuation models. It expressed concern that those valuations were not examined assiduously enough to determine whether they provide a true and fair view. That contrasts with the tenor of the Australian Treasury's 2010 and 2011 Audit Quality Reviews suggesting that everything here is fine in that regard. We are not as convinced, as is shown in chapter 4.

It's time to note that, in Australia and elsewhere, catching wrongdoers is not *consumer protection* of the kind now perceived as necessary in the USA and UK. At issue is whether Australia and other jurisdictions might be well advised to have regulators that are predominantly proactive, rather than reactive, and can demonstrate greater perspicacity in deciding who to pursue.

After each period of boom and bust the predictable reaction has been a changing of the form of the investor and prudential regulatory mix. That, however, is missing the point. Consumer protection requires a more fundamental rethink. We note with some concern that this is lacking in the main reform proposals (albeit with different specifics) in the USA, UK and Europe: the so-called Volcker rule as part of the US Congress Dodd-Frank Act, the UK government's reforms following the recommendations of the Sir John Vickers Independent Banking Commission and the ECB reforms following recommendations of Erki Liikanen's Commission of Inquiry. Apart from recommending a Glass-Steagall-like split between investment and 'ordinary' commercial banking services, they look very much to be patches, amounting to more of the same reform rules and sanctions model that had appeared in previous decades, and failed.

Now that the GFC fog is lifting we might usefully review how effective ASIC's and APRA's protection has actually been. Did Australian financial institutions weather the GFC because they were well regulated and hence more financially sound than their overseas counterparts? Or was it the case when several institutions were rumoured to be in financial difficulty that the Australian government acted promptly with a substantially higher financial guarantee than elsewhere? It seems that the generally positive assessments of the regulators' performances overlook what occurred in the HIH, One.Tel, Westpoint, Allco, Babcock & Brown, Centro, ABC Learning and other shadow banking affairs. For instance, an opinion piece at the end of 2010 suggested ASIC was wounded in its abortive litigation of One.Tel executives, and then again when 10 James Hardie executive and non-executive directors successfully appealed in the New South Wales (NSW) Supreme Court against the earlier lower court decision in favour of ASIC. That earlier ruling held directors had breached provisions of the Corporations Act, namely that they had signed off on a misleading press release that suggested that the Medical Research and Compensation Foundation had sufficient funds to meet any long tail asbestos claims. Indeed, as we show in Box 3.1, Australia's ASIC has limped along like a wounded kangaroo.

Box 3.1 ASIC is wounded – time for a rethink

Corporate regulation has been shown once again to be more than difficult. The successful appeal by James Hardie directors against the decision in favour of ASIC has brought deserved increased criticism of the regulator's performance. It adds to other events this year highlighting why society needs to contemplate seriously the future of traditional corporate structures and the current means of regulation.

It may well be that it is time to question whether a group of companies (the major form of big business activity to which we have become accustomed) is capable of being effectively regulated.

ASIC's win against James Hardie non-executive directors in August 2009 had been welcome news for the regulator. Not so happy were its earlier costly losses: the One.Tel affair; Fortescue Metals Group; its oversight of Centro, Storm and Westpoint; and the AWB case.

All of that was on top of concerns about the future of its US counterpart, the Securities and Exchange Commission. The SEC's poor handling of Markopolos's revealing submissions to it during the decade before the Madoff affair put the skids under it.

The SEC survived that crisis intact but the creation of a Consumer Financial Protection Bureau after the global financial crisis implied traditional SEC-style regulation was considered insufficient protection of US public interests.

A similar message might be implied by the plan to have a Consumer Protection and Markets Authority in Britain. There, the rethink of regulation promised the scrapping of the Financial Services Authority after its less-than-stellar performance leading into, and during, the GFC.

In contrast, here, ASIC's questionable performance has been rewarded with regulatory oversight of the ASX.

It's arguable whether ASIC's style of corporate regulation works. Iterations of Australian regulation over the past half century have had individual State Companies offices, a National Companies and Securities Commission, the ASC and now ASIC all applying a rules-and-sanctions regime of the kind the SEC has championed since President Roosevelt initiated it in 1933.

And each time there is a change, more resources are provided to the regulator.

But corporations are no longer the relatively simple commercial vehicles they mostly were then – corporate group structures and asset-shifting tactics they facilitate are now the rule (often to the peril of employees' termination payments) rather than the exception. We now have the too big to fail (rather than a too big to save) syndrome, which raised its ugly head during the GFC and is a card Australian banks are playing against efforts to curb their practices.

Risk of apprehension and the threat of penalties are no problem for the large modern corporation. Notwithstanding the proposed federal initiatives regarding executive remuneration, neither the risks companies' managers take nor their executives' remuneration are controllable by rank-and-file shareholders, any more than were the practices of banking companies and their affiliates on the US stock exchanges in the 1930s. Little is new. Past corporate misbehaviour and past inept modes of regulation all too frequently endure.

Calls to scrap capitalism are misplaced. But it may be that some of its artefacts have passed their use-by date. Corporations as they are now – many with

> balance sheets far bigger than sovereign nations, hundreds of subsidiaries and other commercial vehicles (trusts, 'special purpose entities', and the like) loosely attached – are obvious examples. Clearly, an emerging view of governments is that consumer and investor protection requires more than ASIC-type regulators and regulations. Virtually none of the regulatory patching has worked. Nor does increasing resources, *per se*, seem to have worked.
>
> Time to act. Time for some serious thought on how best to change the regulatory mechanism or how to change the accepted corporate structures to something more controllable.
>
> *(AFR, 29 December 2010–1 January 2011, p. 55)*

ASIC later appealed the decision and won a High Court judgment on 7 May 2012 (*Australian Securities and Investments Commission v Meredith Hellicar and Ors* [2012] HCA 17), upholding the original lower court decision that the directors had breached the Corporations Act. Predictably, ASIC lauded its success in the Australian financial press. However, its moment of self-congratulation was typically short-lived. The NSW Court of Appeal reviewed the penalties to be imposed on directors following the High Court ruling, and in mid-November 2012 held that they be reduced by about half in most instances (*Gillfillan & Ors v Australian Securities & Investments Commission* [2012] NSWCA 370). This was viewed by many as a slap on the wrist for those directors, evidence of regulatory 'lite' in action, but the appeal judgment did confirm the initial basic ruling that the non-executive directors could not delegate their primary obligations, nor generally rely on others (such as the executive directors or, say, auditors) in fulfilling those obligations.[16] This aligns with the judgment met earlier in the Centro case about not necessarily relying on experts – in that case, the auditors. Interpreting what is good governance is clearly not easy.

In focus in the opinion also was the way corporate regulators go about their investor protection task. In the USA inadequate regulation was shown to be in focus when Bernie Madoff's Ponzi fraud went unnoticed for over a decade by the SEC. One assessment is that the regulator was loath to proactively shut the scheme down. Rather, the SEC waited and then sought an arguably ridiculously lengthy gaol sentence, by far exceeding a normal lifetime, against Madoff. It was a very public instance of focusing on the individual. Perhaps more important is Markopolos's claim that the SEC was not only inactive because of internal ructions, but that few of its officers had the technical expertise necessary to pursue Madoff. Fraud is clearly not abating – as is made clear by the evidence reported on the websites of the US Committee of Sponsoring Organizations of the Treadway Commission (www.coso.org), the UK National Fraud Authority (www.homeoffice.gov.uk) and Big Four practitioner surveys (www.kpmginstitutes.com and www.deloitte.com). However, it is inherently difficult to draw lessons from fraud. It seems that many fraudsters are technically ahead of the watchdogs, whether they be regulators or auditors. We question in chapter 4 why this should be so.

It does seem that ASIC and the SEC have similarities in the way they respond to such finagling. Underpinning that view is a concern about the repetitive nature of the cycle of collapses and public angst aroused by the inept governance of corporate activities. Many of the companies hosting such individuals are household names: in the USA, Fannie Mae and Freddie Mac, Lehman Brothers, Citigroup, Goldman Sachs; in the UK, RBS, Barclays Bank; and in Australia, James Hardie, Baycorp, Fincorp, Westpoint, AWB. Three relevant opinion pieces appeared in the years preceding the apogee of the GFC: 'Watchdog's Bark has Hollow Tone' (*AFR*, 28 July 2008) (see Box 3.2), 'Harsh Light May Shine on Non-executives' (*AFR*, 12 March 2007) and 'Bay and Westpoint Show Up Regulators' (*Newcastle Herald*, 31 May–1 June 2006). The 'Watchdog' opinion prompted a favourable *AFR* editorial response the next day, 'Protecting Investors'. Those pieces contest some regulatory chestnuts, such as the need for 'director and auditor independence' as conventionally defined, and the recurring suggestions that *more* regulation is better than *less*.

Box 3.2 Watchdog's bark has hollow tone

ASIC will be in the hot seat this reporting season. ASIC's proposed, close scrutiny of companies' financials this reporting season ('ASIC warns of reporting season blitz', *AFR*, June 25) is a curious approach to its responsibilities.

It seems that the Australian Securities and Investments Commission holds the view that market turmoil makes companies' balance sheets less reliable than they normally are. Debt classification, asset values, fair-market values, going-concern assumptions, off-balance sheet arrangements and the like are mooted as likely to receive additional attention. But these are matters no more relevant now than they were in happier times to determining whether companies' financials show a true and fair view of their financial positions and performances.

The point is, the threat of closer attention to such things now invites the inference that ASIC's surveillance has possibly been less in the past than we might expect from a vigilant regulator. For, whereas the decline in companies' balance sheets has been rather dramatic over the past six months, the fall is from equally dramatic increases reported when they were on the way up.

Australia's Corporations Act is unequivocal in that companies' financials are to show a true and fair view of the financial positions and latest performances. That they are drawn up 'in accordance with the Accounting Standards' offers no relief from that obligation.

We are entitled to expect ASIC to be as vigilant in respect of that at all times.

Classification of debt is no more an issue now than it was in the past. Just as misclassification might be used to enhance impressions of current compliance with debt covenants, it could be used in the past to increase the borrowing for which the cover is now so critical.

The current focus seems to be drawing on a fear that assets may be overstated. But are we to presume that previous understatements apparently did not receive the same scrutiny?

Discussion of ASIC possibly turning up the heat has brought some interesting observations that imply little awareness of financial niceties. We're told that valuation is a problem because some assets don't have active markets.

Elsewhere, that simply means that there isn't any evidence of a market value.

Elsewhere it would be thought untrue to declare a market value when none exists. How is it any different in accounting? It has to be called as it is. Disclose the existence of the asset by all means, but without a market value attached.

How can serviceable debt-to-equity ratios be determined without evidence of the money's worth of assets and liabilities? If they don't have any, then that is it – and, moreover, precisely the only serviceable information.

How can solvency be assessed without *inter alia* such information?

Data in companies' financials are used habitually to determine their wealth and progress, and to determine their salient financial characteristics – solvency, asset backing, debt to equity, interest cover, whether they have satisfied debt covenants, the nature, composition and money's worth of their assets, the amount of their liabilities, and the like.

Unless ASIC surveillance has established that the data in their financials are serviceable for that, ASIC couldn't possibly be confident that the financials show a true and fair view and satisfy the legislation. The issues that ASIC seems to consider a problem now were no less deserving of attention, of diligent surveillance, when things were on the rise. Are we to assume ASIC did not evaluate whether companies were showing a true and fair view in the past?

Significantly for Australia, recently the UK Financial Reporting Council sought a QC's opinion as to the relevance of the true and fair view criterion in today's globalized (presumably), more uncertain world.

The result, reported in UK Financial Reporting Council's May 19, 2008, press notice 222 confirmed a series of earlier QC opinions (1983 by Hoffmann and Arden and in 1988 by Arden) that the true and fair criterion persists as the cornerstone of the British system of corporate financial disclosure.

It is high time that Australian regulators, directors and auditors also recognized this point – in good times and in bad.

(AFR, 28 July 2008, p. 63)

In the years since the GFC, ASIC has rolled out what amount to boilerplate media warning announcements like 'ASIC Warns of Reporting Season Blitz'.[17] These releases iterate warnings to directors and auditors to be on the alert that there are several areas (impairments, revenue recognition, deferring expenses, off-balance sheet arrangements, solvency matters – standard fare for those familiar with creative accounting) that are on ASIC's watch list.[18]

ASIC, it seems, does not need a crisis – it also rolls out such edicts regularly in normal times. Likewise, the SEC is quick to encourage and for companies to then embrace a new accounting standard in the wake of the exposure of the latest corporate financial disclosure caper. As with ASIC's annual announcements, the effectiveness has thereby been blunted: in Australia because of the predictable nature of ASIC's pre-emptive threats and in the USA because by the time each new rule is promulgated the bird has already flown. Neither protects.

We contest why such a warning is needed by Australia's corporate regulator. One would imagine that this is the regulator's *raison d'être*, for it not to be keeping a close watch on protecting investors' (equity holders and bondholders) interests would be incongruous. This is not to say that the areas noted in the opinion piece are unimportant – indicators of insolvency and debt classification (as in 2012 Centro found out to its detriment) are critical as interested parties need to be informed of such matters to facilitate their ongoing adaptive strategies – (see chapters 2 and 4).

In late 2012 ASIC's perceived ineptitude was again illustrated when the Australian High Court ruled against it in its long-running case considering whether Twiggy Forrest had misled the Australian public, initiating substantial erratic share price movements. The negative legal decision is estimated to have cost ASIC upwards of $30 million.[19] On top of its loss in this and the earlier One.Tel case, ASIC's desire to earn brownie points has resulted in the investing public viewing its performance as possibly at its lowest point. ASIC is now placed in the position of either accepting it is merely not up to the task or that the task is too difficult for everyone – that corporations in their present form cannot be regulated so as to protect what ASIC perceives to be the public interest.

The above opinion pieces suggested that all is not well with the present regulatory frameworks of business generally, and in the finance sector in particular. The type of regulatory responses to numerous finance sector market failures has been shown to be flawed. Examples noted here have included setting Basel-type targets rather than having leverage ratio data and other risk indicators disclosed, and issuing more and more corporate governance rules as evidenced in the myriad governance codes promulgated worldwide. *Patching* the existing legislative or regulatory rules persists.

This malaise is evidenced in the area of debenture financing of property by the non-banks (so-called shadow banks), and this regulatory deficiency exists worldwide. We describe in chapter 6 the nearly universal concerns about the shadow banking sector. Here we consider briefly some recurring episodes over the last five decades in Australia. Estate Mortgage Trust's 1990s capers involving complex inter-entity financing of borrowing companies (separate but related investment trusts) have been repeated since 2000 at Westpoint, Baycorp, Australian Capital Reserve, Fincorp, Provident Capital, City Pacific, Prime Trust and, as this book goes to press, in the Banksia and LM Investment Management Ltd collapses.[20] Regulatory patches are revealed to have failed repeatedly to cover the real issues. Several of our opinion pieces suggested that a lack of focus on underlying (often used as collateral) asset valuations was a fundamental deficiency in those regulatory responses.

Debenture and other forms of mortgage financing are commonly used to finance property investments in Australia and elsewhere, many of which have produced minimal or no returns. Accounting, as noted in chapter 2, has failed generally to mark such investments to market. Regulatory responses following those shadow banking sector collapses requested borrowing companies to make adjustments voluntarily to their capital to liabilities ratio (similar to the mandated ratio requirements under the Basel accords for banks). Where these are not put in place, the non-banks are to disclose that in any prospectus.

With some reports suggesting collapses in the last few years in Australia's shadow banking sector have resulted in losses of $10–15 billion, several concerns have been expressed about those voluntary measures, and more generally the performance of the relevant oversight agency, ASIC. At an ASIC Forum in March 2013 the ASIC Chair Greg Medcraft declared in respect of the LM Investment Management collapse that a global response was needed to redress the present regulatory deficiencies. His SEC counterpart was attending the conference and was reported to agree. It seems to us that this is missing the point: what is required is a fundamental review of accounting for investments in the shadow banking sector. We return to this point in chapter 6.

For some it will come as a surprise that ASIC was aware of major solvency issues in many shadow banks. It had identified 15 at-risk debenture borrowers in 2007 (at the height of the boom prior to the GFC) but failed to intervene with public announcements – eight have subsequently collapsed. Banksia reportedly was placed on an ASIC alert in late 2011, and an on-site visit occurred in 2012,[21] but some general points about the voluntary measures suggested by ASIC overlook other critical factors. First, the reported calculus used to measure capital often has non-financial amounts included. In contrast, the denominator (liabilities) in the ratio is a straight monetary amount. This issue was discussed in principle in chapter 2. Second, in other cases some of the relevant debts may be held off-balance sheet, as occurred in several overseas cases (see chapter 6 for further discussion).

An inappropriate regulatory model?

Here, we have observed that recurring failures and regulatory responses reveal the need to consider whether what is being regulated, governed, is appropriate. Amongst other things, is the corporation in its modern corporate group form still a suitable – the best – vehicle for conducting commerce? Is the existing form of accounting for groups appropriate? In several opinions we suggested (as had the Bank of England's Andrew Haldane) that more of the same regulation is not better than less. Moreover, the US and Australian experiences also support this. What is required is a more focused set of regulations, one that includes a fundamental rethink of the nature of the modern corporation. From 1844 to 1855 unlimited liability industrial companies existed, with little fundamental change – for the next 150 and more years no liability (mining) public companies have been permitted to operate. Also companies can operate in a 'limited by shares' or 'limited by guarantee' form. There is nothing sacrosanct about the present 'limited liability within limited liability' corporate group form – its appropriateness should be continually reassessed.

Heartening are other radical suggestions such as those in Anderson (2012) to revisit the utility of the corporate veil by suggesting that even when fraud is absent, parent company fault should be the basis of liability, even if this necessitates piercing the veil. This draws on the present Australian liability for parent companies as shadow directors and their existing fiduciary duty to act with care and diligence and in good faith. Our proposed reforms relating to corporate groups and their accounting, hinted at in the above opinion pieces, are more radical and are discussed in chapters 1 and 6 and the Epilogue.

It is difficult to be particularly sanguine regarding the effectiveness of corporate regulation in Australia, the UK or the USA. Even if starved of funding, what is forthcoming presently from the corporate regulatory agencies is a long way from value for money. Those national regulators have demonstrated over a long period and certainly while under pressure during the past decade that they cannot control the complex group structures that now dominate corporate arrangements. They cannot control corporates' financial disclosures, their 'earnings management' accounting disclosures or the audit of them; and certainly they provide little to no protection to the investing public, or to the employees of those corporations. Overall, the UK, US and Australian regulatory agencies are failing to protect those members of society who, by virtue of legislation, would otherwise be able to access with relative safety the undeniable benefits from incorporation.

Notes

1 The US PBS *Frontline* programme shown on ABC's *Four Corners*, 17 March 2013, 'The Untouchables', noted earlier.

2 Matthew Drummond, 'Judges Demand Say Over Settlements', *AFR*, News, 25 March 2013, p. 10. Consider also the ASIC Senate Inquiry announced in late July 2013 following concerns being raised about ASIC's actions regarding CBA's failure to act on whistleblowers' information.

3 IMF Country Report No. 12/310, *Australia: Financial Safety Net and Crisis Management Framework – Technical Note*, November 2012.

4 As demonstrated in Dean, 2005.

5 Brooke Masters, 'Regulators Peer into Financial Shadows', *Financial Times*, 18 November 2012.

6 It has been similarly suggested that accounting academics became too close to the corporate sector and the government, leading to claims that private sector funding is producing biased research design and conclusions (see Chabrak, 2012).

7 An overview of the role of gatekeepers generally is provided in Coffee, 2006.

8 Shahien Nasiriipour and Alice Ross, 'Forex Swaps Win Waiver from New US Rules', *AFR*, 19 November 2012, p. 20; see also Rivlin, 2013.

9 Patrick Durkin and Matthew Drummond, 'ASIC Handcuffed', *AFR*, 17–18 November 2012, p. 41.

10 See also the folly of banking rules explained by the UK academic John Kay, 'The Law that Explains the Folly of Banking Rules', *AFR*, 13 September 2012, p. 27.

11 Respectively: *SMH*, Business, 23 July 2012, p. 7; *AFR* letter to the editor, 19 July 2012, p. 51; *AFR*, 27 July 2012, p. 33; and *AFR*, 27 July 2012, pp. 1, 10, 11.

12 G. Liondis and Patrick Durkin, 'APRA No Good in a Crisis: Treasury', *AFR*, 13 September 2012, pp. 21, 25.

13 Intriguingly, in the post-GFC low interest rates environment, junk bond financing is again to the fore as parties seek higher yields. It is unlikely that any form of regulation will prove effective in preventing a repeat boom and bust outcome.

14 See Clarke and Dean, 2007, especially chapter 1, pp. 27–32.

15 The April 2013 Parliamentary Banking Commission report about the HBOS failure, *An Accident Waiting to Happen*, shows that this failure, like many before (and most likely

many after), is the failure to understand the intertwined nature of accounting, finance and management – coupled to greed.

16 Samantha Hutchinson summarizes this saga in 'Rocky Road after Hardie', *AFR*, News, 17–18 November 2012, p. 6.

17 Consider the ASIC website, which records the following media announcements: 10–147MR, 'ASIC Focuses Attention on 2010 Financial Reports'; 11–139MR, 'ASIC Focuses Attention on 30 June 2011 Financial Reports'; 12–140 MtoR, 'ASIC's Areas of Focus for 30 June 2012 Financial Reports'; 12–292MR, 'ASIC's Areas of Focus for 31 December 2012 Financial Reports'. Respectively, these are available at: www.asic. gov.au/asic/asic.nsf/byheadline/10147MR+ASICfocusesattentionon2010financialreports ?opendocument (accessed 25 September 2012); www.asic.gov.au/asic/asic.nsf/byhead line/11E28093139MRASICfocusesattentionon30June2011financialreports?opendocument (accessed 25 September 2012); www.asic.gov.au/asic/asic.nsf/byheadline/12-140MR +ASICE28099Sareasoffocusfor30June2012financialreports?openDocument (accessed 25 September 2012); www.asic.gov.au/asic/asic.nsf/byheadline/12292MR+ASICs+areas +of+focus+for+31+December+2012+-+Financial+reports?openDocument (accessed 1 December 2012).

18 For those seeking an overview of creative accounting, see McBarnet and Whelan, 1999; Clarke *et al.*, 2003, esp. chapter 2; and Jones, 2011.

19 Patrick Durkin, 'How Regulator Blew $30m on Twiggy', *AFR*, 6–7 October 2012, pp. 50–51.

20 M. Drummond, 'ASIC had no Prudential Role: Regulatory Hole Allows Lender Failure', *AFR*, News, 27–28 October 2012, pp. 2–3; Chanticleer, 'Another Zombie Crawls Out of the Shadows', *AFR*, 26 March 2013, pp. 48, 43.

21 C. Joye, 'Local Bankers, Blessed, Not Brilliant', *AFR*, 1 November 2012, p. 63.

4

MISSION IMPOSSIBLE

Auditors on the rack

Effective company audits became virtually impossible long before the GFC. Post-GFC, things have deteriorated. Scandals involving financial institutions and large corporations reemphasised the need for improved audit governance mechanisms for major corporations. The tasks of internal and external auditors again have been front and centre. For auditing is regarded as a necessary gatekeeping function, integral to ensuring a market economy functions properly. It is a key to ensuring corporate disclosures made to the securities markets can be relied upon. A June 2012 International Auditing and Assurance Standards Board Invitation to Comment, 'Improving the Auditor's Report', sought responses on a proposed changed format of the audit report post-GFC. It aims to tighten the scrutiny of companies' books and improve investor protection, similar to the US Treadway Commission proposals several decades earlier.

For nearly a century 'independence' has been deemed critical to the gatekeeping function of auditing. The 8 December 2012 issue of *The Economist* carries a story, 'The Big Four Auditors Accountable', detailing claims of conflicts for the Big Four because of contiguous provisions of non-audit and audit services to their multinational clients. Nothing new there.

Also there is nothing new in the recent UK Competition Commission's proposed reforms to auditing following a parliamentary inquiry into the competitive nature of auditing in the UK. In sum, the Commission found that, while a Big Four oligopoly undeniably exists regarding the audit of the largest listed companies, effectively competition was not compromised.[1] The USA's Public Company Accounting Oversight Board (PCAOB, 2013) also reported in February 2013 that its review of large audits over the period 2007–10 had revealed fewer audit deficiencies than the previous review covering the period 2003–06. This general view of present-day auditing not being in need of a major overhaul is consistent with the Australian Treasury's conclusion in its relevant 2010 and 2011 reports of inquiries into auditing, but it is at odds with Australian regulator ASIC's December 2012 review and report (discussed below), which was very critical of present-day audits.

Over 50 years ago in the US practitioner pieces such as Wise's *Insiders: The Stockholders' Guide to Wall Street* (1962), plenty of comments appeared about the independence of auditors. Robert Mautz, a US professor in the early 1950s, noted the need for the auditor to possess an 'independence of mind'. Regulators, like the SEC had proscribed forms of client–auditor relationships much earlier. With his co-author Hussein Sharaf, Robert Mautz argued the need to discriminate 'independence of mind' from 'independence of appearance' in their *Philosophy of Auditing* (Mautz and Sharaf, 1961), but contestably then suggested both were critical. That has spawned an enormous literature on independence, drawing on all sorts of research methods.

In many studies, either explicitly or implicitly there is a suggestion that non-auditing services (and fees) are cross-subsidizing audit services work. Auditing is perceived by many to have thus been commoditized – it is no longer primarily a professional task. A recent example using a large sample of US companies is the 2012 study by Christensen *et al.*, *Pork Bellies and Public Company Audits: Have Audits Once Again become Just Another Commodity?* The authors observe an association (a 'correlation') between audit fee levels and audit quality. This, like most of the empirical papers to date in this area, did not provide compelling evidence for regulators to promulgate sound policy. Thus, academic research has generally resulted in little effective change to practice or improvements in consumer protection. This chapter notes in particular that there has been a misplaced emphasis on independence, distracting from the pursuit of effective reforms.

Repeated financial collapses through the first decade of this century demonstrate the unresolved difficulties facing auditors. Bookending the opinion pieces examined in this chapter are major audit inquiries in several Anglo-American countries: the so-called Blue Ribbon Audit Committee inquiries in the USA, in particular the committee's audit quality review in 1999 coupled with the post-dotcom and Enron inquiries resulting in the Sarbanes-Oxley Act. The UK's Combined Code consolidates work in a number of reports from prior governance inquiries. These include those chaired in the 1990s by Sir Adrian Cadbury (1992) following UK corporate scandals at Maxwell Communications and Polly Peck. Cadbury's later reports followed the Bank of Commerce and Credit International (BCCI) and other major company failures, as did Sir Ronald Hampell's (1998) report, and reports of inquiries such as Nigel Turnbull's (1999). More recently, Sir David Walker's (2009a, 2009b) 'Stewardship Code' was preceded by the GFC collapses of Northern Rock, Bradford & Bingley and other financial disasters. On 30 November 2011, the European Commission proposed new rules to the statutory audit of public interest entities specifying that there be a six-year time limit for an audit engagement (extendible to nine) and prohibiting the provision of non-audit services to audit clients. As note 1 records, the UK Competition Commission sought submissions on draft audit reforms provided in its February 2013 issues paper. Unfortunately, little is new in those draft proposals. There is thus no real likelihood of much improvement on the consumer protection front in the foreseeable future.

In Australia a decade earlier, the federal government, needing to be seen to be doing something after the One.Tel and HIH failures, rushed headlong to put in place the reforms suggested in the Ramsay inquiry into auditor independence and the Joint Parliamentary Committee on Accounts and Audit inquiry into registered auditors. Both reports suggested auditing independence reforms. Unfortunately, these were to be more regulation of the same old rules (or recommendations) and sanctions variety, with little imagination and with predictable outcomes. There was an overemphasis on the independence of appearance notion, and a desire in some jurisdictions to give auditing standards (as well as accounting standards) the force of law.

We saw in chapter 3 that not long afterwards Australia introduced its CLERP reforms, and, like many countries in the Western world, it agreed to adopt the international financial reporting standards by 2005, but again this entailed more of the same. Fast forward to 2010 and Australia (and other countries) again witnessed unexpected collapses and financial dilemmas like those occurring at its beginning – failures in the non-(shadow) banking sector like Storm Financial, Banksia and LM Investment. The common mantra of 'Where were the auditors?' was quick to reappear and it was suggested auditors had not been sufficiently alert to red flags. Commenting on Banksia's troubles, ASIC chief Greg Medcraft was reported to lay much of the blame on the auditing profession: 'Failed non-bank lender, Banksia, which collapsed in October 2012, incurring about $650 million of losses for its 3000 investors, had been given the tick of approval by auditors only weeks before.'[2]

By 2010 economies worldwide remained affected by the GFC and related euro-zone debt crises. Government and private sector initiated enquiries into specific collapses ensued. An early one was the several thousand-page March 2010 report by leading Chicago lawyer Anton R. Valukas, the examiner into the 2008 collapse of Lehman Brothers, which was soon followed by the House of Lords' 2010–11 Economic Affairs Inquiry into 'Auditors: Market Concentration and their Role'. Further, there was the contiguous EU review about whether auditors and their clients are 'too close' because of the often simultaneous provisions to a client of audit and non-audit services by the same accounting firm (see note 1). Various government reports into financial institution scandals appeared worldwide: the Royal Bank of Scotland report in 2011, the UK HBOS report in 2013 and the 2012 HSBC report in the USA, the various 2012 reports in the UK, USA and Europe into the Libor and Euribor manipulations during the GFC, with the Royal Bank of Scotland and Barclays Bank fined for their part in the affair, and a slew of other banks implicated. These financial imbroglios again beget the question 'Where were the internal and external auditors?' Where were they, indeed!

The events confirmed the need for verification of what is being reported by corporations. This entails that independent auditing (in the sense described below) and independent, sceptical and honest auditors should be up to the task. Auditors are to express an independent opinion on the 'truth and fairness' of an entity's accounts, an opinion about whether there are material misstatements in the accounts. Those statements may arise through unintentional error or fraud. Truth and fairness in accounting was the focus of an earlier chapter, so here we consider mainly matters of what is entailed in an independent audit opinion. In what follows it is essential to develop a proper understanding of what is meant by 'independence' per se, and the interdependence of the true and fair view opinion, and independence.

Auditing's devil

Accounting in accord with the current mandated IFRSs is auditing's devil. *Indecent Disclosure* (Clarke and Dean, 2007, chapters 4 and 5) drew on the inherent uncertainties of the accounting standards-based accounting practices that have caused auditing to be, in our view, a mission impossible. Those uncertainties expose auditors to difficulties in verifying what is reported publicly by managers of major corporations. There, recent reforms to auditing practices were shown to be misdirected, with inquiries in some countries producing mandated professional standards – some having the force of law. The impression often created is that the problems all lie with auditing processes, rather than with the inherent defects in the accounting data auditors confront and the need for auditors to have maximum discretion to apply their specific wisdom and judgement, presumably gained over many years on many audits.[3] Straitjacketing auditors by mandating auditing and accounting standards to follow is the antithesis of professionalism. It *hobbles* auditors' activities. We return in this chapter to that theme in the last opinion piece.

One might have expected that, had audit as a quality control mechanism been improved by all of the recent regulatory reforms, unexpected corporate collapses would largely have been eliminated. In fact, a 2006 international public gathering of the Big Four accounting firms had that optimistic proposition included in its communiqué. However, evidence abounds that material misstatements due to fraud and related unexpected collapses persist (Clikeman, 2013). Recent fraud, and also difficulties in assessing material misstatements where fraud is absent prior to the GFC, have been noted (Lee *et al.*, 2008). One high-profile Australian case early in this century involved the telecommunications company One.Tel. While nearly a decade separated the collapse and the judgment, some of the affairs at One.Tel were eventually revealed. In particular, the judgment exposed matters addressing accounting and auditing's interconnectedness, and problematic factors related to determining an entity's solvency within an economic group. The 3,105-page NSW Supreme Court judgment by the Hon. Robert Austin in November 2009 (*Australian Securities and Investments Commission v Rich* [2009] NSWSC 1229) motivated the opinion piece in Box 4.1.

Box 4.1 One.Tel ruling proves solvency a thorny issue

The judgment provides food for thought on fashionable corporate governance.

Companies might rethink how they assess their solvency now that judge Robert Austin has ruled that the Australian Securities and Investments Commission failed to make its case that One.Tel had traded while insolvent.

The judgment emphasized that much more forensic evidence was needed to gain a conviction. This observation led to the following headline in the *Australian Financial Review*: 'ASIC slated in One.Tel court defeat' (*AFR*, November 19). Such observations recur in major commercial cases where problematic notions such as solvency and true financial state are involved.

Management's inclusion of anticipated capital contributions from James Packer and Lachlan Murdoch-connected companies was a disputed aspect of the failed action against One.Tel's Jodee Rich and Mark Silbermann.

Austin's 3,105-page judgment adds another dimension to the solvency algorithm. A decision earlier this decade somewhat extended the potential sources of funds to include potentially whatever funds the borrower might reasonably be expected (based on past experience) to be able to source, to assess its capacity to pay its debts as and when they fall due. These could be from related or unrelated entities.

Timing and its related impact on the certainty of the sourcing of the funds is potentially now a more critical issue than it was even when ASIC found fault recently with Centro's directors regarding the accounting classification of their companies' liabilities.

While yet to be adjudicated in court, the directors allegedly misclassified short-term liabilities (those due for payment within the ensuing accounting period) as long-term and by implication due and payable some time in a more distant future.

It works both ways. Long-term liabilities incorrectly classified as short term might evoke unjustified impressions of likely insolvency and precipitate all that goes with it – possible share price declines, loss of potential orders, unjustified disinvestment or even non-investment.

Of course, someone has to 'win' financially and someone must 'lose' irrespective of whether the misclassification is deliberate or accidental.

While an entity might be temporarily illiquid, insolvency suggests a much more permanent concern about an entity's net asset position – including not only consideration of shortfalls in working capital, but also the relation of fungible longer-term assets relative to longer-term liabilities and the ability to source funds as and when required.

Assessing solvency where expectations are embedded thus creates headaches for directors and auditors. This judgment seems to re-emphasize the importance of the role of the reasonableness of expectations regarding the future sources of funds. One.Tel's prospect of raising $132 million in a rights issue has emerged to have met that criterion.

The One.Tel judgment also raises reasonable questions regarding the usefulness of non-executive directors (NEDs).

A prevailing notion seems to be that NEDs are essential, the more the merrier, and better performing the board will be. The positive argument runs that they bring a greater level of independence, a most valuable form of detachment, than might the other directors.

One.Tel demonstrated that high-profile NEDs might rate brownie points as far as the connections lauded in the annual report are concerned, but arguably, they frequently might be seen as having competing loyalties for the attention they can give to their non-executive responsibilities.

Importantly, they appear dogged by very poor memories. In their evidence, One.Tel NEDs James Packer and Lachlan Murdoch both explained that they couldn't recall many of the matters put to them.

We saw Meredith Hellicar having similar difficulties when giving evidence in the recent James Hardie case, curiously better able to recall what she did not do than what she had. Such memory lapses led in the One.Tel case to Austin placing much greater reliance on Rich's account of the critical solvency events in January to March 2001 than those of others.

This One.Tel decision possibly clarifies for ASIC issues often arising in its pursuit of directors signing financial and the related solvency assessments. It has been already noted that this case might allay the fears of some directors as it clarifies aspects of their ability to rely on the business judgment rule.

Further, it enhances existing criticism of corporate governance regimes that specify majority non-executives on boards, comprising key board groups such as 'audit committees', and, indeed, the almost incessant lauding of the virtues of non-executive directors.

A supposed superior, higher level of independence that non-executive directors are claimed to possess might be less a virtue than imagined.

In this extensive and clear judgment, Austin has provided much food for thought. Notions of which entity is to be considered when assessing solvency and of 'solvency' itself are under the spotlight. Solvency is no easy matter to assess.

That is something for ASIC and directors to ponder. The supposed virtues of non-executive directors is food for thought for the corporate governance gurus.

(AFR, 20 November 2009, p. 59)

Analysis there noted that determining a verifiable indicator of solvency is critical for auditors and directors performing their required tasks. In that, a major problem for both is the manner in which physical assets are valued and usually reported under conventional IFRS accounting standards now operative in Australia, the UK and the other EU countries. That accounting usually entails an agglomeration of asset valuations – initial (historical) cost, cost restated as at some date prior to the accounts, cost (whether written up, down, or not) but written down by an amortization of the book value, a current value, impaired values and an actual cash amount, or their current selling prices. This problem is exacerbated when the assets are held and financed by entities within a complex corporate structure. Solvency is entity (not group) specific unless guarantee covenants are in place. To many it seems that assessing the capacity to meet one's debts as they fall due presents insuperable difficulties. 'As they fall due' seems to be a major stumbling block. True, the future is uncertain. It is also the case that estimating the amount for which physical assets might now be sold is not easy, even if there is a market currently in which prices are displayed. Every price may well differ in the future. Of course, the plot thickens when a debt is due at some distant future time. Some assets saleable now may well not be at that future date. Or, if still saleable, it is likely that they will be for a greater or lesser price. Several matters are important there.

First, in respect of 'current solvency', whatever prices exist *now* for assets sold in the ordinary course of business are indicative of their current money's worth. They are by far the best evidence of how much immediate cash can be realized from those physical assets. Those amounts plus liquid (cash) assets are surely easily compared with the amount of debt now due to get an approximate assessment of *current* solvency.

Second, in respect of debts due in the future, solvency assessments draw upon the professional quality of the auditors and management. A physical asset's future money's worth in its market is likely to differ from what it is now. However, every proposition regarding its likely future price generally implies knowledge of its current price, for that is the starting point, the point of departure for estimates of possible future prices. It is impossible to estimate reliably the future without an understanding of the present. Clearly, historical cost data – or supposedly a financial quanta drummed up for the occasion with an algorithm based on several expectations-based inputs (such as occurs in the impairment calculus) – could not be as serviceable for solvency assessments as are the best estimates of the current selling prices.

Any management worth its salt knows such things, and has the acquired skills and business nous to find them out. Every auditor who knows the client's business well and understands its assets has (or at least should have) a developed knowledge of the markets in which it deals. This is the accumulated wisdom, the *differentia specifica* so lauded by professionals. That exercise (discriminating between: estimating the future from the current position) is merely what the public are entitled to expect from 'professional' auditors using their knowledge acquired from years of experience of making practical observations and in exercising their judgement.

A similar tale highlighting the inherent difficulties in relying on conventional accounting to determine solvency had been in our focus a decade prior to One.Tel's collapse when Bond Corporation went to the wall. It was evident again in the 2002–03 revelations following the 2001 HIH collapse and noted in the 2003 HIH Royal Commission's Report. Those solvency and related issues at HIH aptly illustrate conventional accounting's lack of serviceability when critical financial assessments and evaluations have to be made:

> HIH was placed into provisional liquidation in March 2001. Initial estimates of the maximum losses by the administrator were $4 billion, subsequently revised to more than $5.3 billion. The administration occurred, incongruously, not long after HIH had reported the 'apparently' successful purchase of FAI for $300 million in 1999, followed by a 112 per cent rise in profits in the first half of 2000. Although detailing an 'emphasis of matter' opinion in note 13 of the

Notes to the Accounts, HIH's auditors had provided an otherwise unqualified opinion in respect of the financial accounts in June of that year, showing a surplus of net assets of $939 million. That exposes the curious state of the auditing game. An 'emphasis of matter' of opinion, though obviously indicative of a reservation entertained by the auditors, is not regarded as a qualified opinion.

There is a view that the 'emphasis of matter' opinion should have alerted any interested parties to possible risks at HIH. Counterbalancing this, the Royal Commission inquiry appears to have revealed questionable accounting [and related financing] practices ... The lore is that HIH was under-reserved. The issue of assessing the amount of an insurer's liabilities is inherently difficult – as many witnesses to the HIH Royal Commission have attested. HIH's provisioning policy did not provide for an adequate prudential reserve margin in respect of its future claim obligations, but rather it sought reinsurance to cover the risk. Allegations before the HIHRC suggest there were undisclosed (at least to many), questionable 'reinsurance side letters' that may have meant that certain reinsurance rearrangements would have been, in effect, loans. If so, reported profits would have been reduced and liabilities would have been higher ...

The failure of the international accounting community to explain the function of accounting (and hence auditing) so that such key notions as financial position and performance are defined and articulated in an unequivocal way provides a challenge to the continuing acceptance of accounting and auditing as professional activities. Imagine what might happen were a judge to demand that true and fair 'as ordinary words' be given their 'ordinary meanings'.

Unless accounting data are serviceable they cannot inform, cannot enlighten. But they certainly can confuse, mislead, befuddle and ... delude. That is exactly what financials generally do when certified as 'true and fair' ...

(Clarke et al., 2003, pp. 227–38)

That non-executive directors would bring to such solvency assessments their broad industry knowledge and specific industry experience and skills was thought to be an imperative. Poor memories would no doubt be a distinct disadvantage. It was the acknowledged failure of board members' memories in several court cases in the early to mid-2000s that caused us to contest the avowed necessity of companies having independent directors, of the non-executive type in particular. More in respect of the obligations of non-executive directors, and especially the extent to which they can rely on others, especially at James Hardie, appears in chapter 6.

A peculiar practice

The notion of a necessary *independence* of directors or auditors is curious. It seems to be a hangover from Adam Smith's 1776 warning in his *Wealth of Nations* that human nature was such that owners were likely to be more careful with their own money than they might be with that of others. This certainly was reinforced by Berle and Means's 1932 development of the idea that professional managers would be self-serving – a notion gradually morphing most recently into full-blown *agency theory*. One way to defend against self-serving behaviour is to offer rewards (a form of bonding) such that behaviour becomes based on the facts, on the evidence, *independent*, we are told, of related assessments and decisions. Auditors too, we are told, must be independent observers and evaluators of the facts. So, when HIH collapsed it was not surprising that the Australian federal government quickly jumped on the independence bandwagon and initiated its Ramsay review of audit independence.

Of particular interest really is how honest auditors actually are when evaluating the evidence before them. *Honest*, that is, not only in respect of whether they allow ulterior motives to drive their opinion on the truth and fairness of their client's statements of financial position and financial performance, but also whether their assessments possess the necessary industry and client knowledge and professional skills to undertake the audit. Such skills differentiate the professional from the journeyman. Thus, one was bound to be somewhat dismayed when the HIH liquidator was in court defending a 'cost blow-out' as a consequence of having to acquire software to unravel HIH transactions with FAI. Our letter to the editor of the *Australian Financial Review* (Box 4.2) thus focused on HIH – this time concerning what underpinned generally a can of worms for auditors revealed in the administration of HIH and related ongoing litigation.

Box 4.2 High cost for audit software a mystery

Your 'Court fight over HIH case cost blow-out' (April 10) reported the NSW Supreme Court case involving litigation by the HIH administrator, Tony McGrath, against several parties. It revealed the liquidator would have to spend 'between $4 million to $6 million in software acquisition costs' to discover the financial consequences of transactions underpinning the 'true financial position' of FAI at the time it was acquired by HIH in late 1998.

This raises interesting questions.

The HIH Royal Commission Report (especially Ch. 21, 'Audit Function', Vol III, p. 86) reveals that in the financial years 1999 and 2000, Andersen's audit (and non-audit) fees of the HIH group were: $2.417 million ($0.757 million) and $1.7 million (and $1.631 million) respectively. FAI companies were included as part of the wider HIH group audit.

How did Andersen do so cheaply what now is going to cost so much more for what, arguably, amounts to only part of the same job?

If Andersen's software is still available, why not use it and save a mint? Indeed, did Andersen have any such software? And if not, how did it do the job?

Even more interesting, as McGrath's task is the sort of thing auditors might be expected to be doing generally to form an audit opinion about the truth and fairness of an entity's financial condition, isn't there standard software available that might be used?

If not, how do auditors undertaking their audits of major corporate groups manage to disentangle what are often complex structures and intertwined transactions?

An interesting can of worms.

(AFR, 17 April 2008, p. 85)

We have more to say about this in chapter 6, drawing on the HIH Royal Commissioner's experiences with corporate groups, but, in the meantime, how Andersen's staff made such an assessment without such audit software, especially when it related to only part of the auditor's task, was not on the agenda. The purpose of the letter was clearly to press the point that the operations of auditors attempting to form an *honest* opinion on the truth and fairness of the financial position and performance of HIH with conventional accounting and without the appropriate software were missions impossible.

Interestingly, auditors' obligations, such as complying with rules-based accounting standards often having the force of law, make it difficult (nigh on impossible) for an audit to be undertaken professionally. Complex group transactions requiring significant effort to trace, revealed for instance at Bond, One.Tel and HIH, were repeated in subsequent Australian cases. Likewise, in many overseas collapses – in the USA at Enron, WorldCom and 'Europe's own Enron', Parmalat, the international dairy product combine that unexpectedly collapsed in early 2003. Parmalat brought European auditing again under the spotlight, resulting in another inquiry and audit revelations. There was a black hole in the audited accounts to the tune of $US15 billion. Upon inquiry, the Parmalat fraud revealed that some of its previously verified reported figures relating to the overseas operations were on such a scale as to border on the ridiculous. In reporting on Parmalat's activities in Cuba, for example, it was claimed that Parmalat was selling more milk powder there than (were it to be converted into milk) the Cubans' yearly milk consumption. Certainly, were the auditors knowledgeable of Parmalat's Cuban operations they either must have suspected such a claim to be false or have been party to the deception. No approval of accounts containing such an error could be *honestly* made without enquiry. When Parmalat's deceptions became public the cry went up: 'Where were the auditors?' Where indeed? Where had they been in respect of myriad other accounting-related audit failures? Not, it seems, protecting the public.

This was the catalyst for a 13 January 2004 opinion, 'Lapping it Up and Ignoring the Evidence' (Box 4.3). Several issues were annoying about the Parmalat affair: first, the directors' commingling private and business affairs was a well-established creator of commercial chaos. This is especially so when large corporate groups are micromanaged by major, often founding, owners of the equity in the controlling companies, as was Parmalat by Calisto Tanzi. As Lee *et al.*'s (2008) analysis shows, an auditor of Grant Thornton's standing would have been expected to be extremely careful when presented by company founder Tanzi's managerial style and the level of family involvement. Second, the Cuban powdered milk fiasco aspect and an alleged botched Bank of America bank balance verification were indicative of an apparent low-level understanding of how and what should be used as evidence supporting financial data put before auditors.

Box 4.3 Lapping it up and ignoring the evidence

The latest financial fiasco in Europe has echoes for corporate reformers in the US and Australia.

Parmalat Finanziaria's fraud and the implications for creditors of its subsidiaries, including its Australian arm, Parmalat Pacific, is a case of *déjà vu*.

Its modus operandi has overseas and Australian precedent: fraudulent reporting, contradicted industry data that myriad observers ignored, mingling of public and private assets and the manipulation of the complexities of corporate groups. Moreover, it exposes the potential impotence of auditor rotation and challenges one of the key planks of governance reform – separation of audit from non-audited services.

Company founder Calisto Tanzi's alleged skimming of funds on a huge scale from the Parmalat public companies and the unexpected collapse provide an object lesson that the more things change, the more they remain the same.

Skimming public company assets into family companies' coffers is an ever-present hazard when public and private resources are commingled in group structures. Recall the notorious Stanhill (property development) Round Robin affair in the 1960s?

There are also inherent risks when affairs are run through large groups of related companies. Parmalat had 200 subsidiaries. Remember the problems caused by Adsteam's convoluted structure and the Spedley, Bond and Enron groups' complexities?

Regulators and other observers appear to have failed to match company claims with publicly available information highly contestable of what has been reported. In Parmalat's case, alleged sales of $US620 million for 300,000 tons of powdered milk to Cuban importer Empresa Cubana should have rung alarm bells. In hindsight, it's said that that converts into 2.3 billion litres of milk, enough for Cubans to 'swim in', and, 'if spread around it would make Cuba look like Switzerland in winter'.

Earlier instances of such failure are legion and universal. Consider how the UK's Royal Mail shipping company during the 1920s created illusions of profits when its competitors were having a rough time.

In the '60s, American Tino De Angelis claimed his Allied Oils was producing, and stored in its New Jersey tank farm, more vegetable oil than the entire US production, according to government agriculture data. Nobody, it seems, noticed.

In Australia in the '60s, electrical retailer H.G. Palmer reported increasing profits when virtually everybody else in the business couldn't make a quid. Observers, including politicians, took it that HGP knew how to bring home the golden fleece.

In 1972, the Equity Funding Insurance group in the US claimed growth in its business at a rate that would soon imply it had written policies over the entire US population, a most unlikely scenario, but Equity Funding was lauded by those in-the-know as a market leader.

We might also note how experienced traders knew that Nick Leeson at Barings could not have been making the profits he was claiming and Barings was reporting from arbitrage activities through SIMEX. All seem to have ignored it when caught up in the euphoria of the moment.

The dotcoms, WorldCom in particular, bought up more bandwidth than ever likely to be marketable at the valuations placed on it. This all passed uncontested by most observers, auditors and regulators.

The premiums at HIH Insurance contradicted industry experience, but it took a long time for that to sink in as well.

Such discrepancies should have been red flags to the observant. Parmalat's crash shows again observers' and regulators' penchant for preferring internally to externally generated evidence, despite their declared allegiance to independence and its related objectivity. Parmalat is a classic case of how the public evidence is ignored and the privately generated information, albeit attested by auditors, is lapped up.

Other Parmalat matters also strike a chord at this moment when corporate governance in Australia is under the spotlight. First, auditor Grant Thornton was 'rotated' out of the audit of the Italian arm of Parmalat under the nine-year rule, which requires the whole firm to be replaced in the auditing role, in contrast to the Australian CLERP 9 proposed reform requiring individuals to be rotated. The apparent manipulation of the Parmalat group structure demonstrates how impotent the rotation rule can be. This questions the virtues of audit rotation being a breakthrough.

Second, that Grant Thornton did not provide any consultancy services to Parmalat shows audit failure is not as dependent upon the audit/consultancy nexus as many of our reformers would have us believe. Independence of mind would seem to be the real issue.

Government knee-jerk reactions have been predictable. The Parmalat affair has prompted Italian Prime Minister Silvio Berlusconi to declare a need to restructure the system of corporate control, despite having decriminalized accounting manipulations several years ago. Shades of US President George Bush and his post-Enron posturing on corporate reform?

Through it all, the need to have the system of verified financial reporting as the real monitor of things seems to have taken a back seat once again.

(AFR, 13 January 2004, p. 43)

Of course, ignorance is no excuse in a professional activity. Even worse in Parmalat's case was the auditor's acceptance of what was presented as a Bank of America 'bank balance certificate' from a Parmalat employee, rather than receiving it directly from Bank of America – a fundamental blunder akin to an elementary Auditing 101-type error.

More significant is not only the unawareness of audit history that underpins comments on audit failings, but also what audit practitioners could learn were they to know of that history. Seemingly, those who teach auditing in our colleges and universities, those who prepare candidates for professional examinations and those who devise curricula that are the basis for professional examinations generally ignore the history of both company and company audit failure. It has been our observation over many decades that few programmes in universities in Australia or elsewhere (we are aware of a few in the UK and the USA) include *detailed* case studies when recourse to external evidence would show internal evidence either to be patently false or at least of being worthy of much closer examination. Yet external evidence is so rich, so instructive. Moreover, it generally is free. In the opinion piece in Box 4.3, examples from incidents of audit failure from the UK, Australia and the USA were drawn upon. In each the *modus operandi* was relevant to appreciating better the Parmalat affair. Clearly so in respect to the manipulations when corporate groups are involved, for they in particular are illustrative of the failure of auditors to draw upon externally generated evidence when assessing a client's wealth and progress.

This point was reiterated in a November 2012 *AFR* letter to the editor (Box 4.4) and another a few months later.[4]

Box 4.4 On the money to study corporate capers

John Kehoe's piece 'Financial crises 101: Just an idea' was absolutely on the money. Inquiry into business in universities is generally out of whack! Only rarely are students confronted with corporate histories, their successes, failures, managers' necessity for constant review and adaptation, their entrepreneurial actions and shenanigans. Too often, when attention is addressed to corporate games, it is as if they are 'one off' anomalies, rather than the ever-present norm. We wrote *Corporate Collapse* in 1997 and *Indecent Disclosure* in 2007 to expose students of accounting and business to the real world of business.

It is wrong, however, if he thinks that such matters are not addressed in any university programs. At least in the University of Sydney's postgraduate course in Advanced Auditing candidates are directly exposed to the corporate capers, at Equity Funding, Bond Corporation, Cambridge Credit, Allied Oil, Enron, Adsteam, McKesson and Robbins, HIH, One.Tel, WorldCom, H.G. Palmer, Parmalat, China Oil, Lehman Brothers, Westpoint, Allco, AIG, and the like, make presentations and write on allocated cases. Whereas we designed the program there for students to examine auditing issues, automatically it entails a critical focus on accounting, financial disclosure, commercial decision making,

> regulation and governance, the repetition of common mistakes, regulation that
> failed in the past being adorned with new labels.
>
> *(AFR, 6 November 2012, p. 43)*

During the 1920s, when world shipping was having a tough time, the Royal Mail Steam Packet Company's balance sheet data (contained in a prospectus) duped the public into believing that it was making huge recurring annual profits. On the basis of this it paid handsome dividends through the 1920s. Further, management bonuses were substantial and based on annual reported profits. Without specific disclosure it was an understandable inference to be drawn. For the balance sheet was the sole disclosure, with no annual 'profit and loss account' being required until the 1929 UK Companies Act (and actually not in operation until 1934). Transfers from reserves into which refunds from the British government of Excess Profits Duties paid by the Royal Mail company during World War I were the source, but not explicitly disclosed. All quite legal of course, though arguably deceptive. There, the Price Waterhouse auditor (a 'Mr Moreland') was not fooled, but the Royal Mail setting illustrates the value of external evidence relative to that created internally. The unlikelihood that the Royal Mail was outperforming *each* year its competitors was to be found *external* to the impression gained from figures in the internally generated balance sheet. It lay in the knowledge and experience at the time of the worldwide depressed shipping industry.

Barings Bank's internal auditors failed miserably to detect Nick Leeson's 88888 manipulations in respect of his illegal securities trades (see the Singapore government's *Report of the Inspectors*: San and Kuang, 1995). Again, ample external evidence was there to alarm every reasonably astute auditor. Those in the industry, not only at Singapore's SIMEX but worldwide, bearing in mind international recognition of his purportedly arbitrage-based trading achievements, were openly incredulous that he could make profits of the magnitude Leeson reported to London. Yet it seems those on the audit trail and the board of directors did not bother to query the mismatch between what the industry was generally experiencing and Leeson's claims.

Likewise, external evidence readily available from the US Department of Agriculture (DOA) would easily have brought down Tino de Angelis's 1960s fraud regarding the amount of vegetable oil his Allied Oil was producing and supposedly held at its Bayonne tank farm. DOA statistics showed that, though only one of many producers, de Angelis's production claims easily outstripped the entire US production year after year. Not until the exposure of his Bayonne tank farm ruse of having otherwise empty tanks fitted with small oil-filled tubes for inventory testing purposes was the discrepancy noticed.

Several external matters in the public domain should have brought US life insurer Equity Funding Corporation of America to heel long before it failed in the early 1970s. First, while the US life insurance industry was experiencing a problem with selling policies, Equity Funding was reporting data that bucked the national trend. Second, Equity Funding was achieving this with premiums that were lower than those charged by the ailing firms. However, by far the most egregious implication was that, were its reported policy sales to have continued for much longer at the current pace, Equity Funding would have 'insured' a 'most improbable' number ... more than the entire population of the USA.

In *Disconnected: Deceit and Betrayal at WorldCom* (2003) Lynne Jeter explains how Bernie Ebbers overestimated future international broadband demand in his acquisition of 75 carriers in a few years, to the point by 2001 of setting up WorldCom to be then the world's largest bankruptcy. No doubt Ebbers was caught short in the fervour of a juggernaut industry, part of the dotcom hype, but the external evidence of the public take-up of broadband usage was not supportive of the projected future usage that drove his acquisitions. His expectations (like all expectations, incapable of being verified) were nonetheless accepted by auditors to justify capitalizing the expenditure related to unused usage, allowing Worldcom to declare huge profits. In contrast, according to the external evidence his projections were found wanting, and consequently the expenditure should have been 'expensed'. That would have had the effect of turning WorldCom's reported profits into gigantic losses.[5]

Indifference to discrepancies between internal and external evidence has a long history as those few instances show. Another notable example was that of a leading Australian post-World War II household electrical goods retailer H.G. Palmer's claim of 15-year continuous (since listing) profitable trading, when everyone else in the industry was having trading difficulties. Palmer would collapse having never reported a loss! Again, auditor McBlane, being a party to the deception, was not fooled, but the public *bought* it, and so presumably did the auditor of Palmer's acquirer, one of Australia's largest insurers, MLC Insurance Ltd. Post-failure inspection at Palmers revealed it had never been profitable. It was an exemplar of creative accounting (see Clarke *et al.*, 2003, pp. 71–84).

Equally inviting scrutiny were the public differences between HIH's claims to profitability in the late 1990s and early 2000 when its policies for general insurance were at odds with industry experience in respect of both risk ranking and premium prices. There, it seems that for a considerable time neither the regulator APRA nor auditor Arthur Andersen compared industry experience with what HIH was claiming, to the point where discrepancies made them uncomfortable.

Similarities with other fraud over many decades and across many countries, pre and post the current increased regulatory regimes, have highlighted the need to understand accountants' recourse to seek an excuse – labelled the 'expectations gap'. Such a label has been used by the profession and most audit textbook authors to highlight how unreasonable the public's expectations are in respect of audit outcomes. In early 2013, an Australian CEO of a Big Four auditor had recourse to it in an *AFR* opinion piece arguing the audit function needed to evolve. Expectations needed to be lowered. This led to our *AFR* letter to the editor response (see note 4). The claim was repeated at an ASIC Forum several weeks later. The fact that such a plea had been used by leading 1930s US practitioner George O. May in his 'limitations of accounts' apologia,[6] and again in 2006 when the then Big Six audit firms held a symposium on auditing,[7] does not appear to be known by many. More importantly for us, it is a plea that does the accounting profession a disservice.

Both the profession and many other commentators appear at pains to tell those other than their accounting colleagues that something in auditing is too complex for the general public to grasp. Too complex, that is, insofar as auditors are not to be taken seriously when they report their opinion that the financials show a true and fair view – that that is what they mean. A persistent proposition is that the general public has it wrong in their expectations of what auditors do, and that there is an expectations gap, but corporate audits are paradoxical. Company auditors are expected to presume and have to place an unreasonable level of reliance on the honesty of senior managers. Thus, let us consider some. They are to accept management's views on the making of consolidation adjustments, on which of each company's assets to bundle into particular cash generating units (CGU), the amounts of future revenues expected from each CGU, and the rate at which each should be discounted to meet the IFRS impairment regime. Managers thus have the 'whip hand'. Auditors are virtually at their mercy, have to rely upon their honesty, and are at the risk of their own inadequacy regarding those matters bringing them unstuck. This complex and potentially damaging situation has its genesis in mid- to late nineteenth-century prosecutions of fraudulent reporting in the UK. As a consequence, the expectations gap continues to be a 'tolerated *professional oddity*', but it ought not to be. To that end Lee *et al.* observed:

> They admit they can do so – but, hypocritically, only as a management advisory service. They claim to do so in a limited way by assessing audit risk in relation to MAM [material accounting misstatement]. But they have never accepted full and direct responsibility for dealing with the disease.
>
> *(Lee et al., 2008: 706)*

> If public accountancy education is to change to permit auditors to assume the responsibility for detecting MAM by DSM [dominant senior management], the programs must incorporate appropriate instruction in the thinking and procedures necessary to identify and assess the red flags of MAM and DSM. These red flags cover managerial characteristics and traits, contractual opportunities and incentives, complex organizational and financial forms, as well as economic and operational conditions. To deal with these matters, more curriculum time needs to be available for relevant aspects of economics, finance, law – perhaps at the expense of technical accounting and auditing matters.
>
> *(Lee et al., 2008: 707)*

Having such an incongruous position in 2008 makes it possible to consider how those projections about auditors and accounting fared in the events preceding the GFC, and when its aftermath hit. In most countries the GFC had greater impacts on the survival of many banks and other financial institutions than in Australia, but Australia was not totally spared, especially, as noted, companies in the shadow banking sector. There were property- and financial institution-related crises – at Westpoint, Baycorp, Fincorp, Allco, Babcock & Brown, Storm Financial, Prime Trust, Banksia and LM Investments, to name a few. One account of the fallout suggests the property and related financial sectors cost shareholders of property trusts and related financial institutions several billions of dollars.[8] At the apex of the GFC in late October 2008, without prompt action by the Australian federal government to introduce a guarantee of up to a million dollars per customer account on all banks' and 'large' credit unions' deposits, it was suggested by some financial press commentators and Barton (2012) that more than one large Australian financial institution would have been in financial difficulty. This would be further supported if revelations published in a recent account of a proposed class action against National Australia Bank's contestable misleading disclosures about its banks' financial position at the apex of the GFC in October 2008 were to be proven.[9]

So, given our audit 'mission impossible' prediction, it was to be expected in early August 2009 when ASIC was telling auditors of Australian listed companies that they would be monitoring closely going-concern opinions, and any 'emphasis of matter' opinions that the professional bodies worldwide have decreed were to be classified not as a qualified but a modified opinion. Such terminological nuances have long plagued accounting and auditing, being another cause of the expectations gap. So that issue was in focus in August 2009 (Box 4.5).

Box 4.5 A 'mission impossible' for auditors

We might well expect to see more uncertainty over going-concern evaluations by auditors this reporting season, as Tuesday's *AFR* editorial pointed out, but we might also expect that their clients will not like it.

So, if auditors let their uncertainty pass without mention they may be personally at risk if a client subsequently strikes solvency troubles, and they may also face the ire of a client's management if it disagrees with the auditor's evaluation.

As directors cannot continue to trade when their company is insolvent, we must assume directors of any ongoing trading client do not harbour solvency doubts.

Squeezing auditors on fees is understandable, but foolish. If interested users want their expectations met, auditors have to be allowed to do their job thoroughly and be properly rewarded for it.

We might also question whether attaching an 'emphasis of matter' tag is a sufficient warning (so-called barking an alarm) to the public in general and investors in particular.

The emphasis of matter tag is peculiar. No matter how much gobbledegook the auditing profession wraps it in, it is a kind of Clayton's qualification – the reservation used when it is critical to protect the auditor's backside, but less than safe to come out and qualify the report.

It does not amount to a formal qualification in the auditor's report, but it certainly expresses doubts on the evidence that was the basis of the audit report. How else are auditors to assess the going-concern basis other than by determining the client's financial position and, drawing upon the evidence, predict how it might perform in the future?

There is a disconnect between what the public expects of auditors and what the profession seems hell-bent on telling the public – that audit is not the function of an audit.

It is true that an audit of a public company which produces an unqualified opinion is not a guarantee that the financials are without a reasonable, workable, degree of error. Nor is it a guarantee that a company will never collapse. But it is more than reasonable for a reader of an auditor's report to expect that the audit opinion means what it says.

Where it says the accounts show 'a true and fair view of the company's financial performance and financial position' it is an absolutely reasonable expectation for it to mean precisely what is said. And that the ordinary, everyday words used have been used with their ordinary, everyday meanings.

What other function can an audit serve? None, as far as we can see.

Auditors face a difficult reporting season. But as it stands, with auditors squeezed on fees and faced with an inept Clayton's qualification system, reasonable expectations of them are being falsely rubbished.

They are damned if they do and damned if they don't.

(AFR, 12 August 2009, p. 63)

The attention on true and fair, solvency and the difficult task facing auditors would soon be examined again, as events of the years prior to the Centro's unexpected (to many) financial demise came before the Australian courts. There, the Hon. Justice John Middleton provided a ruling in 2011 about the actions of directors in signing off on the 2007 Centro accounts. The role of the audit was also mentioned in *obiter* regarding the case. The class action followed this ruling, and in July 2012 Justice John Middleton approved a proposed settlement by the parties.

We have discussed Centro particulars in chapter 2, and in the conclusion to this chapter it is appropriate that we again focus on the belief that an auditor must comply with the auditing standards and, of course, the accounting standards currently in vogue, but that auditors also be subject to the overriding necessity to report on whether the accounts show a true and fair view. It was the consequence of having to comply with accounting standards that underpinned the letter to the editor reproduced in Box 4.6, relating to Justice John Middleton's Centro settlement decision. A week earlier the *AFR*'s Agnes King had nailed auditors' gatekeeping role in respect to accounting rules.

Box 4.6 Standards hobble auditors

The decision by Agnes King is right enough in her assessment of *gatekeepers failing* in the Centro-PwC affair (*AFR*, 14 May). Antony Robb's letter ('Incomplete IAC standards in Centro', *AFR*, 23 May 2012) supports King's claim, contesting the view of some that there was not a systemic accounting failure at Centro. King was also right in that accountants do not like bad publicity. But we question whether PwC will remain the poster-boy of 'auditors behaving badly' for long.

Importantly, following the Cambridge Credit collapse in the 1970s, the introduction of class actions in corporate matters has made a mark. So the importance of this brouhaha is that the action demonstrates an effective method by which disgruntled corporate investors can chase compensation from inept corporate directors and auditors. Here, it seems there was a rather elementary costly error underpinning PwC's current troubles. But we can assure the public at large that accounting is so chock-full of unnecessary complexities, inconsistencies and commercial contradictions leading many to question in future class actions that this affair was (at a technical level) near to child's play.

As soon as those who use the accounting data reported in company's financial statements trying to assess a company's wealth and progress realize that they are being led up the garden path by standards-based compliant financials, the rush of class-actions will come.

Auditors must express an opinion on whether the company has complied with the standards currently in use but, most importantly, they must express an opinion as to whether those compliant financials show a *true and fair view* of the company's *financial position* and *financial performance*. Curiously, neither 'true and fair view' and 'financial position', nor 'financial performance' are defined in the legislation.

Perhaps not, because it was thought that commonsense would prevail. But it hasn't! Accountants generally seem to have the view that complying with the standards will meet the 'T&F' test. In the Centro case and in many others (see our *Corporate Collapse ...*, 1997 and *Indecent Disclosure ...*, 2007) it doesn't. Indeed, creative (misleading) accounting is demonstrably more the result of complying with the standards than it is deviating from them.

In our books we made that observation. It remains unchallenged. There, we also explained that auditors were on a *mission impossible*, predicting that somewhere, someday, somehow, someone was going to challenge auditors and accountants as to the validity of their 'standards compliant/true and fair statements'. They depart from the standards at their peril – damned if they do, and almost certain to one day be damned if they don't.

Happily this class-action likely brings that day ever closer.

(AFR, 21 June 2012, p. 63)

Compliance with accounting and auditing standards dominated the Centro case. Subsequent financial press reports saw ASIC and the Centro auditor, PwC partner Stephen Cougle, agree to an enforceable undertaking that he be suspended from undertaking audit-related work for two and a half years for 'breaching the accounting standards'. This notwithstanding, Cougle objected to certain aspects of ASIC's claims.[10] Our concern is that this latest regulatory push for another head on a pole, drawing on mandatory standards compliance, has detracted from the systemic deficiencies revealed at Centro.

ASIC's Greg Medcraft publicly released a dismal December 2012 'audit report card' showing his concern over auditors neither obtaining sufficient appropriate evidence nor showing sufficient scepticism to support their opinions. One can hardly disagree. Banksia's clean audit report just weeks before its failure brought on the regulator's latest outburst.[11] ASIC's inquiries showed (from a contestably small survey) 18% of audit firms not obtaining sufficient evidence, up from 14% at the previous year's measure of audit quality. This contradicted the Australian Treasury's edict in its 2011 biannual review of audit quality that quality continues to be very high, but it was closer to the concerns that had underpinned the overseas inquiries into the auditing noted at the beginning of this chapter.

Maintaining auditing under the spotlight as this monograph goes to press was the release by the accounting firm PPB Advisory of its administrators' report to creditors into the collapse of the large Australian engineering group Hastie.[12] A major criticism there was that the accounts did not show a true and fair view of the entity's financial position and performance, thereby questioning the roles not only of directors, but also of the auditor. Regarding the latter, the PPB Advisory Report (p. 67) also observed: 'Based on our initial investigations, it appears the Hastie Group's auditor may not have fully complied with a number of his obligations under the Australian Auditing Standards. We are concerned that the auditor may not have: [1] notified the Board of the underlying control and management issues within the Hastie Group; [2] made appropriate recommendations regarding the write down of certain asset values.'

Auditors need to lift their game, was Medcraft's clear message. Yet ASIC may well be a cause of some of the problems. For, as noted, it has regularly warned accountants that they must comply with the accounting standards, and almost without exception has accepted accounts with auditors' opinions that show a true and fair view. This encourages the false belief that compliance alone will meet the requirements of the Australian Corporations Act. It seems that auditors can't win.

To err is human

The last decade has confirmed the view formed in earlier work that the recurring nature of the inquiries and regulatory responses over many decades entail essentially a mere tinkering with longstanding regulatory and governance structures and a rules-based mentality that does little to address bad auditing practice. Opinion pieces in the period 2001–12 canvassed arguments underpinning the proposition that forming an audit opinion of whether the director-prepared financial accounts show a true and fair view of the entity's financial position and performance necessitates that an auditor act with independence of mind. In essence, it is suggested that they draw on their years of accumulating professionally acquired wisdom. Continuing to focus on expectations gaps, in particular on whether auditors are 'independent *in appearance*' as well as 'independent *of mind*', are distractions for regulators and other market participants.

Chambers in his 1973 *Securities and Obscurities* aptly noted an audit's quality control function:

> To err is human. Hence the practice of one man checking the work of another, particularly where the consequence of error may be serious or costly. In the command of aircraft and seacraft, in medical diagnosis and surgery, in building construction and industrial processes, in scientific inquiry, testing or checking is commonplace ... tested is the *result* of some previous action, not that action itself ... [it is] to do with the way in which the thing tested will 'fit in with' other things, or will do what it is expected to do [that is, how 'serviceable' or 'fit-for-use' is that thing]. In effect all testing is a form of quality control ... The tests that auditors should apply, therefore, are tests of the fitness of the financial figures for use in further calculations and in making judgments about the past or decisions about the future on financial grounds.
>
> *(Chambers, 1973, p. 145)*

At the end of the day it is a reasonable expectation that accounting produces reliable data. Yet it is unimaginable that any self-respecting person, certainly not a professional accountant, would ever consider many of the conventional accounting data *fit for use* in the assessment of their own wealth and financial progress, related indicators of solvency, and their capacity to adapt financially.

There is nothing new or unusual about an audit per se. Indeed, virtually everybody experiences and possibly benefits from audits from time to time. Evidence is tested against predetermined norms or calculations – mothers dipping their elbows in babies' bathtubs to test the water temperature; in ticket inspections on public transport; everybody who has undergone a surgical operation has experienced (been the beneficiary of) operating theatre nurses counting swabs, surgical instruments, drugs and blood supplies used before and after the operation; and everybody flying has benefited from the pilots working though their pre-flight checklist. All those are examples of audits in one's common experience. All were adopting a commonsense, cautious approach. Making observations and verifying against expected external referents. In that exercise they apply their professional wisdom to the task, but financial audits appear to depart from that mould. Company auditors are placed in the unenviable position of being continuously wrong-footed by often expectational data provided by managers (which by definition are incapable of being verified) and the need to comply with mandated rules prescribing such data. Company auditors are thereby robbed of their professionalism. They are hobbled.

Clearly mistakes can occur. Human judgement can be erroneous. However, observations are common to each: testing evidence, drawing on external sources, is paramount. What is needed is acceptance that an audit is a warrant, that audit processes are a form of quality control – where the audit is the quality control mechanism – and that an audit report must mean what its contents say.

Mistakes are inevitable, understandable and forgivable. Not following sensible, truly professional practices certainly is not.

Notes

1 The Commission released its summary findings, *Audit Market not Serving Shareholders*, 22 February 2013, and requested submissions on draft reforms, which will look to 'create a situation where tendering and switching become the norm, and where greater transparency and information increase both contestability of the market and the ability of shareholders to judge the service they are getting. We also want to increase their influence – and that of the audit committee – over the choice of auditor'. The academic findings on this and related matters such as the costs and benefits of dual auditor activities are mixed (see Clarke and Dean, 2007, p. 41, fn 3), and, as this book goes to press, Svanstroem (2013), which concludes that there is a net benefit from knowledge spillover effects when an auditor undertakes audit and non-audit services for the same client.

2 Jonathan Heath and Patrick Durkin, 'Sharpen Up, ASIC Warns Auditing Sector', *AFR*, News, 4 December 2012, p. 9.

3 There have been major changes in Australian (ASAu) and international (ISA) auditing standards in the last decade. In some jurisdictions, like Australia, they have the force of law. Within Part 2M.3 of Australia's Corporations Act (2001) s. 307A requires since early 2006 that auditors comply with the Australian auditing standards promulgated by the Accounting Professional and Ethical Standards Board (APESB). Interestingly, this was introduced as part of the CLERP 9 reforms.

4 In an *AFR* letter to the editor, 'Auditors and Quality Control', 24 February 2013, Clarke and Dean argue that a better-focused accounting system with independent testing (in the quality control sense discussed here) by auditors would better inform shareholders and the market.

5 Other instances of those types of fraud in many other jurisdictions are documented in Lee *et al.*, 2008.

6 For more details, refer to Clarke *et al.*, 2003, pp. 50–51.

7 See Symposium Report, *Global Capital Markets and the Global Economy: A Vision from the CEOs of the International Audit Networks*, November 2006.

8 John Kavanagh, 'After a Period of Shocking Results Property Securities Doing Well', *SMH*, 29 August 2102.

9 The action was settled out of court as this monograph went to press. See www.smh.com.au/business/nab-pays-115m-to-settle-class-action-20121109-293i3.html#ixzz2DIlvbiM2 (accessed 29 July 2013). The conundrum persists as such settlements obfuscate lessons, prevent precedents.

10 These matters are well covered in Agnes King's 'Centro Auditor Suspended', *AFR*, News, 20 November 2012, p. 7; and in Chanticleer's account of the same date, 'Plaudits for Tightening Audits', *AFR*, p. 56.

11 Jonathan Heath and Patrick Durkin, 'Sharpen Up, ASIC Warns Auditing Sector', *AFR*, News, 4 December 2012, p. 9.

12 Joint and Several Administrators, Ian Carson, Craig Crosbie and David McEvoy, *Report by Administrators into Hastie Group Limited and Specific Subsidiaries Pursuant to Section 439A of the Corporations Act*, January 2013.

5

EXECUTIVE SNOUTS IN THE TROUGH

That there is a disconnect between executive and worker remuneration – who gets paid what – has again become a major corporate issue. Importantly, too, it has again become a major public issue. The notion that a fair day's pay for a fair day's work is a reasonable basis for remuneration for all, for executives as well as line workers, seems lost. The GFC highlighted the chasm between executive rewards and line workers' wages. That that needed to occur was evident for the former's compensation was shown to be clearly out of kilter and the gap between the two ever widening. Reports of golden handshakes for executives edged off comfy seats on the boards of failed companies appeared more than generous and hit at the proposition that, like those who sweat to earn a living, executives should be paid a fair amount based substantially on the basis of reported performance. In agreement with the general argument developed here about the need for a fair remuneration, a recent article by Rost and Weibel (2013) draws on social norm theory to argue that executives should be paid a fair remuneration for their services.

How executive remuneration is to be disclosed seems to be high on the critics' list of post-GFC reforms – whether as separate components, or singly as proposed in a 2013 UK reform. In Australia, the federal government in its December 2012 draft reforms seems to be contemplating the separate component approach, causing one commentator, Ownership Matters co-founder Martin Lawrence, to note: 'Oddly enough the United Kingdom, with its single take-home pay figure has already done the work for us. I don't know why we don't just steal the UK idea.'[1]

Several concerns of the executive remuneration debate are notable for the insights they allow into human character. First, hostile reception by executives to union claims for a greater share in company spoils during the good times were shown to be not too smart. For once business turned sour, either because of failure or other market disruptions in the GFC fallout, ordinary employees were far less than sym-pathetic to corporate executives getting huge payouts under their contracts of appointment. Second, shareholders, other investors and the general public were all strangely vocal regarding the financial terms under which executives and boards had been appointed and received their legal dues. They had had little to say, and generally showed no interest, when times were financially buoyant.

Numerous government inquiries have addressed the remuneration issue, in particular assessing whether it was a cause of, or at least exacerbated, the GFC (Gregg *et al.*, 2012). They presaged numerous proposals for change. For instance, in the USA in early 2011 the SEC in a split vote allowed shareholders at AGMs to have a non-binding vote on executive salaries. Section 439 of the UK Companies Act 2006 mandates a vote on director pay at the yearly accounts meeting, with disclosure of directors' remuneration packages provided in a Remuneration Report (s. 420). This has been the case since the early 2000s. The London Stock Exchange Listing Rule 9.4.1 and the Combined Code require that all listed companies must comply with or explain why they do not have a binding vote on approval of long-term investment plans. Since 2009, a similar opportunity has existed in Australia through a non-binding vote on the executive remuneration report.

Regarding the issue of disclosure, currently the focus is on whether multiple or single director remuneration disclosures are the best ways to provide the market with information. While this is important, we show below that measuring and disclosing performance accurately is an equally pertinent and equally slippery matter. This has gained focus with the reported release of Rio Tinto's CEO, Tom Albanese, for poorly performing investment decisions. It followed ongoing major aluminium impairment write-downs following its Alcan aluminium acquisition in 2007 (at the height of the GFC) and also coal write-downs following its 2011 Mozambican coal acquisition.

Interestingly, conventional accounting's impairment method produces highly contestable results. It fails to mark up such long-term investments if they increase in value and has dubious expectational inputs underpinning the impairment approach when there is a fall in value. The issue was further highlighted in the PPB administrators' report to creditors into the Hastie Group collapse (2,700 workers losing their jobs). One of the criticisms was that the accounts did not show a 'true and fair view' of the entity's financial position and performance. As well as inadequate controls, a major cause of this was the way impairments related to goodwill had been calculated.[2] We mentioned earlier the contestable nature of the IFRS-mandated impairment calculus, with its unverifiable estimations.

Late in the last decade concerns re-emerged about the level of remuneration paid to directors and CEOs. A prime example in Australia was the golden handshake paid in 2009 to Frank O'Halloran, CEO of one of the largest Australian insurers, QBE. At the time the estimated $AU7 million payout was criticized by many, including a leading proxy adviser. This resulted in a QBE press release to the ASX rejecting the proxy adviser's analysis, but, interestingly, soon afterwards the board announced that it had halved the payout.[3]

In the period just prior to the release of the 30 June 2012 reports of some of the largest Australian listed companies, an interesting phenomenon occurred. Before their

AGMs, CEOs were quick to announce publicly that they would be forgoing bonuses in this year. It was as if a PR team had won the contract for all those announcements. Not long after that it was revealed in an Australian Council of Superannuation Investors (ACSI) survey of the 2011–12 annual bonuses of the CEOs of the Top 100 listed companies that 'Top CEOs Take a 20pc Cut in Bonuses'.[4] In this environment it seemed as if spin doctoring had tried to circumvent the obvious question as to why there had been any contemplation of a bonus when those companies' performances had been so poor.

Consider some instances in other countries. In particular, the pay-for-performance mantra emerging in the context of the decision in late 2012 by J.P. Morgan to inform the market of the reduced pay to CEO Jamie Dimon of $US10 million (down from over $20 million the prior year). The catalyst was the billion-dollar losses incurred by Morgan's special head office investment unit (the 'London Whale') when engaging in proprietary trades that were outside the Volcker rule restrictions on short-term investments (and certainly were contrary to its spirit). The pay-for-performance mantra clearly has some strange interpretations.

In the UK similar concerns about executive remuneration in 2009 saw their banking sector regulator, the Financial Services Authority, initiate two major inquiries. One resulted in the Turner Report and the other produced the interim and final Walker Reports, *A Review of Corporate Governance in UK Banks and Other Financial Industry Entities* (Walker 2009a) and *A Review of Corporate Governance in UK Banks and Other Financial Industry Entities: Final Recommendations* (Walker 2009b).[5] These had followed earlier reports on executive remuneration, such as Richard Greenbury's in 1995 following public concerns over perceived unjustifiable executive pay outcomes, particularly in several public utilities that had been privatized.

Gregg *et al.* (2012, pp. 91–92) provide an overview of inquiries worldwide into executive remuneration following the GFC, noting that, 'At the international level, remuneration policy has been taken forward through two main channels'. These are the Financial Stability Forum (FSF, subsequently renamed the Financial Stability Board) and the Committee of European Banking Supervisors. The FSF (2009) contained principles 'for sound compensation practices, with similar themes to the Walker Report'. Not all countries followed these principles, producing a lack of a level playing field, possibly causing problems in the future for EU-based banks competing in non-EU markets. Three years later the same concerns surfaced as the EU legislated to limit executive bonuses in respect of EU banks to a multiple of one year's salary.

Showing that the issues are pervasive, and certainly not limited to the financial sector, in 2010 the Australian Productivity Commission provided a preliminary report on its inquiry into director and executive remuneration. In April and May 2009 public debate on executive remuneration arose in the *Australian Financial Review* and other press outlets.

Remuneration rorts have a long history

Memories and a knowledge of history were as scarce in the 1930s as they are now. The 2010 Productivity Commission white paper opened the way for an explanation in a 15 April 2009 *Newcastle Herald* opinion that executives having their *noses in the trough* (despite the financial anguish of others) was nothing new. When Ferdinand Pecora issued his 1934 Report into pre-Depression US banking practices including executives' remuneration he exposed publicly what most in the industry knew: that many company executives received very large compensation packages. Pecora no doubt wanted his report to be sensational. It is rumoured that when accepting the role to head President Franklin D. Roosevelt's inquiry into stock exchange practices Pecora had high hopes of becoming the first commissioner of a likely Securities and Exchange Commission. A tough, relentless approach would do that ambition little harm. History shows he did not get the SEC appointment. Questioned as to why the patriarch of the Kennedy family, Joe Kennedy (then a modern-day robber baron of the kind the Pecora Commission was pursuing), got the job when the SEC was created, Roosevelt is said to have replied that one 'has to set a thief to catch a thief'. According to Michael Perino's 2011 cause célèbre *The Hellhound of Wall Street: How Ferdinand Pecora's Investigation of the Great Crash Forever Changed American Finance*, Pecora conducted his inquiry with the relentless vigour of a commercial inquisition, in particular into the remuneration rorts by investment bankers.

Pecora's account of the Commission, *Wall Street Under Oath* (1939), noted some of the executive remuneration excesses he had unearthed. We suggest that they are comparable in size (purchasing power adjusted) with current executive compensation packages. The opinion in Box 5.2, 'Golden Handshakes Have a Strong Grip', pointed to how then, as now, what were thought reasonably large salaries were frequently supplemented with liberal bonuses, often putting the total beyond most workers' wildest imaginations. Charles Mitchell, the president of the National City Bank, was a case in point. Even at present-day levels his compensation was quite staggering. The $US60 million (equivalent 2009 $AU), while a rough and ready calculation, is sufficient for our purposes to indicate the scale of the payments. Bearing in mind that it did not allow for any difference between the $AU and the $US at the time, or for differences between the US and Australian CPIs or changes in them, the calculation possibly understated the current equivalent. Importantly, he was not alone in sharing in that largesse.

The notion of executive officers voting on how to divvy up between them a 'management fund' comprising half the earnings of their company was apparently common practice. Like those who received bonuses during and after the GFC, nothing paid out to Mitchell and his colleagues during 1929, when the National City Co. incurred huge losses in the crash, had to be repaid.

Queried whether he thought it a 'good system to set up for a financial institution', Mitchell replied, 'Yes; I think so … it establishes an *esprit de corps*'. For those able to gild their own nest, doing so is nothing new.

A GFC upside?

Perhaps the most significant upsides to the GFC were the legitimacy of a kind it gave to the Occupy Wall Street movement and the way it switched the Occupy emphasis from globalization to a focus upon corporate behaviour per se. In particular, there is the way in which it highlighted the outlandish remunerations being paid to company executives, especially when payments were so out of line with the company's reported performance. This illustrated once again accounting's critical role in all of this. The cry was loud and clear that executive rewards should be better aligned to shareholder interests – that is, executive remuneration should be better aligned to corporate performance over an extended period.

In this respect the 2009 post-GFC Wall Street bonus season illustrated the point so vividly that nobody could ignore it. This especially, when it was revealed that the $US170 billion TARP payment (taxpayers' monies) to AIG was used to repay debts that AIG owed to other financial institutions like Goldman Sachs, and in particular to pay AIG executives' bonuses related to the GFC period – ostensibly to executives who were accused of having played a major role in facilitating the global financial meltdown.[6]

In March 2009 AIG paid bonuses of up to $US6.4 million to senior executives, and 22 others are reported to have received $US2 million each in this corporate welfare. Neil Barofsky recounts in *Bailout* (2012) – his account of time spent as the inspector-general trying to ensure some semblance of honesty in the TARP allocation and payment systems – the platitudinous justification given was to the effect that the bonuses 'were necessary' – so that AIG would retain the 'personnel necessary to wind down AIG's complex transactions', of which they were the arch designers. AIG executives were receiving bonuses for attempting to stop the financial haemorrhaging from the wounds they had in fact inflicted (Barofsky, 2012, p. 182). Few have ever been so richly rewarded for such incompetence.

In Australia the same sentiments abound. Recall the O'Halloran uproar at QBE and the more recent focus on the remuneration levels of senior public-sector bureaucrats. In Western Australia, increases in executive remuneration within Western Power and LandCorp (both government trading authorities) have been met with community, media and political disbelief.[7] Attention on executive remuneration proved to be an ongoing core focus for the 2012 reporting season. The chief executive of Fairfax, Greg Heywood, for example, proposed that he forfeited half of his bonus in response to poor performance results. However, this failed to appease investors sufficiently.[8] Increased scrutiny and questioning of remuneration does appear to have had some recent impact in driving management to revise bonuses slightly downward in the face of poor reported performance. In its 'CEO Pay in the Top 100 Companies: 2011',[9] the Australian Council of Super annuation Investors observed that reported or statutory pay for the top 100 chief executives fell to an average of $AU4.724 million in 2011, driven by tougher market conditions. Egan Associates report that the rate of growth of non-executive directors' fees has also declined in recent years and is now more closely aligned with the rate of growth in weekly earnings.[10]

There is a mixed set of views about remuneration developments in Australia. These range from concerns that proxy advisers have had too much and too great an influence, that bonuses are still too excessive and do not marry with actual performances, to concerns that the whole remuneration issue is too complex to be understood properly. There are numerous possible explanations for these contrasting perceptions.

Attempts to align executive rewards with managerial performance (at least on the upside) hark back to the idea of reining in professional managers perhaps doing more to feather their own nests than looking to shareholders' interests. That makes some sense, were it possible to do so, but the GFC brought into stark reality a fermenting uneasiness regarding the manner in which executives were contracted with such high remuneration packages – generally on the advice of well-paid remuneration experts appointed in the main by corporate boards through their remuneration committees. Prima facie at least, this is all very cosy. Even if the recipients do not vote on their own package, generally their mates do.

Prior to the Australian government's *two-strikes rule* being enacted in 2011, under the Corporations Act 2001 there was already a non-binding vote arrangement. Shareholders could exercise a non-binding vote against payments, but it did not have any real effect. As AGMs were increasingly recording opposition votes to remuneration packages presented to them, it was not surprising that the Labor government's Prime Minister Kevin Rudd attempted to beef up its requirements with its two-strikes legislation (Corporations Amendment (Improving Accountability on Director and Executive Remuneration) Act 2011). Under it, were a company from 1 July 2011 to incur two successive votes greater than 25% against its remuneration packages, 50% or more of those with eligible casting votes could requisition an extraordinary general meeting of the company at which the entire board would spill, with all directors facing re-election. In the first year after its enactment over 100 Australian publicly listed companies recorded their first strike. In the 2012 financial reporting period in Australia four listed companies received their second 25% negative remuneration vote and were eligible for a board spill if the shareholders were so inclined. In one of the few spill votes to date (Prentice Soda), no board members were removed.

Consider another remuneration matter. The 2009 Australian Commonwealth Budget spelt the death knell for ordinary employees receiving free shares in incentive schemes. Up to then the general situation was that employees with incomes of less than $60,000 could defer their income tax on bonuses until they disposed of the shares, and also claim $1,000 rebate on their tax bill. It is reasonable to suggest that neither the Australian Taxation Office nor taxpayers were sure which individual schemes were 'eligible share schemes' under the legislation. The 2009 budget set out new Eligible Employment Schemes (ESS) rules: payment of any discount 'up front' on the ESS bonus to those with adjusted taxable incomes of less than $180,000 per year and a $1,000 rebate off the tax paid. The point there is that the free (or heavily discounted) shares were intended to be an incentive for employees to align their interests with those of shareholders.

Fundamental there was the idea that an incentive was necessary for an average employee to do the work contracted for under formal or informal agreements. This resulted in an opinion response, reproduced in Box 5.1.

Box 5.1 Share scheme proposal exposes salary setting

Proposed budget changes to the employee share tax scheme, and then the weekend backtrack by the Government, do little to address the real problem.

Share and flexible salary schemes are rarely what they seem. Usually they are 'too smart by far', protecting employers' cash flows in exchange for uncertain outcomes for the recipients. Of course, at high remuneration levels that risk is well compensated for. The budget inadvertently exposed a questionable salary-setting tactic masquerading as an ordinary employee benefit. It's time to scuttle wobbly thinking on remuneration matters.

Share schemes are a contestable wage-setting tactic. We are told they are to align employees' interests with those of the shareholders in the companies employing them. But what evidence is there that they and other flexible wage arrangements achieve greater 'alignment'?

Provided pay is the appropriate reward contracted for the work undertaken, it's likely that incentives are unnecessary. Contracts of employment ought to specify the maximum tasks required and the 'just' payment for them.

Present workplace arrangements seem to inject a notion of 'standard tasks' or 'effort' for which a fixed sum is contracted, and a variable voluntary 'further performance' attracting incentive payments or payment flexibility.

There is no good reason why a fair day's pay for a fair day's work needs inducements. Is there evidence that such schemes induce enhanced alignment? We suspect not. Indeed, the uncertainty they introduce is as likely to breed contempt and induce unnecessary competition between otherwise equals.

So, while many understandably lament the prospect of losing a tax break, they really are also the losers as it currently stands. Were their employment contracts to compensate for the potential tax break now at risk, their workload clearly specified and properly paid for, they would be faced neither with tax uncertainty, nor thought to be in need of inducements to perform well. Though addressing executive remuneration, some submissions to the Productivity Commission inquiry seem to pursue that theme.

Importantly, employee schemes are possibly used to justify questionable executive remuneration practices. The rub is that performance bonuses and flexible remuneration alternatives accrue faster for executives than for those at the $60,000 point. Employee schemes are certainly in executives' best interests. But there too, why high-flier executive performance is not to be expected and forthcoming without extra incentives is inexplicable.

Performance incentives of the kind now being so hotly defended are alleged to have led to management short-termism, encouraging excessive risk-taking. Eliminating that makes sense, as does rolling rewards into a package, certain in amount, certain regarding exposure to tax, and certain regarding the performance required in return.

It looks as if the budget was pre-emptive regarding the possible outcomes of the Productivity Commission's current inquiry into the Regulation of Director and Executive Remuneration in Australia. Perhaps the budget aim was to ensure that Treasury captures the considerable tax entailed. It might also be interpreted as indicating uncertainty that the commission will find in accord with government thinking, or to ensure that the rules are set in concrete before the commission reports.

Requiring companies to 'expense' option components was rejected several years back in the Corporate Law Economic Reform Program deliberations, primarily because taking-up the options could 'cost' the shareholders (not the company) through diluting their capital. Similar to the alignment imperative put in support of employee share schemes, generally the cases for share issues and granting options in executive remuneration packages draw on the alleged incentive issue.

Some submissions to the commission's current inquiry appear sympathetic to our theme that for the most part alignment doesn't need such incentives.

It was 230 years ago that Adam Smith suggested inducements might be necessary to offset outsiders being less likely to care for others' property as carefully as their own. And 75 years ago Adolfe Berle and Gardiner Means put to Roosevelt's 'new dealers' much the same line in their *The Modern Corporation and Private Property*. Since then the need for alignment inducements has been mostly assumed, virtually never evidenced.

Whereas the Government's motives underpinning its take on employee share schemes might differ from the argument here, were employees to be properly rewarded, their uncertainty removed, both they and shareholders might emerge better off.

(Newcastle Herald, 26 May 2009, p. 9)

The idea that alignment of the interests of those who worked for a corporation and its shareholders was necessary, implies that it does not automatically exist. Berle and Means seem to have held such a view as early as 1932. Over 70 years later Lucian Bebchuk and Jesse Fried in *Pay Without Performance* (2004), written in the wake of the Enron, WorldCom, Tyco and Conseco US financial entanglements, thought it wise to pursue. They found that mostly bonuses and executive loans were decoupled from performance of any description. WorldCom's Bernie Ebbers, for example, is unlikely to repay the $US408 million he received (as he is more than 60 and according to his sentence will be in gaol for the next 25 years); Conseco lent and promised more to its executives in 1999 than its earnings for the year to purchase company stock; and Tyco's Dennis Kozlowski received $62 million in relocation costs. Bebchuk and Fried (2004, p.113) noted that in 2002 30% of the top 1,500 companies in the USA lent on average $US11 million per company to their executives. The total insider indebtedness of the top 500 that year was $US4.5 billion. *Forgiving* executive loan repayments also featured strongly in the USA. It was estimated that up to $1 billion lent prior to Sarbanes-Oxley would eventually be forgiven (Bebchuk and Fried, 2004, p.116). Importantly, those making the decisions and those who received the benefits in the corporate setting are often one and the same.

A similar situation was evident in a recent paper, *Money for Nothing and the Risk for Free: Pay in Large Cap Financials,* by proxy-advisory firm Ownership Matters (2013). It details the Australian pay-for-performance mismatch in the Big Four Australian banks, noting that the GFC had little impact on pay levels and structure: annual bonuses at most large firms are not variable.

Humbug replaces morality

Submissions to the Australian Productivity Commission's inquiry into executive remuneration from industry and commerce mostly did not like the possibility of a two-strike rule. The most balanced view was from consultants ISS, pointing out the fact that, in any event, under the existing companies legislation only a voting share-holding of 5% was needed to call an extraordinary general meeting at which aggrieved shareholders could attempt to move whatever resolution they chose. However, the press did not appear to comprehend that in any event a board spill did not give shareholders any capacity to upset retrospectively remuneration arrange-ments. Those remuneration packages already in place could stand untouched. *Threats* of a board spill were, at best, equally immoral, as was the conferring of the unfair remuneration complained of.

A notable example of sensitivity to criticism of executive bonuses being paid to those heading Australian companies experiencing recent setbacks included BHP Bil-liton's CEO Marius Kloppers announcing that he would forgo a 2012 bonus. BHP Billiton generated a \$US15.532 billion profit after taxation in the year ended 30 June 2012, but the sensitivity to proceeding with agreed bonuses was driven by concerns about having to write down goodwill relating to two of its subsidiaries by \$3.284 billion. Similarly, BHP's major competitor Rio Tinto generated a profit after taxation of \$6.765 billion in the year ended 31 December 2011. Yet because that profit was after recognizing impairment losses of \$9.766 billion (including \$7.405 billion with respect to goodwill), its chief executive, Tom Albanese, agreed to forfeit his approved bonus for that year. Each example indicates the fragility of conventional profit cal-culations as a measure of performance. Of course, neither Kloppers nor Albanese was reported as offering to repay bonuses paid in the years before the impact of the write-downs was brought to account. Write-downs rarely impact only on the year in which they are made. In any event, as 'proxy advisers' Ownership Matters' Dean Paatsch pointed out, both Kloppers and Albanese had done quite well out of equity compo-nents of their remuneration packages, which were possibly helped along by what now are the subject of the write-downs in any event.[11] BHP and Rio were amongst 13 top Australian companies reporting executive pay cuts or bonus forgoings at the beginning of the 2012 reporting season (*AFR*, 20 August 2012). So perhaps, notwithstanding the legal position, the psychological effect of the publicity the two-strikes might attract has weighed heavily on those who have happily banked huge compensation in the past.[12]

In 2009 the Australian Productivity Commission's inquiry and the submissions to it prompted considerable public discussion and several opinion pieces. Three years on, in the middle of the 2012 financial year, 108 companies with nearly 500 board members faced a second strike at their forthcoming AGMs. However, the likelihood of large shareholders voting down any motion for a spill (thereby putting flesh on to James Packer's threat to vote down any Crown Casino 'spill' motion with his own Crown Casino shareholding) just about negated the likely adverse impact of a second vote against that remuneration report.

In a May 2009 submission to the Productivity Commission, Clarke and Dean explained the inherent conflict arising from using the conventional accounting standards to determine the financial characteristics of wealth and progress:

> Whilst various definitions relate to corporate performance, for example: various measures of profit, EBITA, share price movements, and the like, one way or another accounting data generally, and accounting components of profits and changes in corporate wealth are almost universally considered inputs to them in whole or in part. And in articulated income statements and balance sheets, each of the financial indicators noted by the Commission ... generally has implications for both statements, insofar as misstatements of expenses, revenues, assets or equities flow through to affect each other of the indicators ... for the most part conventional balance sheets drawn up in accord with the AIFRSs comprise some data indicative of actual cash and its equivalent (cash balances, deposits, and the like); amounts of money spent in the (sometimes distant) past (assets stated at cost and capitalized expenses) – that is money gone; the market value of some assets (listed securities, and other assets *marked-to-market*, etc.), money equivalents; assets stated at their estimated discounted future income streams (where both the streams and the discount rate are arbitrarily selected and based on expectations) – never money in the past, money at balance date or necessarily equal to any equivalent money sum guaranteed to be acquired in the future; purely fictitious items such as 'deferred tax debits' – purely the fallout from using a technique known as tax effect accounting – never money in the past or necessarily money in the future; goodwill – and similar items – the difference between the market value of assets acquired and the larger amount paid to acquire them – money gone, surely a loss by everybody's [sensible] reckoning!
>
> In that brief explanation the financial aspects of the essential cash linkages of wealth and progress are examined. For without such a cash focus financial accounting serves no purpose. Business starts with cash and ultimately ends with cash – balance sheets are approximations of the interim positions along that cash continuum. *Performance* is sensibly the assessment of the *progress* (or the *regress*) between those interim cash and cash equivalent positions.
>
> To that list we must inject the complication that mostly consolidated (that is *group*) accounts are used to determine corporate wealth and progress ... The financial indicators of corporate performance noted in the Issues Paper cannot be calculated properly with conventionally prepared data.[13]

There, accounting data prepared in accord with the (then) standards was argued to be 'not serviceable' for making the calculations of the kind habitually used to determine corporate financial performance. The position then was prescribed in the AIFRS. Although in several places above we show that a little has changed, the overall effect has not. In the USA, the FASB standards produce data even less serviceable.

Ownership Matters' Martin Lawrence expressed reservations publicly on several occasions about the inadequacy of relying on conventional accounting to derive performance measures for bonus calculations. One example was the way in which revenue was calculated for listed property companies, involving revenue increasing 'face rents' – these face rents do not factor in incentives paid by landlords to tenants such as for fit-outs and rent holidays.[14] More recently others have expressed broader concerns, such as those about the use of conventionally calculated depreciation charges to obfuscate matters in respect of whether bonuses are appropriate, and, of course, we demonstrated earlier the subjectivity inherent in the standards-driven impairment calculations. Such accounting serviceability concerns involving reported numbers based on 'mere calculations' that have no external referent go wider than their use in supporting bonuses. Using a similar creative accounting method, lengthening the useful asset lives of the US Waste Management's truck fleet allowed it to report a $US100 million profit in the 1990s.[15]

Free-fall, golden parachutes and golden hellos

While ongoing remuneration packages caught the public's eye well and truly post-GFC, huge termination payments also became a subject of scrutiny. In Australia an early example was the 2009 golden handshake/parachute recommended to be paid upon retirement to QBE's CEO, John O'Halloran. Many golden parachutes were given to free-falling executives who (it seemed) were on the way out of companies that had not fared too well in their recent past, or to encourage others to jump anyway. Golden circumstances properly captured attention. It seems there that golden parachutes may be a means by which executives were rewarded for poor performance. For others they were merely used to replace otherwise lucrative employment contracts, but the point is that these should not have been written in the first place.

Similar payouts are evident in the UK and in the USA. The Economist Intelligence Unit – Executive Briefing summarized on 11 October 2012 (p. 3) that Leo Apotheker, the former CEO of Hewlett-Packard, resigned in 2011 after just 11 months' employment with a $US13.2 million payout; Craig Dubow, the former CEO of newspaper publisher Gannett, resigned in 2012 with a $US32 million payout; and Eric Schmidt, who led Google for a decade, resigned in January 2011 with an astounding $US100 million golden parachute. In the UK, the chief executive of Marks and Spencer, Marc Bolland, was paid a golden hello of £15 million in 2012 while also having to defend the company's worst clothing trading result in three years.

In Australia, notable golden parachute payments post-GFC include the payout to former chief executive of Transurban, Kim Edwards, of $15 million in 2008 and the payout to the former chief executive of Artists and Entertainment Group, Ben

Macpherson, in 2009. The former Foster's chief executive, John Pollaers, enjoyed 2011's best golden parachute. After having been in that post for only seven months, he walked away having vested an estimated $4.66 million worth of share options, along with a $114,389 cash bonus and one year's fixed pay of approximately $1.6 million.[16]

Boards endorsing such bailout arrangements prompted publication of a 15 April 2009 account of the long history of such corporate largesse in the *Newcastle Herald* (see Box 5.2).

Box 5.2 Golden handshakes have a strong grip

Executive and director remuneration appears well in the sights of the Australian Government with the Productivity Commission's recent release of its White Paper on the matter.

Quite appropriately so, bearing in mind the arguably excessive remuneration packages and golden parachutes received for running companies whose performances leave a lot to be desired.

It might be a mistake however to expect too much to come from the current probe. What happens elsewhere ought to interest us, for the executive remuneration issue is truly a global phenomenon, evoking common allegations and equally common responses.

Of particular interest ought to be the US Government's proposal to impose a 90% tax on bonuses paid out by companies receiving Troubled Assets Relief Program bailout money by US insurance giant AIG for example, and its claims that the payments were 'to retain' key personnel which from a distance seems highly improbable.

We can possibly expect the same claims here. Already the claims are that the market for skilled executives is thin, and that executive remuneration is to establish and retain 'status' in some kind of contestable executive pecking order.

Nor, in the light of such nonsense, should we lose sight of the present hullabaloo repeating what Ferdinand Pecora unearthed 75 years ago when presiding over the US Senate's banking and currency committee's examination of financial executives' remunerations in Roosevelt's New Deal enquiries.

Pecora was 'after the Wall Streeters', J.P. Morgan and Richard Whitney (president of the New York Stock Exchange) in particular. He nabbed Whitney, who ended up in gaol. Pecora's vigour appears to have been driven by seeing himself as the likely first commissioner of Roosevelt's securities and exchange commission, a job that went eventually to alleged bootlegger and speculator Joe Kennedy (the famous father of JFK).

Today's excesses more than had their parallels in Pecora's time. In his *Wall Street Under Oath* he explains the tangled web of remuneration schemes in US banks at the time, and the magnitude of the money they entailed.

As now in the Productivity Commission's enquiry, Pecora had focused on possible connections between managerial risk-taking, short-termism and rewards. Although the terminology has changed, the notions underpinning the issues have not.

And the amounts involved were mind-boggling. Typical, for example, was the remuneration received by Charles Mitchell, president of the National City Bank in the years leading to the 1929 crash 1927, 1928 and 1929. Unbeknown to the shareholders he received in total $US3,481,732 over the period through a series of bonus-paying 'management fund' accounts, though only a disclosed annual cash salary of $US25,000.

But Mitchell was 'no ordinary $25,000 man', Pecora explained. No indeed. In terms of current Australian dollars, 'on the side' he had received the equivalent of $60 million. Pecora's observation has a current resonance: 'And had there been full disclosure [these schemes] ... could not long have survived the fierce light of publicity and criticism.'

Public exposure and criticism might still prove to be the strongest change agents.

(Newcastle Herald, 15 April 2009, p. 9)

Of particular interest is Pecora's role in unwinding the arrangements that J.P. Morgan and Richard Whitney had organized for themselves, and later in the similarity with AIG executives' notion of their individual worths. The idea that AIG executives were essential to recover the insurer from potential bankruptcy echoes Bebchuk and Fried's (2004) complaints that the idea that the skills necessary for recovery lay with the malefactors beggars belief.

Though outrageous, the UK multiples are nonetheless outdone by those in the USA. According to Greg Farrell's *Corporate Crooks: How Rogue Executives Ripped Off Americans ... and Congress Helped them Do it!* (2006), though no saint on any scale, J.P. Morgan is reputed to have said that US executives should get a multiple of 20 times average weekly earnings. In the early 1980s US executives' haul was a multiple of 42, of 85 by 1990, and of 531 in 2000. Charles Wang of Computer Associates received $US698 million in 2000, while it is said (Farrell, 2006, p. 35) that Michael Eisner, the Walt Disney CEO, 'pulled in' $US69.9 million. New York Stock Exchange (NYSE) chief executive Dick Grasso was embarrassed when his total salary over the years 1999 to 2002 was revealed to have been $US81 million and $US190 million in deferred payments. When Grasso was forced to resign his NYSE post, he was replaced by the 'eased out CEO' of Citibank, John Reed, who is reputed to have received $US293 million in 2000.

In the USA the more recent Dodd–Frank recommendation to tax golden parachutes, hellos and termination payments at perhaps 90% is perhaps a move in the right direction. However, the 1930s experience showed that in this area we have learned little about corporate governance in the last 80 years. Executives' noses were equally in the trough then, according to Pecora, while Bebchuk and Fried observed similarly that the situation is unchanged. Similar experiences are evident in the UK. Former academic and NSW Supreme Court Judge Bob Austin ('Austin Legal') noted that in 1988 CEOs in the UK received a yearly average of £1 million and ordinary workers £17,000 – a multiple of 69. By 2007 CEOs were picking up an average of £9 million compared with workers' £24,000 – a multiple of 161. CEOs' average remuneration had increased by over 300% compared with the workers' increase of just over 30%.

A little more on the current state of play in Australia and elsewhere is now provided. By late 2012, there was a reduced use of stock options and bonuses were being deferred. This made sense as the markets around the world were still languishing five years after the nadir of the GFC. The deferred bonuses are another contestable way to align executive pay with performance, to align managers' and shareholders' interests.

As noted in the introduction to this chapter, the Australian government has implemented a formal review of the 2010 remuneration changes. On 24 December 2012 the Treasury released for discussion its *Corporations Legislation Amendment (Remuneration Disclosures and Other Measures) Bill 2012* – 'Corporations Act amendments: executive remuneration and dividends'. Key executive remuneration measures proposed included:

- requiring listed disclosing companies whose financial statements have been materially misstated either to disclose whether any overpaid remuneration to key management personnel (KMP) has been 'clawed back', or, if no reduction, repayment or alteration of overpaid remuneration has been made, an explanation of why not;
- removing the requirement for unlisted disclosing entities that are companies to prepare a remuneration report. The Bill will require only listed disclosing companies to prepare remuneration reports;
- requiring listed disclosing companies to include in the remuneration report a general description of their remuneration governance framework;
- requiring the disclosure of details in the remuneration report of all payments made to KMP upon their retirement from a listed disclosing company; and
- requiring listed disclosing companies in the remuneration report to disclose for each KMP:
  - the amount that was granted before the financial year and paid to the person during the financial year;
  - the amount that was granted and paid during the financial year; and
  - the amount that was granted but not yet paid during the financial year.

Submissions are likely to be varied and it will be interesting to see which of these proposals are legislated. In this way, perhaps the GFC at least has brought into the public arena what previously really wasn't even canvassed openly behind the closed doors of AGMs.

Initial public reactions to the proposals have noted that in the UK and EU recent actions related to banks regarding capping bonuses and related measures may have pre-empted Australia's response. In the EU there is a new reform to limit bonus payments for bank executives to one year's salary. This potentially has spillover effects to UK banks, but notably there is no proposal for the wider application of such reforms to the broader business community.

Governance – and non-executive paranoia

Appointing more lower-paid non-executive directors is a theme consistent with reducing the overall remuneration bill. Folklore has it that non-executive directors also inject boards with a level of business acumen ensuring better decisions and overall better governance. Such was the finding in the report of the UK Higgs Committee. Australia was quick off the mark and soon corporate boards had their quotas of non-execs. Striking a blow to that proposition were proceedings that began in September 2008 in respect of ASIC charges against James Hardie non-executive and executive directors that they had breached the Corporations Act by signing a misleading press release (see Box 5.3).

Box 5.3 Harsh light may shine on non-executives

The James Hardie charges could weaken the argument for independent directors. Proposed legal action by the Australian Securities and Investments Commission against 10 past and present James Hardie directors might produce some unintended consequences. It could inadvertently reveal that one of the cornerstones of corporate governance rhetoric is without foundation. ASIC's charges mostly allege misstatements regarding the estimated funding to compensate asbestos diseases victims.

By including seven non-executive directors (NEDs) among the accused, ASIC threatens widely held ideas regarding corporate governance. Previously, NEDs have been promoted as the honest brokers on corporate boards, the means by which boards are injected with the alleged virtue of independence said otherwise to be missing. Conviction of the non-executives in this high profile case would place a major question mark over the virtue claim that is reflected in the independence fetish. And acquittal on the grounds of a likely defence that, as part-timers, non-executives are at the mercy of what they are told by the executives, puts paid to the supposed value added by having them dispensing their accumulated business wisdom, unfettered by their predilections.

At issue is whether NEDs have all that much to offer. ASIC's action against One.Tel's Jodee Rich and Mark Silbermann has already exposed several notable, internationally experienced, non-executives claiming they were profoundly misled.

And, according to commissioner Neville Owen, HIH's non-executives didn't fare too well either.

The push for public company boards to comprise a majority of non-executive directors has arisen through a questionable line of reasoning. Part of the thinking has drawn on executives featuring in notorious recent company collapses receiving remuneration disproportionate to the poor performances of their companies.

Claims are made that the collapses were the result of the executives managing companies on a short-term basis, to their own advantage, rather than for the benefit of the shareholders, especially long-term.

Aligning directors' remuneration with the shareholders' returns is reasoned to have backfired. A general thrust has been that part-time non-executive directors, with remuneration not linked in that way, inject board deliberations with an element of independence otherwise missing.

It has been claimed, and generally accepted without compelling evidence, that the non-executives inject boards with the benefit of the individual independence that the other directors are presumed to lack. It has never really been explained why. Nor has exactly what director independence means, and consequently why it is such a board virtue. Part of the implied reasoning appears to be that there is virtue in not being aligned to any particular view, in not having any commitment to a school of thought. It follows that, at the extreme, the less informed the directors, the greater their independence is presumed to be. Uninformed independence emerges as a dubious virtue!

Independence is the catch-cry of the corporate governance community. It is supposed to be an element missing in circumstances that influence making decisions contrary to what one really believes or knows. Non-executive directors are taken to be insulated against such circumstances because their remuneration is not directly linked to the reported short-term performance of the company. But, of course that is nonsense, for at the end of the day if a company performs poorly, or there are actions against the board over various matters, non-executives are also accountable. Curiously, the push for non-executives has been an about-turn from deliberate attempts to link executives' remuneration to the shareholders' main interest, their company's performance and particularly how the share price reflects it.

Australian companies have been pushed into the non-executive caper. Listed companies are expected to conform to the Australian Stock Exchange's corporate governance council guidelines that press for a majority of the board to be non-executives, for key committees to contain non-executives, and [a listing rule] the audit committee to be solely composed of them.

In the popular tick-a-box exercises rating companies' corporate governance performances, having a swag of non-executive directors scores highly. Following the argument above, the greater the number of uninformed directors, the higher the rating.

That's a mind-boggling proposition. Paradoxically, success by ASIC in the James Hardie litigation has the potential to kneecap the primary board component in the popular corporate governance regime.

> Then again, that might not be such a bad thing. To the contrary, it may bring some commonsense into the debate about improving how companies are run.
>
> *(AFR, 12 March 2007, p. 63)*

An *AFR* letter correspondent responded the next day to the opinion in Box 5.3, disputing our unhappiness with the focus on non-execs, as this extract shows:

> The saga of James Hardie is an unhappy chapter in Australian corporate history. The role of an independent board includes providing an effective check and balance with respect to the management of the affairs of a company … In … James Hardie, the events … may bring into question the issue as to whether the board of the day failed to fulfil that role. However, failure on one occasion does not mean our system of corporate governance is broken. During the past 15 years, Australia has experienced sustained economic growth and vigorous corporate activity. There are examples, including HIH and One.Tel, of failure of corporate governance during this period, but what is striking is how few failures there have been. By and large, Australian companies are well managed, and our standards of corporate governance compare favourably to those of any of our global competitors.[17]

Yes, James Hardie was undeniably an unhappy chapter, but to us the matter of corporate collapse is not one of statistics. Against the statement that there have been so few failures is how disturbing it is that many listed companies – often large ones – have 'unexpectedly' failed in the last five decades. *Unexpectedly* in the sense that their financials did not reveal the failure coming. Every listed company has numerous shareholders and the failure of their company is a 100% problem for them – there is no statistical comfort there at all. This is especially so if the failure has not been flagged in the audited financials. In any event it is likely more listed companies have failed (many unexpectedly over many decades) than most can, or care to, remember.[18]

Now, nearly every Australian superannuation contributor (that is, nearly all Australian workers) and superannuated retiree has an equitable interest in listed companies. Similar situations apply elsewhere. In the end most of the companies that failed were thought by some interested parties to be in trouble. For the most part as far as the general public was concerned, they failed unexpectedly. At least, their prior years' financial reports gave little indication of a trend or drift towards failure. Conventionally based distress prediction models would not have detected their financial travail.

'All are well managed', it is suggested above. Well, who knows? Few allow one into their centres to witness whether optimal decisions have been made. The claim that 'standards of corporate governance compare favourably with those of our global competitors' is faint praise in the light of the numerous unexpected large failures elsewhere. Unfortunately, we can agree on an international basis that the Australian Wheat Board-banned deals with Iraq rank *favourably* against alleged employees' actions resulting in Barclays' Libor manipulations, HSBC's money laundering and Standard Chartered's Iran dealings.

This chapter has recounted a lengthy history of executive snouts in the trough and covers many jurisdictions. Governance and other regulatory actions have failed to stem the tide of public concerns about those excesses, both in respect of ongoing bonuses and severance golden handshakes. Past experience suggests the latest proposed regulatory actions in many countries are likely to prove ineffective in preventing excesses in the future and as a consequence that public discomfort will endure. As this book goes to press, a report by Australian proxy advisers Ownership Matters provides evidence that indeed this is occurring.[19] However, all of that misses a major issue in the executive remuneration debate. If remuneration is to be linked effectively to performance, then accounting as conventionally mandated needs a major overhaul. This was addressed in chapters 2 and 4 generally, but it is considered in the next chapter in respect of corporate groups and group accounting.

Notes

1 Patrick Durkin and Mercedes Ruehl, 'Executive Pay Disclosure Rejected', *AFR*, 11 March 2013, p. 5.
2 Joint and Several Administrators, Ian Carson, Craig Crosbie and David McEvoy, *Report by Administrators, into Hastie Group Limited and Specific Subsidiaries Pursuant to Section 439A of the Corporations Act*, January 2013.
3 Matthew Drummond and Ruth Liew, 'When Prudence is at a Premium', *AFR*, 4 March 2013, p. 18; note that this is the only time an ASX company disclosure announcement has been used to 'take on a proxy adviser firm'.
4 Australian Council of Superannuation Investors, 'CEO Pay in the Top 100 Companies: 2011', www.acsi.org.au/publications/research/annual/ceo-pay-in-the-top-100-compa nies/777-ceo-pay-in-the-top-100-companies-2011.html (accessed 1 November 2012); Patrick Durkin, 'Top CEOs Take a 20pc Cut in Bonuses', *AFR*, 18 September 2012, p. 13.
5 Financial Services Authority, November, www.hm-treasury.gov.uk/walker_review _information.htm (accessed 15 September 2012).
6 A detailed analysis of TARP appears in a 2010 APRA working paper by Grant and Ellis, 2010.
7 Paul Plowman, 'Government Pulls Wrong Rein on CEO Pay', *WA Business News*, 1 November 2012.
8 Kate Mills and Andrew Heathcote, 'Fairfax Media Feels the Heat', *AFR*, 1 November 2012, p. 45.
9 Australian Council of Superannuation Investors, 'CEO Pay in the Top 100 Companies: 2011', www.acsi.org.au/publications/research/annual/ceo-pay-in-the-top-100-companies/ 777-ceo-pay-in-the-top-100-companies-2011.html (accessed 1 November 2012).
10 Egan Associates, 'KMP Edition 4 November 2012: Remuneration of Non-executive Directors Among the ASX 300 and NZ Top 50', www.eganassociates.com.au/key-reports/ (accessed 1 November 2012).
11 E. Sexton, 'Bosses Sacrifice Bonuses to Avoid Shareholder Revolt', *SMH*, 18 August 2012, p. 6. As this book goes to press both Kloppers and Albanese resigned from their CEO positions – seemingly, the impairments had been too much for their boards to tolerate.

12 Dean Paatsch, 'Disclosure Helps Curb Perverse Incentives', *AFR*, 26 November 2012, p. 28.

13 Frank Clarke and Graeme Dean, 'Submission to the Australian Government Productivity Commission Enquiring into: Regulation of Director and Executive Remuneration', submission 67, www.pc.gov.au/projects/inquiry/executive-remuneration/submissions #initial (accessed 1 November 2012).

14 Mathew Dunckley, 'Property Giants Slated Over Use of "Face Rents"', *AFR*, News, 7 November 2012, p. 3.

15 A. Countryman, 'Companies Have Plenty of Leeway to Get Around Complicated Accounting Rules', *Chicago Tribune*, 27 June 2002.

16 Scott Rochfort, 'The Magnificent Seven: Winners Who Stood Tall Amid the Ruins', *SMH*, 24 December 2011, p. 6.

17 John Story (Chairman Australian Institute of Company Directors), 'Non-exec System isn't Broken', *AFR*, letter to the editor, 14 March 2007, p. 55.

18 Each financial year, ASIC produces its 'Insolvency Statistics: External Administrators Reports', summarizing details of external administrator statutory reports in the preceding 12 months. In its 2011/12 report, ASIC notes that lodged administrator reports increased consistently in the three years to 30 June 2012, from 8,494 reports lodged in 2009–10 to 10,804 reports lodged in 2011–12 (p. 12). The latest ASIC, 'Report 297 Insolvency Statistics: External Administrators' Reports 1 July 2011–30 June 2012', is available from www.asic.gov.au/asic/asic.nsf/byheadline/Reports?openDocument#rep297 (accessed 2 November 2012).

19 Georgia Wilkins, 'Leading CEOs Take Home Nearly 70 Times Average Salaries', *SMH*, 20 September 2003, pp. 25–26.

6

GROUP ACCOUNTING SHENANIGANS

Consolidated financial statements are the conventional (professionally mandated) way to account for the cumulative commercial impact of related entities, but such statements are based upon fiction, unrealistic assumptions, contain items and balances not found in any of the related companies said to form the economic group, and fail to respect the separate legal entity principles fundamental to the centuries-old corporate form. In today's global commercial environment the arrangements of companies to form an economic group, and to account for them with consolidated statements, is an habitual means to bewilder and confuse. Such statements betray the trust in mandated corporate financial disclosure.

In chapters 2 and 4 a radical rethink in respect of the way trust and financial information underpin an orderly commerce was suggested. Reviewing group accounting and related auditing as it is conventionally undertaken is part of that. Any suggestion to outlaw or otherwise to cease what has been a major part of conventional accounting for nearly a hundred years is too radical. The group accounting techniques we propose entail a not too severe departure from the conventional disclosure ethos of the UK Companies Act of 1844 and subsequent reforms to enhance it. Transaction costs have increased as the use of complicated group activities using off-balance sheet vehicles has increased. They include the costs of group accounting misinformation and altered financial intermediation in respect of the costs to creditors of increased recourse to the 'limited liability within limited liability' rules in modern corporations. This has been shown to be an issue especially in the shadow banks' use of off-balance sheet entities in developing financial intermediation innovations.[1]

Our suggestion to eliminate group accounts in their present form of conventionally prepared consolidated financial statements – namely to eliminate consolidated balance sheets, consolidated income statements and consolidated cash flow statements – is not made lightly. Nor is it made without due regard for the current manner in which corporate affairs are usually arranged. For, notwithstanding the repeated criticisms of the modern corporation noted in this monograph, the immediate intention is to improve the current state of corporate group reporting rather than dismantle what we have before developing a workable idea regarding what might usefully replace it.

Commenting on the position in Australia, van der Laan and Dean (2010) confirmed that corporate groups play a major role in business, a feature revealed a decade earlier in the data compiled by Ramsay and Stapledon (1998). 'Many businesses in Australia are conducted not by one company standing alone but as a group structure of several companies over which a parent company has control', observed Austin, Ford and Ramsay (2007, p. 139). The situation is similar elsewhere, for it is common for corporations to imbed themselves in complex groups with networks of majority and minority holdings (Hadden, 1992; see also Ramsay and Stapledon, 1998, 2001).

Bakan (2004) and the OECD (1999) observe that global groups of related companies are the norm rather than the exception. Over three-quarters of a century earlier, corporate America in the period during which Berle and Means made their observations was characterized by the growth in monolithic private utility companies and the railways, against which the few Carnegies, Vanderbilts, Morgans and Goulds stood out. Corporate America was relatively isolated. We indicated in the Prologue that things have shifted since then. Multiple and dual listings of company shares on the international exchanges, multinational monoliths and the number of significant international mergers and acquisitions of the magnitude witnessed by the modern mergers of, for example, AOL and Time Warner, or Daimler-Benz and Chrysler were not common previously. Shareholdings are less dispersed now due to substantial institutional holdings. Furthermore, financing arrangements are changing constantly, with generally greater complexity.

As such, the expression 'corporate group' has evolved into a broad concept that embraces a large number of varying corporate combinations (CAMAC, 2000). In respect of this the HIH Royal Commissioner Justice Neville Owen noted: 'The reality of modern public companies is that they are managed and controlled at a group level … the group structure can be complex' (HIHRC, 2003, vol. 1, p. 129). One example is that groups often have a central banker company, and another for central administration and accounting functions. In a later interview Justice Owen responded to a proposition that related to the size, complexity and control features of corporate groups today. Specifically, he was asked whether, first, corporate groups had become unmanageable and, second, the task of auditors had become a 'mission impossible'. He responded: 'Sadly, that is, sadly from a commercial perspective, I must agree with the "mission impossible" lament.' Then he suggested: 'People have thought it's just too hard, leave it alone. That is an area where I think we are going to have to make some inroads.'[2] From such an experienced and knowledgeable commercial judge this is a sad indictment of the present financial reporting system, but his concerns provide strong support for a way forward, as proposed in this chapter.

The claimed group tax avoidance manoeuvres of multinationals such as Apple, Google, Microsoft and Amazon have resurfaced with the purported use of what a US Senate Committee investigation referred to as a 'complex web of off-shore entities' –

referred to allegorically as 'ghost subsidiaries' – entities technically having no residence for tax purposes (King, 2013). This highlights the difficulties of what is meant by profits, assets and liabilities within a large corporate group operating across many jurisdictions.

Enron utilized complex group transactions and financing arrangements, facilitated through off-balance sheet vehicles described as 'special purpose entities'. However, it is not unreasonable to suggest that SPEs and the like have been facilitated not only by the less than honest exploitation of group arrangements, but also by the fact that consolidation accounting has failed to meet financial disclosure needs. Such ploys as SPEs and creative group accounting practices were not new. Nor, apparently, are they thought outmoded, for they have been used since. Justice Owen in that same interview argued that, as a result of that complexity, 'it's very, very difficult to have an audit system that is going to fulfil the [community] expectations that seem to have arisen …' In the discussions post-Enron, reference is often made to other acronyms for off-balance sheet entities: SIVs and VIEs are just two. Always these are associated entities (in a loose, not literal sense of the word *associated*) engaged in off-balance sheet activities, such as complex, intra-group financing and other transactions.

The prevalence of such group ploys during the GFC resulted in the UK and US standards setters considering changes to the regulatory approved (since about the 1980s) conventional 'control-based' consolidation accounting regime. The concerns related to off-balance sheet debt and effectively keeping 'bad news items off the balance sheet' (Gordon, 2012, citing Ernst and Young, 2011), with many mortgage-backed securities, collateral debt obligations (and the CDO-squared variants) being operated through SPEs that entail unregulated activities of the shadow banking sector. Presumed to increase systemic risks, the sector includes the activities of money market funds, monoline insurers, and Enron-type off-balance sheet investment vehicles. Use of the sector, for example, facilitated another cause célèbre when Lehman Brothers reportedly was able to keep $US49 billion of debt temporarily (at balance date) off its consolidated balance sheet through the use of Repo 105s and 108s.

Gillian Tett's *Fool's Gold* (2009, especially pp. 114–17) is again instructive as she observes that, unbeknown to many even in the industry, the related parties of the banks, 'SIVs were proliferating like mushrooms after a rainstorm' (Tett, 2009, p. 116). Further, she shows how they were used to circumvent Basel rules by raising most of their funds (the main banks provided the balance) to purchase bonds before then slicing and dicing them further into CDOs. All of this because of the nature of the financing meant they did not have to be reported on the main bank's books. Indecent group disclosure at its best.

Repo and similar types of financing led a Sydney PhD student to opine:

> Conforming to various accounting rules (notably SFAS 140 and FIN 46R in the U.S.A.) banks and other financial institutions could arrange their financial statements such that certain assets and liabilities were held off the balance sheet. This created a belief, based on financial statements, that such risks faced by the financial institutions were far lower than was in fact the case.
>
> *(Tuite, 2013, p. 41)*

The late 2009 FAS 167 included the following summary of the latest professional responses to such ploys:

> The International Accounting Standards Board (IASB) has a project on its agenda to reconsider its consolidation guidance. The IASB issued two related Exposure Drafts, *Consolidation* and *Derecognition*, in December 2008 and March 2009, respectively. The IASB project on consolidation is a broader reconsideration of all consolidation guidance (not just the guidance for variable interest entities).

Although this statement was not developed as part of a joint project with the IASB, the FASB and IASB continue to work together to issue guidance that yields similar consolidation and disclosure results for special purpose entities. The ultimate goal of both boards is to provide timely, transparent information about interests in special purpose entities.

IFRS 10 was finally released in May 2011. It proposed strengthening the conventional control criterion. More tinkering. As the following extract from antecedent ED 10 reveals, it covered proposed changes to IAS 27 and SIC-12 re-emphasizing the 'control' criteria for consolidation:

> SIC-12 *Consolidation – Special Purpose Entities* is an interpretation of IAS 27 and, accordingly, states that a special purpose entity (SPE) is consolidated when the substance of the relationship between a reporting entity and the SPE indicates that the reporting entity controls the SPE. However, SIC-12 includes four indicators of control, two of which refer to the majority of risks and rewards, and two of which focus on the purpose of the SPE and the decision-making powers in the context of who benefits from the activities of the SPE. Because many of the decision making powers are predetermined in a SPE, it appears that SIC-12 is applied in practice with a strong emphasis on risks and rewards.
>
> We agree that presenting information about a reporting entity's exposure to risks provides useful information. ED10 proposes however that the only basis for consolidation should be control (which requires both power and returns) and that information about the risks and rewards to which a reporting entity is exposed (without having any means of managing or influencing that exposure through decision making) is disclosed in the notes to the financial statements.

The IFRS 10 control criteria potentially widen the ambit of companies qualifying as subsidiaries, thereby increasing the parent's capacity for using consolidation techniques to hide assets and debts, resulting in a concomitant reduction in leverage; and increasing the capacity for general obfuscation and masking reality. Also in May 2011, the IASB issued IFRS 12, *Disclosure of Interests in Other Entities*, a new and comprehensive standard on disclosure requirements for all forms of interests in other entities – joint arrangements, associates, special purpose vehicles and other off-balance sheet vehicles. Commenting on the reported improvements announced in IFRS 10, 11 and 12, Sir David Tweedie, then chairman of the IASB, said:

These improvements tighten up the reporting requirements for the consolidation of subsidiaries and special purpose vehicles, and require the substance of joint arrangements [such as occurred in the GFC through off-balance sheet vehicles, like SIVs] to be revealed. The comprehensive disclosure requirements will help investors to understand better risks associated with the creation or management of special purpose vehicles. As a package, these changes will provide a check on off-balance sheet activities and give investors a much clearer picture of the nature and extent of a company's involvement with other entities.

(www.iasb.org, accessed 28 June 2012)

Tweedie's view is contestable. There is no demonstration of how the changes amounted to improvements. How they make consolidated data 'better understood' and in what way the disclosure requirements assist investors to understand business risks associated with off-balance sheet entities (as described in the shadow banking ploys above) are also not demonstrated.

Off-balance sheet financing and/or complex transactions with related entities continue to be to the fore – and couched in the jargon of the need to ensure accounts were based on 'substance over form', standards setters have sought quite rightly (through the 2008 IASB Discussion Paper on *Reducing Complexity*) to simplify reporting. However, that is seemingly an intractable matter where such group complexity persists, for if there is to be form there *must be* legal substance.

Generally, the technical way in which reported financial data about groups is derived, namely the use of worksheets, eliminating intra-group transactions and the use of control rather than share ownership criteria for determining a subsidiary has changed little over the last 50-odd years. At best there has been little more than the usual patching by standards setters (as evident with the recent tweaks to the control criteria) as myriad business crises have come and gone. It is useful to reconsider some of those financial events in the last few decades underpinning standards setters' concerns about conventional consolidation reporting (see Clarke *et al.*, 2003; Clarke and Dean, 2007). During the first decade of the new century the matters re-emerged. At Enron, it was observed that Kenneth Lay and his cohorts:

> *bent* the applicable US GAAP group accounting rules. A well-publicised aspect of Enron's operations was the use it made of those SPEs, allegedly to keep debt off the group consolidated balance sheet and to hide numerous losses. This was possible because US GAAP worked within an ownership criterion to determine which entities are subsidiaries and when their financials had to be consolidated. It was relatively easy for Enron to manipulate the ownership level of the SPEs below the statutory 3 per cent benchmark. It is to be noticed that that *deconsolidation* tactic is similar to mechanisms that supposedly were employed by Spalvins in respect of Australia's Adsteam in the late 1980s. Then, as recently with Enron, the weight of the criticism has been more directed at the alleged manipulation of the rule, than at the ineptness of the rule being so

manipulable, and in any event with consolidation not having any direct relationship with showing the financial consequences of transactions between the related entities.

(Clarke et al., 2003, p. 261)

One might well argue further that the problems lie more in the notion of one company controlling another than in the rule by which that control is determined. It is worth considering Weiss, who provided this account of Enron CFO Andrew Fastow's reflected thoughts after a period in gaol. 'Why did a bright, aspiring, stereotypical MBA cross the grey line and present what some have described as a "foozle" – others a fraud?' According to Weiss, Fastow responded that 'greed, insecurity, ego, and corporate culture all played a part'. However, the key was Fastow's proclivity to rationalize his actions through a narrow application of 'the rules'. Weiss observed further:

> Fastow's message, an important one for all managers and potential managers, has two key points. First, the rules provide managers with discretion to be misleading. Second, individuals are responsible for their actions and should not justify wrongful actions simply because attorneys, accountants, or corporate boards provide approval. Compare Enron's deals with the structured finance innovations we've seen since the passage of the Sarbanes-Oxley Act: Enron's prepays (circular commodity sales which moved debt off the balance sheet and generated funds flow) look very similar to Lehman's Repo 105s (short-term loans secured with a transfer of securities treated as a sale of securities). The mispriced investments and derivatives at Enron look similar to mortgage-backed securities at banks or companies with a disproportionate amount of Level 3 fair-value assets (illiquid assets with highly subjective estimated values). Enron's $35 billion in off-balance sheet debt looks puny compared to the $1.1 trillion of off-balance sheet debt at Citi in 2007. Enron did not pay income taxes in four of its last five years, and GE pays little today. Banks are now engaging in 'capital relief' deals that inflate regulatory capital in advance of the new Basel standards. Are these deals true risk transfers or are they cosmetic?[3]

When the global economy again went south, culminating in the GFC, the shadow banking activities of uncontrolled and poorly reporting subsidiaries, like AIG Financial Products, the London subsidiary of AIG, featured strongly. Shadow banking, briefly touched upon earlier (see the observations of Tett, 2009, pp. 82–83, 143), is little known to the general public. Pozsar *et al.* (2010, revised 2012) defines shadow banks as:

> financial intermediaries that conduct maturity, credit, and liquidity transformation without explicit access to central bank liquidity or public sector credit guarantees. [This means that the shadow banks operate outside the banking regulatory system.] Examples of shadow banks include finance companies,

asset-backed commercial paper (ABCP) conduits, structured investment vehicles (SIVs), credit hedge funds, money market mutual funds, securities lenders, limited-purpose finance companies (LPFCs), and the government-sponsored enterprises (GSEs).

We noted earlier that off-balance sheet entities were integral to the shadow banks' financial intermediation activities. For example, Lehman Brothers' use of Repo 105s and 108s involved related entities.

Observations by two commentators detailing the off-balance sheet operations of banks in the lead-up to the GFC explain well the integral nature of those operations:

> Many examples of shadow banking are sponsored by banks or are operated by them, or both. They are effectively part of their 'parent' bank. In the run up to the present crisis, prominent examples were Structured Investment Vehicles, ABCP conduits, and money funds. Many benefited from financial support from their 'parent' during 2007–8.
>
> *(Tucker, 2010)[4]*

> First, perhaps taking a cue from Enron, which used off-balance-sheet-entities to conceal the risk, the banks created many new special purpose entities (SPEs), structured investment vehicles (SIVs), and the like, which were used to transfer risky assets off their books. They lobbied heavily for these entities to receive favourable treatment by the Financial Accounting Standards Board (FASB), by auditors and by regulators, and they won.
>
> *(Ferguson, 2012, p. 221)*

New data noted earlier from the Financial Stability Board shows that the largely unregulated shadow banking sector has grown to about $US67 trillion as at the end of 2011. The Board continues, suggesting that, as well as reforms already in place for the mainstream banking sector, 'Appropriate monitoring and regulatory frameworks for the shadow banking system need to be in place to mitigate the build up of [systemic] risks'.[5] Reforms contested by the sector include disclosure of the extent of derivatives trading and related matters. One critical matter in this area is the perceived need to have a better understanding of the collateral value (fair value, or some form of market price presumably) underpinning repurchase agreements and securities lending arrangements. This is a fundamental rethink of how best to provide critical information for related companies, which we will demonstrate below and which we have been proposing as essential for several decades.

All of this implies that the current (longstanding) consolidation accounting system is inadequate, but, to reiterate, we do not oppose the provision of group accounts per se. As noted, groups of related companies are unquestionably the common business arrangement in modern, Western-style commerce. Nor should there be entertained any doubt that both management and investors need reliable, orderly, aggregative financial information about related companies, preferably arranged so that the input of the separate companies to the group performance can be sufficiently identified. An aggregation of the accounting information of controlled entities, along with parent data, has significant logic given the assumption that comes with the concept of control that there is some cohesion of strategy and focus across these entities. However, without strict regulation public protection is impossible. Conventionally prepared consolidated financial statement data fall short of such a specification. Overall, professionally mandated consolidated statements are grossly misleading, as they rarely contain pure aggregations. By virtue of highly contestable elimination assumptions, they remove the legally based financial impact of many of the most fundamental commercial transactions of the individual (albeit related) entities of the group. As such, consolidation techniques contradict the reality of modern commerce and generally fail to meet the information claims made of them.

Toxic consolidations

Central to those consolidated financial statements is the idea that, where one company controls another by virtue of share ownership or some other control criterion, the companies combined form an economic group (though not a legal entity) and therefore an accounting entity. Such a group is per se an accounting convenience, an absolute fiction. It takes little imagination to envisage that such a belief, being only a convenience for accounting purposes, will be swept aside when the law necessitates that the legal position should prevail. Nor is it surprising that unscrupulous operators will quickly use the accounting fiction or alternatively the legal position when benefits accrue to them from doing so. Corporate bankruptcy is such an occasion. As Australian corporate lawyers Baxt and Lane (1998) noted in an article addressing directors' obligations, the recourse generally to the corporate veil in bankruptcy and its piercing in day-to-day operations amounts to a form of 'directors' schizophrenia'. This has arisen on numerous occasions in countries where that *group* mentality prevails – in particular, the USA, UK and Australia.

Australian cases in which abusing the group notion has been the means of not only producing false accounts but also of, for example, manipulating employees' termination benefits demonstrate well how groups have been used to the detriment of the public. A salient example of the law prevailing is electrical retailer H.G. Palmer (mentioned in chapter 4), which failed in 1963. Analysis reveals that Palmer's *front end-loading* accounting manipulations were similar to those used a decade later by Australia's Cambridge Credit Corporation, and worldwide by Enron half a century later. The MLC insurance company in 1963 acquired H.G. Palmer in lieu of foreclosing on it because of Palmer's indebtedness to the MLC, but, when push gave way to shove upon the H.G. Palmer subsidiary's bankruptcy, MLC quickly pointed out that Palmer was a separate company. While clearly controlled by the MLC and hence included for consolidation reporting purposes as a subsidiary, in liquidation the MLC dumped its wholly owned subsidiary. It was surely directors' schizophrenia in action. All quite legal and proper for it to do so. It would be neither the first nor last parent company to do so.

The MLC did not stand 'financially behind' the Palmer group of financially distressed companies. Indeed, it financially stood well back. Unless cross-guarantee arrangements had been in place, legally creditors of each Palmer group company would have been expected to be left to access the funds of only that relevant group company. Yet, arguably this was not the impression that had been created by the Palmer and MLC groups in their published financial reports. Especially so when the Palmer group had emblazoned the image of MLC headquarters building on a Palmer's prospectus just prior to its collapse, inviting a belief (though definitely not saying so) that an investment in H.G. Palmer was like investing in MLC itself. In its bankruptcy, Palmer's liabilities were truly its own. The corporate veil was drawn tightly around each separate *Palmer* company.

The Palmer and MLC affair serves to illustrate that at the end of the day, where separate companies have transacted as such, the law will prevail. It always should, if commercial chaos is to be avoided. It appears that use of the corporate veil to end up selecting whom it benefits may not always have been so innocent. An early 1950s and 1960s Australian instance involved the unsuccessful attempt by the parent company in the CSR group to quarantine liability related to its subsidiary Midalco, which operated CSR's Wittenoon asbestos mine. Allegedly seeking to avoid a piercing of the corporate veil, it was suggested in court, unsuccessfully in this case because of the specifics, that Midalco was an independent entity from its parent.[6]

Take another Australian example, the late 1990s Australian case of a Newcastle company Steel Tanks and Pipes (STP), which failed in 2000. The subsidiary company within the STP group in which employees' benefits were supposedly held was bankrupt — it had insufficient assets to pay out employee termination benefits. Similar corporate capers were addressed in Box 6.1.

Box 6.1 Group structures win the corporate games

Corporate Australia is unlikely to appreciate the ruction over the estimated $2 billion shortfall in James Hardie's funding of the Medical Research and Compensation Foundation (MRCF).

It has opened a can of worms highlighting corporate activity's dark side, the downside of corporate limited liability, and how the corporate veil may legitimately quarantine assets from creditors' claims.

Corporate games threaten the claims of asbestos-related disease victims who worked for the Hardie group companies that manufactured asbestos products.

The push by the ACTU [Australian Council of Trade Unions] for the corporate veil to be pierced in 'special cases' and unions' banning Hardie products may be useful stopgap tactics. But, broaching James Hardie NV's Netherlands jurisdiction, extending the circumstances in which the corporate veil might be lifted legally, and boycotting Hardie products do not remove the possibility of group structures quarantining assets.

[In the previous decade] Hunter region workers suffered that in the STP and Nardell affairs, as had Cobar, and Woodlawn mine's employees, and those in the MUA/Patrick waterside kafuffle.

The problem lies in corporates operating through a 'group structure'. Irrespective of the circumstances of Hardie's estimates of the necessary MRCF funding, the current imbroglio is endemic of the corporate group structure.

Neither manipulation nor deception is necessary. Quarantining assets from creditors can be a natural and unavoidable outcome of operating through group structures.

Hardie's recent offer of additional funds requires approval by its shareholders. In the absence of a Deed of Cross Guarantee, appropriation by James Hardie NV of its assets to meet the claims of other than their own creditors would likely be a breach of the directors' fiduciary duties.

What, indeed, is the likely outcome in this case were James Hardie NV shareholders to say 'no'?

In the ordinary course of events lifting the corporate veil only in 'special circumstances' would not protect creditors. In the absence of 'fraudulent manipulation and special circumstances' employees in insolvent companies could still find themselves 'out of the money' for their employee entitlements.

Corporate groups are inherently misleading. The 'group' does not have a legal status. The myth of 'group accounts' perpetuates the illusion that it does.

Despite references to 'group assets and liabilities, financial performance and financial position', there are no valid metrics for such things. The profits, losses, assets and liabilities referred to are those of the parent company and its separate subsidiaries.

Most financial information attributed to corporate groups is utter humbug, bunyip-like pure fiction!

No doubt James Hardie's possible legal immunity from liability in the asbestos affair surprises many. Allegedly Hardie's asbestos was manufactured by its separate subsidiaries Abaca Pty Ltd and Abada Pty Ltd, and in the absence of fraud, that is where any liability for compensation lay.

That is the automatic outcome of operating through a 'group structure'. That consequence peppers the fallout from corporate failures. In 'things corporate', the 'devil is truly in the detail'.

Corporate groups are the ultimate risk-management mechanism but they are rarely employed with the public interest in mind, as the Hardie case and those referred to above aptly illustrate.

It is testing to identify what purpose arranging corporate affairs in group structures serves other than to partition liability. Despite the ACTU's striving to pierce James Hardie NV's corporate veil and the Hardie products boycott, a more permanent solution is required.

Proscription of the corporate group structure is a possibility, or permitting it only if accompanied by a Deed of Cross Guarantee requiring the related entities

> to guarantee one another's debts. It would be interesting to observe whether the group structure retained the appeal it currently enjoys.
>
> Certainly claimants such as the asbestos-related disease sufferers in the Hardie case would be better placed. As would employees seeking their entitlements when the insolvent employer companies go belly-up, and the related 'asset rich' companies survive unscathed.
>
> Perversely, some good may come from the Hardie asbestos tragedy, were the NSW inquiry to see corporate group structure the vehicle of the inherently darker side of corporate games.
>
> *(Newcastle Herald, 7 August 2004, p. 19)*

That opinion referred to similar events relating to employee benefits at risk to those at STP in the contemporary Cobar and Woodlawn mines' closures, and a few years earlier at the Gazal group. The particular message there was that the corporate group was a fiction – and, as such, no *group* could own assets or incur liabilities, for both the notion of 'asset' and of 'liability' entail the idea of property rights under the British-based legal system. Although in the end it is understood that acceptable settlements were reached with employees, the STP (and the other affairs) nonetheless illustrated the false impression that the group possessed any reality. Moreover, it was false to continue as if the ultimate parent or another group company would likely automatically stand by to meet any financial shortfall of a group company in financial distress.

Importantly, corporate regulators either do not appear to understand or choose to ignore the inherent defects in the group concept in respect of how it is so frequently manipulated. Certainly, from our observations of the particulars in several high-profile Australian cases, when the group notion has been found to have been abused no lessons appear to have been learned. The 'capital boundary' has proven to be a repetitive problem that corporate regulators consistently fail to comprehend.[7]

Such a strong allegation is more than justified when for over half a century group structures have been at the centre of corporate wars. We noted also in the *Newcastle Herald* piece that that should have been a focus for both company watchers and those watching over them, such as the regulatory authorities, governments and the public. Generally, notwithstanding the publicity that they spawned, whether high or low profile, national or global, the many major financial muddles have resulted in little effective regulatory reform of group operations. While the James Hardie affair showed group operations at their worst, nothing seems to have changed, other than to imbed further the fiction causing the problem.

Cases alluded to have involved many high-profile companies. Being 'high profile', however, doesn't seem sufficient to initiate real action. One such high profile was the now Australian cause célèbre, the Patrick Stevedores/MUA waterfront dispute of 1998. Clarke and Dean (2007) provided a diagrammatic portrayal of what are known as the Patrick Corporation 'September Transactions' of 1997 (Figure 6.1).

That affair highlights the capital boundary problem. Essentially, assets of several of Patrick Corporation's subsidiary companies (F, G and H – to which the employees were contracted) were relocated within a corporate group to the detriment of the creditors generally and employees in particular. The latter were dismissed and were potentially denied the financial satisfaction of their holiday, superannuation and leave entitlements. Approximately $228 million of bank finance raised by one or more subsidiary companies within the Patrick and other sub-groups was used legitimately for transactions within the parent, Lang Corporation Group. Elsewhere, Clarke *et al.* made the following observations on those intra-group transfers:

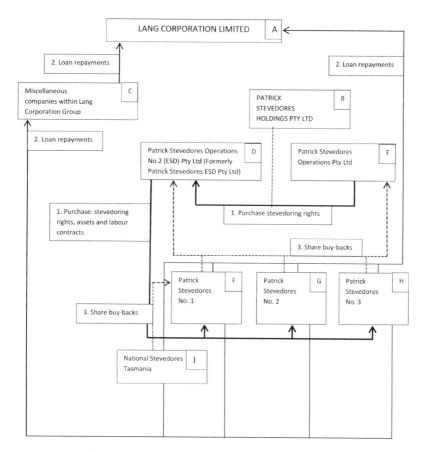

FIGURE 6.1 Preliminary analysis of the Patrick Corporation/MUA 'September Transactions'

Source: HCA judgment, May 1998; Lang Corporation Annual Report for the financial year ended 30 September 1977.
Note: Each company is 100% owned by companies on a higher echelon in the same sector, except company I. The arrows represent cash and cash-equivalent flows between the companies for the following purposes: box = loan repayments; thin line = share buy-backs; thick line = purchases including stevedoring rights. Companies B, D, E, F, G, H and I are part of the Patrick Stevedores Group. At the time of the waterfront dispute $228 million (approx.) was owed to external financiers by various Lang Corporation companies, excluding the parent.

MUA/Patrick's intra-group therapy

Industrial and legal disputes in the 1990s provide illustrations of the complexities resulting from selective recourse to the group and separate legal entity
notions in the management of corporate affairs. They highlight the *capital
boundary problem*. Examples involving the entitlements of employees from
insolvent operating companies include employee dismissals at Cobar and
Woodlawn mines, Steel Tank and Pipes, and the attempted dismissals at Patrick
Stevedores.

Press speculation suggests a situation similar to that at Patrick Stevedores had
occurred in the Australian textiles industry in 1990. On that occasion it was
reported that employees in a Gazal group company discovered after a 'major
event' that 'a separate company that had no assets and only massive debts'
employed them. Allegedly, the employees were frustrated from obtaining
suitable financial redress against any specific 'asset rich' separate legal entity
within the Gazal group due to the separate legal entity impediment to accessing
the 'pool' of group assets. This impediment is endemic to the holding com-
pany/subsidiary company's structure, which is a feature of Australia's [and many
other countries'] corporate sector.

The Patrick affair is a prominent example of the effect of restructuring on
creditors' rights and the limited potential for their protection through provision
of consolidated accounting data and the potential protection afforded by group
financing cross guarantees.

Obfuscation of the domicile of the assets and liabilities of the separate companies is characteristic of consolidated accounting data – indeed, it is an essential outcome of applying the group entity concept. In accord with the group
convention, Notes to Lang's 1997 Accounts (p. 25) revealed that security for
the externally raised finance included charges over tangible and other assets of
the various entities within the economic entity. This further demonstrates the
ongoing potential for and practice of a commercially motivated selective
balancing of the separate and group entity principles.

Consistent with legislatively and professionally endorsed practices, consolidated financial statements neither revealed which companies within the
larger Patrick's economic group or the smaller Patrick Stevedores sub-group
owed moneys to one another. [Nor did the consolidations] reveal which of the
related companies were in debt to external financiers. What consolidation disclosed in respect of the parent's accounts were the aggregate (after netting off)
of the loans made to and from Lang Corporation Limited to its subsidiaries.

(Clarke et al., 2003, pp. 258–59, minus footnotes)

Events often resurface. Yet they may appear new to many. Such was the case in 2004
with the public attitude towards the NSW government's Jackson Inquiry into the
viability of the asbestos compensation fund set up by James Hardie to compensate
asbestos victims of its purported asbestos manufacturing subsidiaries, Amaca and
Amaba. The opinion in Box 6.2 appeared.

Box 6.2 Group system more hindrance than help

We need to take a good, hard look at corporate group structures. The NSW government commission of inquiry into the formation by James Hardie of the Medical Research and Compensation Foundation to compensate people with asbestos-related diseases highlights that the 'corporate group' is a potentially troublesome structure.

The issues paper illustrates how group transactions may be perceived to legally quarantine corporate liabilities and assets under common management.

Evidence before the inquiry has focused on whether assumptions under-pinning the calculation of the required magnitude of the compensation fund were realistic and whether the significance of transactions, such as intra-group dividends and asset transfers, was widely known.

But the alleged isolation of the liabilities in two James Hardie subsidiaries (later merged into the MCRF trust) and asset transfers highlight that the group structure may have been the means by which assets of other Hardie group companies were to be quarantined legally from claimants if the fund were insufficient to meet claims.

If so, it will be a familiar story. Not so long ago we saw the MUA waterfront dispute and numerous similar worker entitlements' imbroglios involving alleged asset transfers and other manoeuvrings through corporate group structures.

Perhaps the James Hardie affair might be another wake-up call for corporate governance reformers.

While corporate performance is invariably expressed in terms of group per-formance the aggregated outcomes of the parent and its subsidiaries when push comes to shove, legal separateness of each of the business entities comprising the 'group' is quickly asserted in line with the century-old Salamon v Salamon rule.

A group structure has frequently been used for allegedly shifting assets around related companies, for legally isolating creditors from assets, and for shifting assets from publicly held interests into promoters' private companies.

Recall the cheque round-robin 'shuffling of funds' at Stanhill Consolidated and Reid Murray in the early 1960s; the laundering of Robe River shares through an intermediary by a Minsec subsidiary to enhance Minsec's 'group profit' in the early 1970s; and Bond Corp's milking of Bell Resources' cash.

More recently, the group structure has also been a primary modus operandi in alleged attempts to separate creditors (often dismissed employees) from the assets necessary to meet their claims.

Initially that was the effect in the waterside dispute between members of the MUA and the Lang Corp group. Creditors were initially left out in the cold in the Woodlawn and Cobar mines disputes, the STP affair in Newcastle and in the Nardell closure in the Hunter Valley.

> Whether deliberate or accidental, the frequency with which assets and liabilities are separated in group corporate structures and the resulting regulatory problems ought to have governance gurus on edge.
>
> The NCSC introduced a voluntary 'deed of indemnity' in 1985, the ASC a more inclusive 'deed of cross guarantee' in December 1991 (altered slightly by ASIC in 1998) as creditor protection devices that would spread debt cover across related companies. But they offer little protection. 'Closed groups' within the 'ultimate group' allow companies to benefit from the deed's quid pro quo, report cost savings and still legally quarantine assets.
>
> It is curious that the prominence of group structures in corporate shenanigans that spawned the current governance fever has not motivated closer attention to managements' alternate use of the group notion when it suits, and the separate legal entity principle when legal refuge is needed.
>
> Corporate groups are a regulatory nightmare. The group structure cuts across the long-established separate legal entity principle underpinning British company law. It is a device that, perhaps unintentionally, facilitates injustices and has been a boon for corporate manipulators keen to defuse and limit liability even further without surrendering control over assets. Arguably, continued use of a corporate group should survive only if there is a demonstrable net benefit to society.
>
> Let's hope the James Hardie matter will be settled equitably. In the meantime, thought might be given to how the group corporate structure is possibly more a governance hindrance than a help.
>
> *(AFR, 1 July 2004, p. 63)*

James Hardie is a more contemporary example of what might underpin the way in which company liabilities are currently managed. Some would argue 'mismanaged', as was suggested with Patrick's 'September Transactions'. There is little new by way of legal principles in the James Hardie dilemma. The subliminal point in our opinion was just that. Group defects are ongoing. Nothing has to change for problems to arise. By reference to the Patrick/MUA, STP, Woodlawn, Cobar Mines and Nardell affairs we were able to illustrate how the group notion meant trouble, no matter the setting. Further, the opinion piece hinted at how the group structure lies waiting to facilitate injustices whether it is used to that end or not. Most importantly, the niceties are largely missed by the public and seemingly by the corporate regulators.

An *AFR* letter in September 2010 considered how consolidation that accords with the traditional control criteria and elimination techniques exacerbates the inherent conventional accounting defects. *AFR*'s Patrick Durkin had aptly noted the latest (annual at least – see chapters 2 and 4) ritual threat by ASIC to 'get tough', to crack down on Australia's accountants by enforcing their compliance with the current batch of accounting standards. The recurring problem at the time was a practice of substituting, at least supplementing, conventional accounts with references to, and in some instances highlighting, what was euphemistically being labelled 'underlying profit' – that is, the results in accord with the accounting standards minus the 'nasty bits'. 'Results' highlighted under the approach used by the companies were said by their executives to indicate better their company's performance than the bottom line outcome of complying with the standards.

Again it was being claimed that deviating from the standards gave a better perception of how companies had performed than did compliance-based results. Not that we argue that such acceptable motives underpin all deviations or all 'underlying profits figures', but, from what was said above about conventional (especially consolidation) accounting, it obviously does not mean that all deviations from standards are necessarily attempts to fool the public. That situation motivated the correspondence to the *AFR* letters editor in Box 6.3.

Box 6.3 Group figures the underlying ferals

Patrick Durkin's 'Crackdown feared on reporting of profits' (August 30) indicates the Australian Securities and Investments Commission again is looking more ready to apprehend and penalize than to prevent default. 'D'Aloisio determined to use war chest' (July 20) boasted a 'war chest' held ready to effect statutory compliance. Examples of reporting 'underlying profits' after excluding the 'nasty bits' implies a disturbing one-way habit of painting rosier outcomes. But, arguably more important is whether the public is much better served by financial position and profit metrics compliant with the accounting standards. While the qualifier 'underlying' might signal a special profit measure, it could mislead on occasions.

Perversely, financials compliant with the standards are almost certain always to do so, especially consolidated financial statements.

Consolidated statements do not relate to any legal entity. The 'group' is an accounting fiction, as are many of the data in consolidated statements, and (by implication) financial indicators derived with them. Consider balance sheets of separate companies said to comprise a mythical group. Almost invariably they include assets stated at past (sometimes amortized) and present costs (money gone), some at estimated fair values (often costs to acquire assets – money wished for), cash balances (money possessed), capitalized expenses (money often long gone), tax-effect debits and credits – artefacts of the accounting system (not money had in the past, guaranteed or committed in the future), debts collectable (likely money in the future), and liabilities owing (money committed).

It's movements in those amounts that come into the calculation of statutory profits. And when consolidated those data undergo another round of massaging, generally removing them even further from commercial reality.

Whereas underlying profit has the potential to delude, conventional group financials are certain to – the ultimate in creativity, about as feral as it gets.

(AFR, letter to the editor, 6 September 2010, p. 59)

That swipe at consolidation accounting again was a golden opportunity to point to the ways in which the conventional, standards-mandated form of group accounts failed to meet its own objectives. Using underlying profits to hide the nasty bits could never be justified. However, equally well is it that, in some instances (for some enterprises), it was useful to expand the conventional idea of accounting profit. The idea of 'underlying profits' also indicated how perhaps, for some, it did not give the whole picture.

In the past commentators addressed this by distinguishing between items as being either everyday *ordinary* items or those considered *extraordinary* to the enterprise. The ordinary/extraordinary dichotomy had appeared to the regulators too open to manipulation to be retained. Regulators seem to have thought it 'too subjective', that it gave the idea that some items were so unusual that those reading the accounts might ignore them, considering them unlikely to arise again. It was thought that that use tended to resurrect the operating/non-operating distinction that had generated similar reservations.

Again the regulators missed the obvious point that what was occurring was, so often, merely evidence that in the ordinary course of business affairs it indeed was the *unusual* that impacts events so greatly. What was considered unusual was not so much so by virtue of its rare occurrence. It was 'extraordinary' rather than unusual mainly as a consequence of its being different from what the ordinarily repetitive events often experienced, their occurrence (though not their nature), easily predicted. What in Nassim Taleb's *The Black Swan* (2007) and *Antifragile* (2012) had been labelled *black swans*. Such events upset auditors for sure. Judgements had to be made whether they were merely obscuring the regular course of things, and that is anybody's guess. The point, seemingly lost on accountants and their regulators, is that most of the big-ticket items affecting business are the unusual events, the infrequently experienced, and often large events, but each rare event is very much part of the multitude of different rare episodes comprising the normal way in which business and life generally operate. The effects of the 'once in a lifetime earthquake' is quickly followed by the 'once in a hundred years flood', followed by the 'five-years-about bumper season', followed by the 'extremely unusual tsunami', followed by the 'once in a decade fashion upheaval', etc. – some good, some bad, but unexpected variety is in the nature of things.

Whether it is the product of one of Taleb's exceptional black swan events is not the issue. The point is that corporates must always be aware of their financial position to be able to maintain flexibility – to be able best to adapt to change, whatever form and scale that change may take.

Mitigating the consolidation problem

Market price accounting for groups is suggested here to be a workable, and more likely to be acceptable, solution. The general mode of mark-to-market accounting can accommodate an effective accounting for related companies, for a commonly declared overall objective of conventional consolidation accounting is to give greater insight into the wealth and progress of related entities than can be provided by their investment cost at acquisition date.

Conventional consolidation accounting sidesteps the more than a century-old *Salomon v Salomon* separate-legal-entity principle. It does this through the aggregation of the physical and financial aspects of the separate entities' assets and liabilities, revenues and expenses of the separate related companies, injecting consolidation-specific data and adjusting legitimate transaction data through the elimination rule, under the umbrella of a supposed group entity. In the wash-up, consolidated data fail miserably to achieve their stated objective.

When in 1966 the Sydney School of Accounting's Ray Chambers proposed 'Consolidated statements are not really necessary', he could not have foreseen the extent to which corporate groups would dominate the business landscape within the next half century.[8] There, he railed about the way in which his understanding of the function of accounting to report the wealth and progress of business entities within a legal, social and economic framework was being frustrated by attributing a legal status to groups of related companies. No such status pertained. The *group*, he explained, was an *accounting fiction*. Subsequently this point was discussed in detail in a legal article, 'Law and Accounting: The Separate Legal Entity Principle and Consolidation Accounting' (Clarke and Dean, 1993).

When Chambers wrote on group accounting, a *group* arose for reporting purposes when one company held more than 50% of the issued shares in another, thereby making the latter a subsidiary of the other. No 'group' could own assets or incur liabilities, earn revenues or incur expenses. Then as now, this was the domain only of legal entities. They were and remain the assets and liabilities *of* the particular separate companies comprising the mythical group. This arises, we noted earlier, because of proprietary rights, which a group does not have. Chambers then outlined a general proposition for an alternative form of accounts that would not only fit in with his Continuously Contemporary Accounting (CoCoA) system. This group accounting format would better provide the aggregative group financial information that consolidation was intended to give when first proposed over 50 years ago (for a discussion of this, see Walker, 1976). However, most importantly, his general proposal would facilitate doing so without improperly attributing any proprietary rights regarding the aggregates of the group assets, liabilities, revenues or expenses that were not their legal due.

Hotly disputed and derided, few critics seemed to realize that Chambers did not claim that aggregative group financial data might not be useful, even necessary, for the effective management of the group affairs. With no support from the profession, his broad description of an alternative group accounting remained just that – a broad description. Chambers would return to this idea in 1973 in *Securities and Obscurities* and again in the 1977 NSW government-approved Accounting Standards Review Committee's Report, *Company Accounting Standards*. Chambers chaired that committee, which held an inquiry for approximately six months and reported in May 1978.[9]

The 1970s Chambers proposal was resurrected in *Corporate Collapse* (Clarke et al., 1997), and fleshed out to a workable mechanism. That was revisited in *Indecent*

Disclosure (Clarke and Dean, 2007). In journal article form this contestable proposal had appeared in the November 2002 issue of the *Australian Accounting Review*. As no refutations of this idea have been forthcoming, a close variant is produced here with a few updates from the 2007 explanation.

An improved corporate group accountability

We have contested whether conventional consolidated data can achieve the objectives attributed to them: show an aggregative financial position of the related entities, assess their overall solvency, determine their potential cash flows, or otherwise evaluate their overall or individual performances. We have suggested that, were there to be a professional and legislative rethink of how to effect the capital boundary in relation to what are currently defined as related companies, Chambers's alternative presentation of the aggregative data provides a workable solution. The overall effect of the features of his CoCoA is to remove most of the causes for the creative group accounting that we have identified elsewhere.

Whereas the specifics differ between jurisdictions and over time, conventional consolidation accounting is based uniformly upon a number of common rules:

- control of one company so that the other is a subsidiary of its parent company;
- a parent company and its subsidiaries comprise an entity (the economic 'group'), which can ignore the capital boundary created by the separate legal entity principle and should be accounted for as if it were a legal unit;
- the data for assets, liabilities, revenues and expenses for a parent and its subsidiaries are therefore combined (that is, *consolidated*) to create a consolidated balance sheet, a consolidated income statement (more recently a consolidated comprehensive income statement) and where required a consolidated cash flow statement. In what follows for ease of exposition we do not address consolidated cash flow statements; and
- generally the applicable accounting standards are applied to the combined data; transaction data are adjusted such that intra-group transaction data are eliminated – presumably to avoid the inclusion of revenues and expenses passing between the related companies, and profits and losses on intra-group sales of inventories and durable assets. It is as if such transactions are to be treated as if they were a sham.

As a consequence of applying the accounting standards in the preparation of the consolidated statements, the consolidated amounts for assets, liabilities, revenues and expenses and the separate items of each classification may differ from the aggregations of those in the separate accounts of the parent and its subsidiaries. Further, the consolidated amounts arising from the use of tax effect accounting may differ, insofar as the net effect may well be a debit in the consolidated statements in contrast with a net credit on an aggregated basis in accord with accounts of the separate companies. That and other consolidation adjustments (eliminations and the like) could have the effect of changing an aggregated net profit in accord with the separate accounts to being a consolidated loss. To top it off, the consolidated statements ordinarily have items for which there is no comparable item in the accounts of the parent or any of its subsidiaries – purely artefacts of the consolidation system. Examples include: goodwill on consolidation, and gain on bargain purchase (previously described as negative goodwill on consolidation or a discount or premium on consolidation).

Presently, under the IFRS regime a company is a subsidiary of another when it is *controlled* by that other. Rules relating to control differ. Indeed, recently we were heartened by an article in Australia's financial press where group accounting matters, other than the control criteria, were to the fore ('ASIC Warns on New Rules'). Concern was expressed over new AASB 10 rules regarding control criteria, namely investment entities with shares in investees below 50% are now required to be con-solidated in some instances:[10] 'investment funds are angry that Australia has opted to deviate from IFRS 10 on this, putting them at a competitive disadvantage' – never mind whether it is helpful to investors. However, later in that piece the appropriate point is made, questioning the 'usefulness' of the new AASB 10 information: 'Fund managers argue that the [consolidation] disclosures are irrelevant to users of financial statements. [ICAA head of reporting Kerry Hicks says:] "These guys manage their business on a fair value basis – what the current market would pay for these investments; they see no use in consolidated statements".' In this respect it is interesting that the IASB is considering whether insurance companies generally should be required to provide fair value rather than historic cost information when measuring assets and liabilities.

Overall the idea underpinning consolidation accounting is that users want aggre-gative information for related companies with a holding (parent) company and sub-sidiary relationship. By doing so they possibly expose misunderstandings regarding the nature of companies being separate legal entities and the property rights underpinning the legal notion of assets and liabilities. In particular, that the assets and liabilities are those that the separate companies own and (in absence of cross guarantees) the amounts that they separately owe. Despite those legalities there appears to be a public perception that consolidated statements will provide information that is useful in decision making. This misunderstanding extends to the securities markets (for exam-ple, in Australia) where moves are to have (as in the USA) only the consolidated financial statement data as the public disclosure requirement of listed 'group' companies. Parent companies' financials would not be required under such a proposal.

Yet nobody owns shares in a group. Nonetheless, financial press analyses regarding corporate rates of return, profits and losses, solvency, gearing and the like almost universally are based upon the consolidated financial statements. As a consequence, investors will receive group information, not data relating to any of the listed companies, data legally manipulated in accord with unsupportable rules.

An illustration

Imagine statements of financial position drawn up showing financial positions in accord with having their assets stated at their current market prices, with their reported profits being determined after an adjustment for changes in the general level of prices. That is, it accords with the CoCoA prescription.

Suppose that H Ltd has a 75% interest in A Ltd and a 60% interest in B Ltd, while A Ltd has a 20% interest in B Ltd. Not only do the data presented below tell it as it is financially, as can best be determined at the time, but they also do so in terms that draw on the common and established understanding of financial matters outside of accounting. The statements of financial position would appear as in Table 6.1. Our group accounting proposal would entail only the parent company statement of financial position and a statistical summary disclosing aggregates for the subsidiaries' various classifications of assets and liabilities, a capital maintenance reserve, paid-up capital and accumulated profits.

Here we have only prepared balance sheet data. It would be a simple matter requiring straight aggregations of CoCoA-style income statements to prepare a sub-sidiaries' statistical summary of revenues and expenses that would give the total retained profits figure of $81 million as shown in Table 6.2.

Of course, whatever detail is thought necessary could be provided as each of the related companies would be required to comply with the disclosure requirements for separate companies under the relevant companies legislation. The statistical summary (as depicted in Table 6.2) gives only the aggregates usually fed to the conventional analytical metrics. Because the current market price data are adjusted by the capital maintenance adjustment the amounts stated for the assets, liabilities and profits are all stated in terms of the general purchasing power of money as at the date of the

TABLE 6.1 Summary of financial positions and aggregative financial performances of H Ltd, A Ltd and B Ltd under CoCoA as at 30 June 2014

	H Ltd	A Ltd	B Ltd
	$million	$million	$million
Non-current assets	251.00	157.20	310.00
Inventories	34.00	16.00	56.00
Debtors	26.80	28.00	31.00
Cash	15.00	15.00	14.00
Investments			15.00
Shares in A Ltd	177.75		
Shares in B Ltd	218.40	72.80	
	722.95	289.00	426.00
Less liabilities and provisions	35.00	52.00	62.00
	687.95	237.00	364.00
Less capital maintenance reserve	163.95	72.00	48.00
	524.00	165.00	316.00
Less paid-up capital	500.00	100.00	300.00
Retained profits	24.00	65.00	16.00

statement of financial position. Being homogeneous in that way they are capable of having mathematical processes legitimately applied to them.

In that statistical schedule we should note that each of the totals for paid in capital, capital maintenance, profits, liabilities and assets are the unadjusted aggregates of the amounts in the subsidiaries' accounts. The amount for the residual equity owned by H Ltd, $396.15, is the aggregate of the amounts shown in H Ltd's statement of financial position as its investment in A Ltd $177.75, and in B Ltd $218.40. The (held by) 'others' amount of $204.85 is the residual equity other investors have in A Ltd and B Ltd, including A Ltd's 20% investment in B Ltd that is also reported as an asset as $72.80 in the statistical summary.

Compared with conventional consolidated financial statements, the H Ltd statement of financial position in Table 6.2, the accompanying subsidiaries' statistical annexure and an inter-entity indebtedness (cross-claims) matrix (like Table 6.3) highlight several features of each:

TABLE 6.2 Parent company statement of financial position and subsidiaries' statistical summary under CoCoA as at 30 June 2014

H Ltd statement of financial position			Subsidiaries' statistical summary[2]		
	$million	*$million*		*$million*	*$million*
Paid-up capital	500.00			400.00	
Capital maintenance adj.	163.95	663.95		120.00	520.00
Retained profits		24.00			81.00
Total residual equity		687.95	H Ltd	396.15	
			Other	204.85	601.00
Debentures		35.00			30.00
Trade creditors					54.00
Provision for dividends					30.00
		722.95			715.00
Non-current assets[1]		251.00			467.20
Inventories[1]		34.00			72.00
Debtors		26.80			59.00[2]
Investments					15.00
Shares in A Ltd		177.75			
Shares in B Ltd		218.40			72.80[3]
Cash		15.00			29.00
		722.95			715.00

Notes: [1] Purchased internally – non-current assets – profit net $9 million; inventories – aggregate profit $6.5 million (at cost (say) $76.1 million); [2] See Table 6.3 for a sample of an inter-entity indebtedness matrix (for Hooker Corporation); [3] Held by another controlled entity, A Ltd.

1 With the proposed alternative mode of group reporting, the fictitious notion of a group entity is dispensed with; the group notion is unnecessary for disclosing the financial affairs of the related entities either separately or collectively.

2 The contentious elimination rule is unnecessary. It matters little under the proposed system whether the transactions are as conventionally assumed, a sham – not at so-called arm's length. It matters little at what price goods and services are traded between the related enterprises, whether it is equal to, above or below the prices otherwise prevailing in the market. It does not matter from whom or when the physical assets are purchased. At least no later than reporting date, each of the physical assets would be restated at the evidenced prevailing market prices as verified by the auditors. It is worth noting that this is a task that the auditors are required to undertake for many assets at present and possibly even more so in the future under fair value accounting, pursuant to conventional accounting (with impairment) and other legislative strictures – clearly much more so than in the 1960s when Chambers first proposed his system in principle.

3 Under the proposed method, the amounts stated in the H Ltd statement for the investments correspond with the proportionate share of the market worth of the underlying net assets of the companies in which the shares are held.

4 Investments in group and 'non-group' entities are stated on the same monetary basis. The expectations of the market embodied in share prices would be disclosed in a manner facilitating a comparison with the current financial state of the relevant company.

5 The outside equity interest of others – the *minority* shareholders – is stated on the same basis as is that of the investment of the parent company. It is unnecessary to resort to the conventional consolidation rhetoric that the interests of the outside shareholders are supplementary data prepared from 'the group point of view', or that the amount of the minority interest is a balancing item. The usual arguments as to whether all or only the 'group share' of 'unrealized profits and losses on intra-group transactions' should be eliminated – whether the outside equity interest in unrealized profits and losses are earned or incurred – are completely avoided.

6 The proposed method automatically takes into account (in our example) the 20% interest of A Ltd in B Ltd, without resort to calculating 'indirect outside equity interests', as would be necessary in preparing the conventional consolidated statement.

7 Were it desired, the data for all the related entities, or for groupings of them, can be aggregated or otherwise arranged in whatever format is desired with complete mathematical propriety, for all the data are indicative of contemporary amounts of actual cash or its equivalent.

8 The parent company's statement of financial position continuously presents a contemporary representation of the worth of the investments in the controlled entities. No additional statement is necessary. The statistical summary of the assets and liabilities of the subsidiaries is required only for the purposes of providing information of the nature, composition and current money's worth of the separate

companies' assets and liabilities. In Australia, many of the companies deemed large would also currently be required to prepare separate accounts and have them audited.

9 The proposed subsidiaries' statistical summary of assets and equities has the potential to provide more information regarding the individual subsidiaries and other controlled entities than the mandated consolidated financial statements, by virtue of its capacity to be arranged to present data about the controlled entities' separate assets and liabilities, or to provide aggregates and sub-aggregates as required. It is to be noted that controlled entities' investments in other entities would be accounted for on the same basis as their parent company has accounted for its investment in them.

10 Aggregate and net inter-company (entity) indebtedness is disclosed, as are the gross and net amounts owed *to* and *by* the related companies through the products of the supporting inter-company debt matrix (as in Table 6.3). Such an NxN matrix would show the amounts owed to and by the related companies to one another and by the related companies to unrelated entities. Whereas the related companies' indebtedness will net out, it would be possible to identify to whom each is indebted (essential to determine their respective solvencies – notably, Australia's prudential regulator APRA requires such company-specific solvency information for insurance companies within a corporate group), the capacity of each related company to offset mutual indebtedness with another related company, and the total indebtedness of each to both related and unrelated companies. Computer spreadsheet mechanisms make this a relatively easy task. It has been suggested to us that the matrix would become unduly messy where the number of subsidiaries is large. For example, consider multinationals News Corporation or BHP Billiton with their many hundreds of subsidiaries. There the number of inter-company claims and cross-claims would be extensive. However, knowledge of those claims and the need to eliminate them is already required as part of conventional consolidated accounting techniques. Under this alternative, all that is being proposed is a listing of those claims via a formal spreadsheet, thereby enabling those legally binding claims and cross-claims to become *transparent* rather than be eliminated, as at present. It is likely with the advent of X-BRL that it would not entail any incremental costs to produce.

11 With corporate liquidations, administrators already need to prepare schedules of cross-claims and others within and outside the group when preparing a statement of affairs. This has been demonstrated in Houghton, Dean and Luckett's (1999) analysis of one of Australia's largest administrations, involving the Hooker Corporation. The type of matrix proposed is illustrated in Table 6.3, drawing on Houghton *et al.*'s data. Similar cross-claim data would apply in ongoing firms (as suggested in point 10 above). A feature of the way the data are presented is the ease of identifying possible cash-flow implications of the intercompany external asset and liability positions of the companies in the group. Similarly, NxN matrices could be prepared for other intra-group elements such as sales, expenses, profits and dividends.

12 Also, with today's technology and X-BRL reporting there would be minimal trouble (cost) in having these inter-company receivables and payables updated and reported continuously to interested parties if necessary. These matrix data could be placed on a company's website and downloaded by those who require it. Indeed, one would presume that the data in this proposed matrix must already exist for auditors to be able to do their job properly and for directors to be able to attest in an informed way to the respective solvencies of group companies.

13 Market prices for listed investments would be the primary basis for statement of financial position reporting, but either when listed or not listed, there would always be a reporting of the proportionate share of the investee's underlying net assets on the basis of their cash equivalent value or approximations to it as evidenced by their current selling prices. The proportionate share in the underlying net assets of the investee would be stated in parentheses immediately below the market price of the investment. Thus all intercorporate investments – irrespective of whether they bestowed a controlling interest – would be accounted for on the same basis, disclosing where applicable both the market price of the shares and the proportionate underlying net assets of the investee.

Déjà vu

The matter of corporate groups and what form reporting for groups should take regained topicality in 2009–10 when the Australian federal government sought to 'Simplify the Regulatory Environment'. One way it proposed to achieve this was to amend the Corporations Act by eliminating the need for parent companies to report. This, coupled to the present reporting exemptions for many subsidiary companies, meant that for corporate groups the only reported information would be what we have referred to as the misinformation in conventionally prepared consolidated group accounts. A submission along the lines outlined above was made to the committee considering that proposal.[11] The continuation of regulators to see virtue in conventionally prepared consolidation accounting is surprising and disappointing. Legislation was passed along the lines proposed in the 2009–10 Bill, but after a year it is again being reviewed, after lobbying saw the initial mandatory rules dropped.[12] Directors of a group retain the option to provide parent entity annual accounts as well as consolidated accounts.

In sum

Our view is that for a group of related entities *more*, not *less*, aggregated information is required to inform the market. The necessary information is already currently collected by the set of related companies as they prepare data necessary for the preparation and auditing of conventional consolidated accounting reports. However, the conventional accounting consolidation process causes pertinent information to be either lost or distorted in that process. This is especially so through the conventional group accounting consolidation elimination procedures for intra-group transactions

TABLE 6.3 Inter-entity indebtedness matrix – Hooker Corporation

Lending company	Borrowing company 1	2	3	4	5	6	7	8	⟋	26	27	Internal assets	External assets
1		24,631,496	2,787,954					7,328,032		1,916,048		109,879,061	76,337,335
2			75,321	336,704			311,857	350,017			719,440	2,609,164	25,523,512
3												0	834,262
4	1,886,487											1,886,487	1,001,833
5	67,792,306	440,846				6,937						68,240,089	22,103,584
6	6,434,972	32,092										6,467,064	1,019,142
7	3,433,477											3,433,477	3,533,127
8						6,249,135						6,249,135	270,403
9												0	25,319
10												0	6,597,296
11												0	3,345,032
12	2,343,810	282						13,451,000				15,795,092	2,745,765
13												0	519,351
14												6,375	28,169,567
15												0	16,334,826
16	93,207,497											93,207,497	612,840
17												2,166	10,036,065
18												12,700,551	22,821,537
19												1,043,415	1,742,448
20	41,512,071											43,365,571	38,815,223
21												0	2,387,578
22												0	1,290,313
23												0	1,928,129
24	6,806,813											6,806,813	19,377,359
25												0	895,583
26												0	976,143
27	3,244,227											3,244,227	7,690,076
Internal liabilities	226,661,660	25,104,716	2,863,275	336,704	0	6,256,072	311,857	21,129,049		1,916,048	719,440	374,936,184	296,933,648
External liabilities	1,644,061,448	35,231	6,438	12,246	57,552,323	762,969	468,067	35,195			891,482		1,983,623,992

Source: Based on Clarke, Dean and Houghton, 2002, pp. 58–72, at 69; the matrix assets and liabilities data are based on particulars in the Hooker Corporation Liquidation prior to the cross guarantee covenants being crystallized. A similar matrix could be prepared for revenues and expenses. Among other things, internal (within-group) assets and liabilities balances must be equal (in this case, $374,936,184). Also, in this liquidation case external assets of $296,933,648 are substantially less than external liabilities of $1,983,623,992.

and balances. They produce the exemplar of creative accounting. Our alternative group accounting approach would see the necessary information (for analyses for specific entities within the corporate group) about a set of related entities provided to the market. With the advent of X-BRL reporting it is likely that it would not entail any incremental costs to produce.[13]

Interestingly, prudential regulators are not convinced of the serviceability of consolidated data, especially for assisting them in one of their main tasks, assessing solvency of financial institutions. They require separate company financial data for any insurance company under regulatory jurisdiction. Gordon (2012) discusses similar reforms regarding superannuation institutions in submissions to a 2007 AASB Consultation Paper on the AASB's proposed requirements in relation to the consolidation of subsidiaries by superannuation entities.

Science proceeds through a process of gradual refinement. In practising disciplines that process is usually a means by which colleagues in academe and practitioners alert one another to errors and possible refinements and improvements in the mechanics, explanation and presentation of them. Practice then changes. Not so in accounting, it seems. In the circumstances we can only assume that we have overwhelming support for our argument and explanation, and that the glitches have not confused anybody.

As Justice Neville Owen (as he then was) observed in the abovementioned interview, *there is a critical need for change in this area.* So our proposals may not be that radical, and they do accord with reforms like those proposed by Haldane (met earlier), who advocated generally that society should strive for fewer, albeit more focused, regulations. Nor are they that far removed from those practices already prescribed by prudential regulators to assist in assessing the solvency of each subsidiary.

Notes

1 The mapping in 2010 by Pozsar *et al.* (revised in 2012) of shadow banking's interconnectedness revealed for the first time the extent of the sector's global reach and systemic risks. Of course, in the general corporate arena such internecine grouping arrangements are quite common. Recent commentaries on pyramidal control structures (critics have endured since the 1930s) include references to the Canadian conglomerate LM Management, with its operations and financings using many intertwined vehicles. Australia's Macquarie Group in the mid-2000s was similarly structured and criticized, as was Australia's failed Allco/Rubicon Group (placed in administration in 2009).

2 Video interview by Graeme Dean of Justice Neville Owen, 14 June 2010, shown on the University of Sydney Business School website under the heading 'Mission Impossible', sydney.edu.au/business/accounting (accessed 28 June 2012).

3 Lawrence Weiss, 'If the Auditors Sign Off, Does that Make it OK?', *Harvard Business Review*, online, 1 May 2012.

4 See also P.M.W. Tucker, 'Speech by Mr Paul Tucker, Deputy Governor for Financial Stability at the Bank of England, at the European Commission High Level Conference, Brussels', 27 April 2012.

5 See FSB, 'Strengthening the Oversight and Regulation of Shadow Banking', November 2012; and the report by Ben Moshinsky and Jim Brunsden, 'Regulators Eye Shadow Banking Sector', *AFR*, 20 November 2012, p. 41.

6 *AFR* commentary, 28 November 2012, on Midalco observes that the Western Australia Supreme Court rejected the independence argument, noting that Midalco directors were

also senior employees of the parent company, and that any expenditure greater than $20 required parent company approval.

7 It would appear that Australia's prudential regulator under the guidance in the mid- to late 2000s of its chairman John Laker, assisted by Charles Littrell, was aware of the problems such grouping creates. Several initiatives involved providing separate entity data to the regulators, unbundling the group arrangements. Overseas prudential regulators, notably the Bank of England's Andrew Haldane, are similarly aware. This is evident in the 'ring-fencing' reforms related to the separate retail and proprietary banking arms recommended by the UK Parliamentary Commission on Banking Standards. They are similar to the US Volcker rule that is part of the Dodd-Frank reforms.

8 The Chambers Archive, sydney.edu.au/business/mpa (accessed 12 December 2012), reveals in private correspondence that Chambers changed his mind regarding support for conventional consolidation statements. Consider the USAP 202 items 8727, 8731, 8733. Another Sydney School of Accounting (SSA) member, Bob Walker, 1976, 1978, provided similar criticisms of conventional consolidated statements.

9 A detailed account of the process and a failure by the main accounting professional bodies to provide input to that inquiry is provided in Clarke, Dean and Wells, 2012.

10 Agnes King, *AFR*, 28 November 2012, p. 40.

11 See Dean and Clarke submission in response to 'Exposure Draft of the Corporations Amendment (Corporate Reporting Reform) Bill 2010', 1 April 2010, archive.treasury. gov.au/documents/1764/PDF/University_of_Sydney.pdf.

12 As this monograph goes to press there is a review by the Australian Treasury of the effectiveness of these 2010 changed reporting and dividend rules. Submissions have been invited from interested parties.

13 The latest initiatives regarding X-BRL are noted on the FASB website, www.fasb.org/ jsp/FASB/Page/SectionPage&cid=1176163248382.

EPILOGUE

(Written more in anguish than in anger)

It is hard not to despair, writing this Epilogue. There are bound to be more than we who bemoan the failure of corporate behaviour to match public expectations. Here mainly we have reproduced and discussed in depth events during the last calamitous decade. Overall we have had little to say about the GFC per se.[1] Most importantly, what we complain of was evidenced well before the GFC, and it continues. A perverse upside of the GFC is the publicity given to the evidence of corporations and their agents behaving badly. The GFC has served to highlight misunderstandings of the function of accounting, the role of auditors in a market economy and the ineptitude of regulators and corporate regulatory agencies. It has brought into the light evidence of corporations' unreasonable political power, their use of corporate wealth against the interests of the public, and the gross imbalances between executive remuneration and the pay of ordinary workers. It has reinforced evidence of the failure of the accounting of the prevailing corporate group form. Whereas the GFC has been the direct focus of so many books over the past four to five years, a generally unreported downside of it is that most of the matters of which we complain existed well before the GFC, and moreover have become worse by virtue of neglect, allowing defaults in the corporate system. That system now is almost beyond repair without a radical, serious and concentrated effort. Unfortunately, there is no likelihood of that on the horizon.

Our analysis reveals precious few authors have concluded that there is anything wrong with the present corporate structure. Yet the evidence suggests to us that the conclusion is obvious: a governance mechanism – in particular, accounting – habitually fails to provide financial information giving a true and fair view of corporations' wealth and financial progress. Conventional accounting data are not serviceable for calculating the financial indicators of a company's financial state of affairs as usually determined; executive remunerations are based on faulty financial performance indicators; auditors are on a mission impossible as they seek to verify companies' accounts; corporate groups facilitate corporate manipulations and deception; and consolidated financial statements relating to those groups fail miserably to meet the information needs claimed of them.

The GFC has strengthened our belief that it is not so much a problem of insufficient governance measures being imposed, or of management being either perverse or inadequate, as it is a case that the corporation in its present holding, subsidiary company form with its limited liability within limited liability feature is possibly past its use-by date. Not a happy thought for many. There appear no ready solutions one would think that are likely to be acceptable to the commercial community with its affairs mostly being organized in complex corporate groups.

Scrapping the corporate format is unlikely to be an acceptable option at the moment. Even in the longer term it may not be an economic possibility due to some ongoing legal impediments. In any event, our analysis has shown that scrapping per se is unnecessary. For, as matters stand, a corporation has automatic privileges not extended to humans. These are not the imperative now that they were in 1844. One way to tame corporates' actions and still retain the corporation's benefits would be to modify, to at least trim, those automatic privileges that have become the avenues for greatest abuse: the creation by mere registration, unlimited life, legal persona, limited liability (especially the prevalent limited liability within limited liability corporate form), and a capacity under existing practice for a corporation to undertake any legal activity it so desires.

Improving a form of group accounts (as outlined in chapter 6) implies that we retain some aspects of the current corporation, but, importantly, we suggest that groups of related companies be accounted for on a different basis than under the prevailing IFRS or national variants. Two matters are important in that setting. First, we believe that aggregated (statistical summary) data extracted from related companies may be more useful than what is provided at present under mandated consolidation in making investment decisions regarding them collectively. Second, for the financial data to be available in a serviceable form we must have the accounts drawn up such that assets are stated at their current selling prices and liabilities at their contracted amount then owing (having an external referent, such amounts are verifiable by auditors), and that an adjustment be made to account for the changes in the purchasing power of money. In short, companies' accounts would have to accord with the basics of what the iconoclastic Ray Chambers labelled Continuously Contemporary Accounting, but it is critical to note that CoCoA is not what others (including regulators and standards setters) currently are calling *fair value* or *mark-to-market* accounting. They are partial systems only, and the mathematical propriety of their data cannot be guaranteed.[2]

As a consequence, some of the data from either fair value or mark-to-market systems are not serviceable for calculating the usual financial indicators found in financial analyses of companies' well-being. This is exacerbated by the recourse in accounting practice to report anticipatory, *expectational*, rather than *factual* data. For, whereas the latter are verifiable, the former are not. Prime examples of this include: a) data produced by the impairment calculation process with its use of myriad forecasts; and

b) in the use of different levels of data when operationalizing fair value in respect of financial instruments in so-called 'thin markets' (see chapter 2).

Any suggestion that the corporation as presently structured is not the best for modern commerce is bound to upset many. No doubt it is seen as an attack on capitalism. It isn't. It may be that the present version of capitalism has developed to the perverse point that separate corporations with their separate legal personae can no longer meet the global demands of modern commerce. Equally so, that the group structures in which commerce is now usually organized are by far too open to mischief, with the shadow banking exploitation of off-balance sheet vehicles in the GFC being the latest example. Enron's use of SPEs a decade earlier was another. Complex corporate groups and conventionally prepared consolidated financial statements are certainly a can of worms.

Clearly the primary social function of accounting is to provide reliable information about a company's wealth and progress. In 1930s US New Deal language, this was expressed as an intention to 'shine sunlight on a corporate's financial affairs'. Without such information investment is no more than a game of blind man's buff. In chapter 2 we argued strongly that conventional accounting in accord with the IFRS, the AIFRS or the FASs fails miserably. Here and elsewhere we have argued separately and collectively that only Chambers's CoCoA does so. Without movement towards the universal adoption of such accounting there is little purpose in attempting to reorganize the many mechanisms in which commerce is prosecuted. That the IFRS have been mandated in many countries (though with the notable exception of the USA) is indicative that the historical cost and modified historical cost systems have had their day in the sun. Neither fair value nor mark-to-market systems make an adjustment for changes in the general level of prices, and fair value (and possibly also the mark-to-market system) admit now a hierarchy of values down to the lowest common denominator – historical cost. Unless accounting is fixed, a fair and orderly commerce is argued here to be unattainable.

Corporate regulation was also demonstrated to be far less than satisfactory. Regulatory agencies seeking to sate their government bosses' demands have sought convictions rather than the development of simpler regimes for the *ex ante* protection of the public. Moreover, as noted in chapter 3, under the guise of a clean broom following the GFC, the USA and the UK have revamped their systems. In both instances the actions were unlikely to be effective.

In the USA this is so because the 2002 Sarbanes-Oxley legislation was introduced as the latest of myriad corporate governance initiatives, which everyone wanted to copy in one form or another, but the legislation failed miserably when the GFC hit. Few who hailed the post-GFC Dodd-Frank legislation seem to recognize that the euphoria accompanying the Bureau of Consumer Financial Protection, the Financial Stability Oversight Council and the Office of Financial Research was really an admission either of failure or of impossibility. Of failure insofar as the SEC perhaps had not maintained the Franklin D. Roosevelt pledge three-quarters of a century earlier to 'put truth in securities'; and of impossibility in as much as corporations are likely as not out of control. In their present form companies are ungovernable. They can no longer be effectively regulated to achieve an orderly commerce. Certainly the

GFC proved that, even if failures over the years – in particular the recent failures at Enron, WorldCom, Tyco, Disney, Waste Management, Xerox – did not. The point is, there is certainly no truth left in the securities markets. Investors are not being protected. Many countries are assessing whether the Dodd-Frank rewarding of whistleblowers has introduced a way to inject US commerce with some degree of consumer protection.

Likewise in the UK the one-stop regulator, the FSA, was given its notice by the newly elected government when in June 2010 the Chancellor George Osborne announced several replacement agencies, a Prudential Regulatory Authority and a Financial Conduct Authority, all of which took effect from 1 April 2013. There, despite lessons over nearly two decades earlier to be learned from the failures of Robert Maxwell's empire and Asil Nadir's high street retail titan Polly Peck, the infamous BCCI Bank, and the hullaballoo surrounding the Cadbury Committee's corporate governance rules (and recommendations of numerous subsequent 'governance' committees culminating in the Combined Code), none apparently produced the consumer protection expected. Increased whistleblowing in the UK is indicative of a growing trend in several countries for the public and insiders to take things into their own hands when those with the responsibility to protect them have failed to do so. Governments worldwide had lapped up and imposed governance regimes with little effect, it would seem.

In Australia much the same story has emerged. ASIC has touted some successes recently with insider trading convictions, but it has enjoyed minimal success in consumer protection. Whistleblowing has been a major source of information in cases like HIH, NAB, AWB and the Securency, but the informants have often been poorly served by the system. As elsewhere, Australian legislators are looking at developments in the USA such as the False Claims Act.[3]

Although not affected by the GFC as much as the USA, the UK or the eurozone, Australian failures and financial crises involving HIH, One.Tel, Opes Prime, Babcock & Brown, the shadow banking failures at Westpoint, Banksia and LM Investment, as well as the AWB, Leighton Holdings and Andrew Forrest debacles, indicate that ASIC's regulation offers little consumer protection of the kind the US and British governments now advocate. While supporting the ideas of one of Australia's leading commercial judges, the Hon. Justice Steven Rares – returning to the previous simplified and principle-based two-line approach under s. 51 of Australia's Trade Practices legislation and the reinvigoration of the true and fair view override – it is argued here that the modern corporation is organized in such a complex form that it is no longer serviceable for society. Bearing in mind the regulatory penchant for seeking heads on poles, some of the regulators' failures still rest with them. For independent regulatory authorities, consumer protection should be their major *modus operandi* by putting *truth in securities*, by preventing rather than apprehending offenders and by not engaging them in 'cash generating no fault settlements'. However, it has not been the case and they have failed miserably.[4]

Of course, individuals make the decisions of which we complain. Understandably, corporate executives and their compensation packages have, post-GFC, become an issue worldwide. However, the GFC has merely highlighted the question of remuneration packages. The present storm possibly would have arisen in the USA following Enron and other failures where 401(k) accounts had invested heavily in the companies that failed. In more recent times bailout recipients using TARP monies to pay bonuses showed little sensitivity to the source of the cash. That alone raises questions about the sensitivity of such demonstrated indifference. In the UK the gap between the remuneration of ordinary blue-collar workers and executives has widened to alarming proportions. We suggested a return to a fair return for all services rendered.

In Australia, given these circumstances, intervention was not surprising.[5] Compulsory contributions to superannuation funds by all employees and by companies brought the issue into focus. It has made virtually every Australian worker indirectly a shareholder in companies on an international basis. Whereas the two-strikes rule with respect to approving executive remuneration has had little impact on shareholder rights, as noted in chapter 5, its psychological impact (seen in the actions' best light) appears to have touched the consciences of those executives who are forgoing bonuses not aligned with their companies' reported poor performances. However, once again accounting is an issue, for what is reported using conventional accounting as a company's financial performance for a particular year is likely as not incorrect.

As a governance mechanism auditing also is at the crossroads. In chapter 4 we extended the idea that auditors cannot win in the present corporate setting. Moreover, the auditors' professional bodies are in error *not* pressing a definition of financial position and financial performance and injecting the notions of serviceability and quality control along the lines we have explained in chapters 2 and 4. Instead, the professional bodies worldwide have persisted in their quest for auditing that is well ordered, with a view that the following of its processing standards (now legally mandated in some jurisdictions) is sufficient for forming their audit opinion. Disclosure rules for accountants are clearly inoperable. The value of testing internally (management) generated evidence against external evidence does not enjoy the prominence that it should if accounting professionals are to be viewed in the same light as other professionals. Yet the regulators and the accounting profession appear happy with the situation. By and large the profession seems content with the notion of an expectations gap – a gap, that is, between what the public expects, protection, and what it gets. The idea that auditors are not expected to detect, other than routine schemes of fraud, is by far too much a let-out clause. With the detailed digital audit trails at their disposal these days, auditors have virtually no excuse other than incompetence for being outplayed by fraudsters, or when confronted by the most ingenious of schemes. If they are incompetent, they should not be appointed auditors.

Honesty, not independence, is the necessary criterion, and honesty in accepting appointment as a company auditor might better be achieved were appointment of auditors placed in the hands of the government – say, by the auditor-general or by the court in a relationship clearly separated from the potential company target, as is the mode for appointing liquidators. This proposal will be resisted, no doubt, by auditors. It will be suggested by them as lacking supporting evidence; that it is an unnecessary and costly intervention by government.

Soulless corporations without a backside to be kicked may have served well when capitalism required a kick-start from the injection of large amounts of capital from individuals who had to be protected with limited liability. Now it is less individuals and more likely other corporations, private equity, investment banks, superannuation funds and other institutional investors that provide the necessary capital. Management structures, too, are possibly ready for a rethink. One critical observer, Gerald Davis (2011), suggests critically that a Copernican revolution has seen manufacturing replaced by finance as the epicentre of the capitalist world, but we suggest that the modern very 'limited liability within limited liability' corporation is the epicentre: perhaps it is time that it should not be, at least in that form.

Certainly, long gone are the days when a few industrialists and bankers ran the corporate world through trusts at the end of the nineteenth century or through holding companies in the twentieth. When those structures were developed they were soon found impossible to control and regulate within their relatively local areas of operation. Corporate regulation has been never-ending – through legislation, then boosted with regulatory agencies, and recently with various governance regimes, 'updated' (patched) after each crisis. Now with globalization we have resorted to another patch, global regulators, and global associations of regulators like the International Organization of Securities Commissions (IOSCO) and the FSB. Repetitively, control measures similar to those that failed in the past have been heaped upon the previous regulatory burden. Nowhere would failed therapies be prescribed seriously except, it seems, in respect to business affairs. It is as if it is thought capitalist business can only function through corporations structured the way they are now. That is not so.

In the British system creation of companies by mere registration in 1844 was without much restriction on structure, activities or financing. This was so, in that *laissez-faire* period, as it was presumed an imperative for British industry to develop rapidly to take advantage of the technical and economic changes that were occurring. Nowadays it is unclear why companies (especially in the form of corporate groups) retain those automatic privileges in the British system, under the various state acts in the USA, or in many other jurisdictions. Why, for example, are companies created at the option of the founders without any evidence of either their economic necessity or what they might otherwise contribute to the social fabric of commerce? This is especially so when we consider the proliferation of subsidiary companies, many with virtually no capital (so-called '$2 companies', or variants such as 'phoenix companies').

Were it, for example, more difficult to create subsidiaries, it would be less easy to organize quarantining arrangements such as were evident with Amaba and Amaca having to shoulder all the asbestos disease liability as the asbestos manufacturers for James Hardie, or the CSR subsidiary Midalco, which operated the Wittenoon asbestos mine in the 1950s and 1960s and was similarly singled out for liability. Nor would dodgy quarantining regarding staff entitlements at Gazal or STP or such as occurred in the MUA/Patrick Stevedores 1997 September Transactions be likely. Permitting parent companies to walk away from insolvent subsidiaries such as the MLC legally did with the H.G. Palmer group in the 1960s, or to create unimaginably complex groups as Samuel Insull and Ivar Kreuger did in the late 1920s and early 1930s, would not be possible. There would be restraints on the capers such as those at BCCI and Maxwell in the 1980s and Enron and others in the 1990s and later that were so complex that when group insolvency hit it took years to unravel.

Companies created for a particular purpose might well have a limit placed on their potential life span. Few companies more than 20 years old now do what they did initially. This is linked to companies being created with a capacity to do almost anything. *Objects clauses* in Articles of Association these days are generally framed so widely as to allow a company to undertake virtually any activity. Without a limit on their life span, they can and do jump from one activity to another. In any event, Articles of Association containing objects clauses can be changed easily. There may be good reasons for this: adaptation must not be inhibited unnecessarily. However, more importantly, it should be that founders and directors of companies have a demonstrated expertise in the declared corporates' proposed functions – property developers in property development, for example – not merely that they have the funding to start the development company.

Legal persona appears a bigger problem in the USA than elsewhere. This is primarily because of the inaccurate Bancroft Davis headnote discussed in chapter 1, attributing Fourteenth Amendment rights to companies, thereby declaring them equal with *human* persons in his reporting of the *Santa Clara v. Southern Railroad* case, and more recently in the judgment confirming Second Amendment free speech for companies in *Citizens United v. The United States Electoral Commission*, which tended to support Davis's error. Free speech has become a major issue in the USA regarding companies' capacity to influence government policy and elections through funding of candidates' election campaigns: in the 2012 presidential election mainly corporate funding is estimated to have been in the vicinity of $US6 billion. Corporate persona had a far more simple function in the nineteenth century. It provided merely a matter of convenience to allow contracts to be signed by authorized staff and to engage in other legal niceties. Outside of the USA it has always been recognized as such.

Limiting the shareholders' individual liability to the amount unpaid on their shares was not part of the incorporation arrangement under the 1844 UK Companies Act. Recall limited liability was introduced in the UK in 1855. In contrast, in the USA it was generally a bargaining point in the charter mongering by the states offering corporate charters, some as early as 1811 by New York state. The point is, limiting shareholders' liability has not always been automatic, but direct financial liability in the event of corporate insolvency in many respects is the minor aspect of limited liability. Shareholders are also protected from liability for crimes or illegalities committed by *their* company, provided they are not a party to it. The use of $2 (often wholly owned subsidiary) companies exacerbates the lines of culpability. Of course, any fines related to corporates' crimes will ultimately come from their company's assets and shareholders may well suffer loss on that score (perhaps also from a consequential share price fall). So, although they like to be considered owners insofar as most shareholders expect to benefit eventually as the residual claimants from their company's actions creating profits, they do not stand to be prosecuted when the company acts illegally. BP shareholders therefore can keep the benefits obtained before the 2010 Deepwater Horizon oil rig explosion. Deaths involved and the consequential environmental damage are not necessarily associated with the actions of any shareholders. Should this be permitted? Should parent companies be protected from such losses due to the acts of their subsidiaries?

Further, no part of the case for limited liability, for example, rests upon there being 'limited liability within limited liability' as undergirds, in the absence of cross-guarantees, a conventional group comprising a holding company and its subsidiaries. An immediate and possible reform would be to have all controlling and controlled companies liable for the debts of one another. This would have been the outcome if the opting-in proposals contained in the UK's 1982 Cork Report proposals had been adopted, and as a possible way forward proposed in Australia's CAMAC *Corporate Groups Final Report* in 2000. That makes our suggested group accounting even more of an imperative. In this respect it has been demonstrated elsewhere that the use of guarantees, while retaining the separate legal entity convention,[6] does not necessarily amount to a pooling proposal.

Perhaps both financial and legal liability protection ought to be removed in risky industries. Property developers in Australia come to mind. So too do those who have poor records, and those investment banks engaged in financial engineering through innovative financial products. You can hear already the moans of those to be affected by such restrictions on the workings of the supposed free-market economy, but very few things operate without any restrictions – it is their degree that should be evaluated.

To distil, the following package of reforms is feasible:

- remove the unlimited life privilege upon incorporation;
- remove the privilege of engaging in virtually any activity by prohibiting open-ended objects clauses;
- modify (perhaps even deny) the limited financial and legal liability privilege for some companies in high-risk/high-return industries;
- scrap conventionally prepared consolidation accounting for subsidiary companies as per chapter 6, and replace it with a much more informative set of group accounting statements (also outlined in chapter 6);
- require companies to drop the IFRS and use a CoCoA system to report annually a true and fair view of financial position and financial performance (chapter 2); and
- related to this is the push in chapters 2 and 4 for auditors to use their professional judgement to audit director-prepared financial statements with more scepticism, thereby providing an independently derived warrant about information contained in them.

Any suggestion that the corporation as presently structured and entailing undoubted economic benefits is ungovernable, 'too big to fail' and 'too big to gaol', and that it is not the best vehicle for modern commerce is bound to upset many. We repeat that no doubt it will be seen as an attack on capitalism. It isn't. It is no more an attack on capitalism than was the introduction of the modern corporation by general incorporation in 1844. Corporations are merely a means to a desired societal end: an orderly, well-informed commerce, where the public has a reasonable chance to evaluate risks and benefits.

Possibly capitalism has developed to the point that separate but related corporations no longer meet the global demands of modern commerce and modern investors' needs, or indeed that they are in the public interest. Corporations incur social costs and benefits, which are continually changing. That they continue to provide a net benefit to society should not be automatically assumed. The time has arrived for a serious rethink of the analysis presented here of how commerce is pursued and, in particular, whether the current corporate form has passed its use-by date.

Notes

1 While there are some spectacular examples of GFC-related corporate collapses and resultant asset fire sales (Lehman Brothers, Northern Rock, General Growth Properties, Bear Stearns), and other corporates that were in sufficient financial difficulties to be propped up through taxpayers' money (Goldman Sachs, AIG), the key losers were investors and holders of financial assets (see chapter 3), who experienced a loss of trust in the system. An overview of the costs and consequences of the GFC is provided in the September 2013 *Dallas Federal Reserve Economic Letter* by Luttrell, Atkinson and Rosenblum 'Assessing the Costs and Consequences of the 2007–09 Financial Crisis and its Aftermath'.
2 This was discussed in detail in Clarke and Dean, 2010.
3 Ruth Williams, 'Warning: Blowing the Whistle Could Mess Up Your Life', *SMH*, 15–16 June, Business section, pp. 6–7.
4 This is aptly displayed in Australia with ASIC's 2012 stoush with the Fortescue Metals Group and its enforceable undertaking with Centro's auditor.
5 Alan Fels (2010) was an early observer to suggest that, and it was discussed in the 2009 Draft Productivity Commission report into Executive Remuneration in Australia.
6 This was shown in several legal and accounting articles. See, for example, Dean *et al.*, 1995; Dean *et al.*, 1993; and Houghton *et al.*, 1999.

BIBLIOGRAPHY

Agostini, M. and Favero, G., 2012, *Accounting Fraud, Business Failure and Creative Auditing: A Micro-Analysis of the Strange Case of Sunbeam Corp*, Universita Ca'Foscari Venezia, Working Paper Series No. 12/2012.

Anderson, H., 2012, 'Challenging the Limited Liability of Parent Companies: A Reform Agenda for Piercing the Corporate Veil', *Australian Accounting Review*, No. 61, Vol. 22, No. 2, pp.129–41.

Arvedlund, E., 2009, *Too Good to Be True: The Rise and Fall of Bernie Madoff*, Portfolio, New York.

ASIC (Australian Securities and Investments Commission), 2010a, *Response to Submissions on CP 150 Disclosing Financial Information Other than in Accordance with Accounting Standards*, www.asic.gov.au/asic/asic.nsf/byheadline/CP-150-Disclosing-financial-inform ation-other-than-in-accordance-with-accounting-standard-submissions?Open-Document &Click= (accessed 27 November 2012).

——2010b, *Regulatory Guides*, www.asic.gov.au/asic/ASIC.NSF/byHeadline/Regulatory% 20guides (accessed 27 November 2012).

——2010c, 'Media Announcement 10-147MR, ASIC Focuses Attention on 2010 Financial Reports', www.asic.gov.au/asic/asic.nsf/byheadline/10-147MR+ASIC+focuses+attent ion+on+2010+financial+reports?openDocument (accessed 25 September 2012).

——2011, 'Media Announcement 11-139MR, ASIC Focuses Attention on 30 June 2011 Financial Reports', www.asic.gov.au/asic/asic.nsf/byheadline/11-139MR+ASIC+focuses +attention+on+30+June+2011+financial+reports?openDocument (accessed 25 September 2012).

——2012, 'Media Announcement 12-140MR, ASIC's Areas of Focus for 30 June 2012 Financial Reports', www.asic.gov.au/asic/asic.nsf/byheadline/12-140MR+ASIC'S+areas +of+focus+for+30+June+2012+financial+reports?openDocument (accessed 25 September 2012).

Austin, R.M, Ford, H.A.J. and Ramsay, I.M., 2007, *Ford's Principles of Company Law*, Law Book Company, Sydney.

Australian Treasury, 2010, 'Simplify the Regulatory Environment', www.gov.au.

——2006, *Australian Auditor Independence Requirements: A Comparative Review*, Australian Government Printing Service, Canberra, archive.treasury.gov.au/contentitem.asp? NavId=&ContentID=1184 (accessed 28 November 2012).

Bakan, J., 2004, *The Corporation: The Pathological Pursuit of Profit and Power*, Constable & Robinson, London.

Banking Commission (UK Parliament), 2013, *Report into the HBOS Failure: An Accident Waiting to Happen*, April, UK Government, London.

Barofsky, N., 2012, *Bailout: An Inside Account of how Washington Abandoned Main Street While Rescuing Wall Street*, Free Press, New York.

Barton, A., 2012, 'Indecent Disclosure: Gilding the Corporate Lily (book review)', *British Accounting Review*, Vol. 44, No. 1, pp.47–49.

Baxt, R. and Lane, T., 1998, 'Developments in Relation to Corporate Groups and the Responsibilities of Directors', *Company and Securities Law Journal*, November, pp.628–53.

Beatty, J. and Gwynne, S.C., 1993, *The Outlaw Bank: A Wild Ride into the Secret Heart of BCCI*, Beard Group, New York.

Bebchuk, L. and Fried, J., 2004, *Pay Without Performance: The Unfulfilled Promise of Executive Remuneration*, Harvard University Press, Cambridge, MA.

Berger, A.N., King, K.A. and O'Brien, J.M., 1989, 'Some Red Flags Concerning Market Value Accounting', *Proceedings, Federal Reserve Bank of Chicago*, pp.515–46.

——1991, 'The Limitations of Market Value Accounting and a More Realistic Alternative', *Journal of Banking and Finance*, Vol. 15, Nos 4/5, pp.753–83.

Berle, A.A. and Means, G.C., 1991 [1932], *The Modern Corporation and Private Property*, Transaction Publishers, New Brunswick, NJ.

Big Six, Symposium Report, 2006, *Global Capital Markets and the Global Economy: A Vision from the CEOs of the International Audit Networks*, November.

Bloom, M., 2008, *Double Accounting for Goodwill: A Problem Revisited*, Routledge, London.

Bruner, R.F. and Carr, S.D., 2007, *The Panic of 1907: Lessons Learned from the Market's Perfect Storm*, John Wiley and Sons, Hoboken, NJ.

Cadbury, A. (chair.), 1992, *Financial Aspects of Corporate Governance*, Gee & Co, London.

CAMAC (Corporate and Markets Advisory Committee), 2000, *Corporate Groups Final Report*, www.camac.gov.au/camac/camac.nsf/0/3DD84175EFBAD69CCA256B 6C007FD4E8?opendocument (accessed 27 November 2012).

Chabrak, N., 2012, 'Money Talks: The Language of the Rochester School', *Accounting, Auditing and Accountability Journal*, Vol. 25, No. 3, pp.452–85.

Chambers, R.J., 1973, *Securities and Obscurities: A Case for Reform of the Law of Company Accounts*, Gower Press, Melbourne; reissued in 1986 as *Accounting in Disarray*, Garland Publishing, New York.

——1978, *Company Accounting Standards*, Government Printer, Sydney.

——1993, 'Positive Accounting Theory and the PA Cult', *Abacus*, Vol. 29, No. 1, pp.1–26.

Chambers, R.J. and Wolnizer, P.W., 1990, 'A True and Fair View of Financial Position', *Company and Securities Law Journal*, December, pp.353–68.

——1991, 'A True and Fair View of Position and Results: The Historical Background', *Accounting, Business and Financial History*, April, pp.197–203.

Chamley, C., Laurence, J., Kotlikoff, L.J. and Polemarchakis, H., 2012, 'Limited-purpose Banking – Moving from "Trust Me" to "Show Me" Banking', *American Economic Review*, Vol. 102, No. 3, pp.113–19.

Christensen, B.E., Omer, T.C., Sharp, N.Y. and Shelley, M.K., 2012, *Pork Bellies and Public Company Audits: Have Audits Once Again become Just Another Commodity?* Working Paper, 4 December, papers.ssrn.com/sol3/papers.cfm?abstract_id=2184413 (accessed 29 July 2013).

Clarke, F.L., 2006, 'Introduction: True and Fair View – Anachronism or Quality Control par Excellence?' *Abacus*, Vol. 42, No. 2, pp.129–31.

Clarke, F.L. and Dean, G.W., 1993, 'Law and Accounting: The Separate Legal Entity Principle and Consolidation Accounting', *Australian Business Law Review*, Vol. 21, No. 4, pp.246–69.

——2002, 'Submission 11 to JCPAA Inquiry', *Review of Independent Auditing by Registered Company Auditors*, www.gov.au.

——2007, *Indecent Disclosure: Gilding the Corporate Lily*, Cambridge University Press, Melbourne.

——2010, 'Commentary: Business Black Swans and the Use and Abuse of a Notion', *Australian Accounting Review*, Vol. 20, No. 2, pp.185–94.

——2012, 'Submission to the Australian Government Productivity Commission Enquiring Into: Regulation of Director and Executive Remuneration', submission 67, www.pc.gov.au/ projects/inquiry/executive-remuneration/submissions#initial (accessed 1 November 2012).

Clarke, F.L., Dean, G.W. and Houghton, E., 2002, 'Revitalizing Group Accounting: Improving Accountability', *Australian Accounting Review*, Vol. 12, No. 3, pp.58–72.

Clarke, F.L., Dean, G.W. and Oliver, K.G., 1997, *Corporate Collapse: Regulatory, Accounting and Ethical Failure*, Cambridge University Press, Cambridge.

——2003, *Corporate Collapse: Accounting, Regulatory and Ethical Failure*, 2nd revised edn, Cambridge University Press, Cambridge.

Clarke, F.L., Dean, G.W. and Wells, M.C., 2012, *The Sydney School of Accounting: The Chambers Years*, University of Sydney.

Clements, J., 2010, *Corporations Are Not People: Why They have More Rights than You Do and What You Can Do About It*, Berrett-Koehler, San Francisco, CA.

Clikeman, P.M., 2013, *Called to Account: Financial Frauds that Shaped the Accounting Profession*, 2nd edn, Routledge, London.

Coffee, J., 2006, *Gatekeepers: The Professions and Corporate Governance*, Oxford University Press.

——2008, 'Turmoil in the U.S. Credit Markets: The Role of the Credit Rating Agencies. Testimony before the U.S. Senate Committee on Banking, Housing and Urban Affairs', 22 April.

Competition Commission (UK), 2013, Summary of Findings, 'Audit Market Not Serving Shareholders', UK government, 22 February.

Cork, Sir Kenneth (chair.), 1982, *Insolvency Law and Practice*, HMSO, London.

Cranston, R.F., 1982, 'Regulation and Deregulation: General Issues', *UNSW Law Journal*, Vol. 5, No. 1, pp.1–28.

Davies, H., 2010, *Financial Crisis: Who is to Blame?* Polity Press, Malden, MA.

Davis, G.F., 2011, 'The Twilight of the Berle and Means Corporation', *Seattle University Law Review*, Vol. 34, pp.1121–38.

Dean, G.W., 2005, 'Editorial: "True and Fair" and "Fair Value" – Accounting and Legal Will-o'-the-wisps', *Abacus*, Vol. 41, No. 2, pp.i–vi.

Dean, G.W, Clarke, F.L. and Houghton, E., 1995, 'Cross Guarantees and Negative Pledges: A Preliminary Analysis', *Australian Accounting Review*, Vol. 5, No. 9, pp.48–63.

Dean, G., Luckett, P. and Houghton, E., 1993, 'Notional Calculations in Liquidations Revisited: The Case of ASC Class Order Cross Guarantees', *Company and Securities Law Journal*, August, pp.204–26.

Ernst and Young, 2011, 'What Do the New Consolidation, Joint Arrangements and Disclosures Mean to You?' *IFRS Practical Matters*, June 2011, www.ey.com/AU/en/Issues/ IFRS (accessed 28 November 2012).

EU (European Commission), 2010, *Proposal for a Regulation of the European Parliament and the Council on the Specific Requirements Regarding Statutory Audit of Public Interest Entities*, Brussels, European Commission, europa.eu/rapid/press-release_IP-08-734_en.htm?locale=en (accessed 29 July 2013).

Farrar, J., Parsons, L. and Joubert, P., 2009, 'The Development of an Appropriate Regulatory Response to the Global Financial Crisis', *Bond Law Review*, Vol. 21, No. 3, pp.1–41.

Farrell, G., 2006, *Corporate Crooks: How Rogue Executives Ripped Off Americans … and Congress Helped them Do it!*, Prometheus Books, New York.

Fels, A., 2010, 'Executive Remuneration in Australia', *Australian Accounting Review*, Vol. 20, No. 1, pp.76–82.

Ferguson, C., 2012, *Inside Job: The Financiers Who Pulled Off the Heist of the Century*, One World, Oxford.

Fisse, B. and Braithwaite, J., 1993, *Corporations, Crime and Accountability*, Cambridge University Press, Cambridge.

Fleckenstein, W.A., with Sheehan, F., 2008, *Greenspan's Bubbles: The Age of Ignorance at the Federal Reserve*, McGraw-Hill, New York.

FRC (UK Financial Reporting Council), 2005a, FRC PN 85, 'Financial Reporting Review Panel Publishes Legal Opinion on the Effect of the IAS Regulation on the Requirement for Accounts to Give a True and Fair View', 24 June 2005, www.frc.org.uk/News-and-Events/FRC-Press/Press/2005/June/Financial-Reporting-Review-Panel-publishes-legal-o.aspx (accessed 24 April 2013).

——2005b, FRC PN 119, 9 August 2005, www.frc.org.uk (accessed 24 April 2013).

——2008, PN 222, 'Relevance of "True and Fair" Concept Confirmed', 19 May 2008, www.frc.org.uk/News-and-Events/FRC-Press/Press/2008/May/Relevance-of-True-and-Fair-concept-confirmed.aspx (accessed 24 April 2013).

Friedman, M., 1970, 'The Social Responsibility of Business is to Increase its Profits', *New York Times Magazine*, 13 September, pp.122–26.

FSA (Financial Services Authority), 2013, White Paper, *Enhancing the Auditor's Contribution to Prudential Regulation*, FSA.

FSB (Financial Stability Board), 2012, *Global Shadow Banking Monitoring Report 2012*, FSB, 18 November.

FSF (Financial Stability Forum), 2009, *Principles for Sound Compensation Practices*, FSF, 2 April.

Gleick, J., 2011, *The Information: A History, a Theory, a Flood*, Fourth Estate, London.

Goodhart, C.A.E., Hartmann, P., Llewellyn, D., Rojas-Suárez, L. and Weisbrod, S., 1998, *Financial Regulation: Why, How, and Where Now?* Routledge, New York.

Gordon, I., 2012, 'Superannuation in Society: What are the Accountability Relationships and is there a Role for (Group) Accounting?' *Australian Accounting Review*, Vol. 22, No. 2, pp.142–54.

Grant, J. and Ellis, K., 2010, *Board Independence, Board Connections and US Government Troubled-Asset Relief Program (TARP) Funding for Banks*, APRA Working Paper, November 2010, www.apra.gov.au/AboutAPRA/Documents/Board-independence-connections-and-TARP-final.pdf (accessed 28 November 2012).

Greenfield, K., 2006, *The Failure of Corporate Law: Fundamental Flaws and Progressive Possibilities*, University of Chicago Press, Chicago.

Gregg, P., Jewell, S. and Tonks, I., 2012, 'Executive Pay and Performance: Did Bankers' Bonuses Cause the Crisis?' *International Review of Finance*, Vol. 12, No. 1, pp.89–122.

Griffiths, Sir P., 1974, *Licence to Trade: A History of the English Chartered Companies*, Ernest Benn Limited, London.

Grossman, R.S., 2010, *Unsettled Account: The Evolution of Banking in the Industrialized World since 1800*, Princeton University Press, Princeton.

Hadden, T., 1992, 'The Regulation of Corporate Groups in Australia', *UNSWLJ*, Vol. 15, No. 1, pp.61–85.

Haldane, A.G. and Madouros, V., 2012, *The Dog and the Frisbee*, paper given at the Federal Reserve Bank of Kansas 36th Economic Policy Symposium, The Changing Policy Landscape, Jackson Hole, Wyoming, 31 August 2012, www.kansascityfed.org/publicat/sympos/2012/ah.pdf (accessed 28 November 2012).

Hampell, Sir Ronald, 1998, *Committee on Corporate Governance: Final Report*, Gee Publishing Ltd, London.

Hannah, L., 2013, *A Global Consensus of Corporations* in 2010, Working Paper, LSE, London.

Hartmann, T., 2010, *Unequal Protection: How Corporations Became 'People' – and You Can Fight Back*, Berrett-Koehler, San Francisco, CA.

HIHRC (HIH Royal Commission), 2003, *The Failure of the HIH Insurance, Vols. I–III: Reasons, Circumstances and Responsibilities*, Commonwealth of Australia, Canberra, www.hihroyalcom.gov.au/finalreport/index.htm (accessed 28 November 2012).

Houghton, E., Dean, G. and Luckett, P., 1999, 'Insolvent Corporate Groups with Cross Guarantees: A Forensic–LP Case Study in Liquidation', *Journal of the Operational Research Society*, May, pp.480–96.

IMF (International Monetary Fund), 2012, *Australia: Financial Safety Net and Crisis Management Framework – Technical Note*, IMF Country Report No. 12/310, www.imf.org/external/pubs/ft/scr/2012/cr12310.pdf (accessed 28 November 2012).

JCCFS (Australian Government, Parliamentary Joint Committee on Corporations and Financial Services), 2005, *Report on Australian Accounting Standards Tabled in Compliance with the Corporations Act 2001 on 30 August 2004 and 16 November 2004*, Australian Government Printing Service, Canberra, www.aph.gov.au/Parliamentary _Business/Committees/Senate_Committees?url=corporations_ctte/completed_inquiries/ 2004-7/aas/report/index.htm (accessed 28 November 2012).

JCPAA (Australian Government Parliamentary Joint Committee on Public Accounts and Audit), 2002, Report 391, *Review of Independent Auditing by Registered Company Auditors*, Australian Government Printing Service, Canberra, www.aph.gov.au/Parliam entary_Business/Committees/House_of_Representatives_Committees?url=jcpaa/indepau dit/contents.htm (accessed 28 November 2012).

Jeter, L., 2003, *Disconnected: Deceit and Betrayal at WorldCom*, John Wiley and Sons, New York.

Jones, M. (ed.), 2011, *Creative Accounting, Fraud and International Accounting Standards*, John Wiley & Sons, Chichester.

Josephson, M., 1934, *The Robber Barons: The Great American Capitalists 1861–1901*, Transaction Publishers, New Brunswick, NJ.

King, Cecila, 2013, 'Apple Avoids Taxes with "Complex Web of Off-shore Entities", Senate Inquiry Finds', *Washington Post*, 2 May.

Kosman, J., 2009, *The Buyout of America: How Private Equity will Cause the Next Great Credit Crisis*, Portfolio, New York.

Langohr, H. and Langohr, P., 2009, *The Rating Agencies and their Credit Ratings: What they are, How they Work, and Why they are Relevant*, The Wiley Finance Series, New York.

Lawrence, Martin, 2013, Discussion Paper, *Money for Nothing and the Risk for Free: Pay in Large Cap Financials*, Ownership Matters, Melbourne.

Lee, T.A., Clarke, F.L. and Dean, G.W., 2008, 'The Dominant Senior Manager and the Reasonably Careful, Skilful, Cautious Auditor', *Critical Perspectives in Accounting*, Vol. 19, No. 5, pp.677–711.

Leibler, M., 2002, 'Submission 50 and Supplementary Submissions 62 and 73 to JCPAA Inquiry', *Review of Independent Auditing by Registered Company Auditors*, AGPS, Canberra, www.aph.gov.au/Parliamentary_Business/Committees/House_of_Representatives_Comm ittees?url=jcpaa/indepaudit/subs.htm (accessed 28 November 2012).

Levitt, A., with Dwyer, P., 2002, *Taking on the Street: What Wall Street and Corporate America Don't Want You to Know*, Pantheon Books, New York.

Livne, G. and McNichols, M., 2009, *An Empirical Investigation of the True and Fair View Override*, Cass Business School Working Paper, www.cassknowledge.com/node/3962 (accessed 28 November 2012).

Llewellyn, D., 1999, *The Economic Rationale for Financial Regulation*, Financial Services Authority (FSA) Occasional Papers in Financial Regulation 1, London.

Luttrell, D., Atkinson, T. and Rosenblum, H., 2013, 'Assessing the Costs and Consequences of the 2007–09 Financial Crisis and its Aftermath', *Dallas Federal Reserve Economic Letter*, Vol. 8, No. 7, September.

Markopolos, H., with Casey, F., Chelo, N., Kachroo, G. and Ocrant, M., 2011, *No One Would Listen: A True Financial Thriller*, Wiley & Sons Inc, Hoboken, NJ.

Mautz, R. and Sharaf, H., 1961, *Philosophy of Auditing*, American Accounting Association, Sarasota, FL.

McBarnet, D. and Whelan, C., 1999, *Creative Accounting and the Cross-Eyed Javelin Thrower*, John Wiley & Sons, Chichester.

McDonald, F., 1962, *Insull*, University of Chicago Press, Chicago.

McGregor, W., 1992, 'True and Fair View – An Accounting Anachronism', *The Australian Accountant*, Vol. 62, No. 1, pp.68–71.

Nace, T., 2003, *Gangs of America: The Rise of Corporate Power and the Disabling of Democracy*, Berrett-Koehler, San Francisco, CA.

Nobes, C., 2009, 'The Importance of Being Fair: An Analysis of IFRS Regulation in Practice: A Comment', *Accounting and Business Research*, Vol. 39, No. 4, pp.415–27.

OECD, 1999, *Principles of 'Corporate Governance'*, Organisation for Economic Co-operation and Development, revised in 2004 and 2010, www.oecd.org/corporate/oecdprinciples ofcorporategovernance.htm.

Ownership Matters, 2013, *Money for Nothing and the Risk for Free: Pay in Large Cap Financials*, Discussion Paper, Ownership Matters, Melbourne.

Parker, R, Wolnizer, P. and Nobes, C., 1996, *Readings in True and Fair*, Garland Publishing Inc., New York.

PCAOB (Public Company Accounting Oversight Board), 2013, *Report on 2007–2010 Inspections of Domestic Firms that Audit 100 or Fewer Public Companies*, 25 February, PCAOB, Washington, DC.

Pecora, F., 1934, *The 1934 Report on the Practices of Stock Exchanges form the 'Pecora Commission'*, 1934, US Senate Committee on Banking and Currency, US Senate Report No. 1455.

——1939, *Wall Street Under Oath: The Story of Our Modern Money Changers*, The Cresset Press, London.

Peláez, Carlos A. and Peláez, Carlos M., 2009, *Regulations of Banks and Finance: Theory and Policy After the Credit Crisis*, Palgrave Macmillan, Basingstoke.

Perino, M., 2011, *The Hellhound of Wall Street: How Ferdinand Pecora's Investigation of the Great Crash Forever Changed American Finance*, Penguin Press, New York.

Pozsar, Z., Tobias, A., Ashcraft, A. and Boesky, H., 2010, *Shadow Banking*, Federal Reserve Bank of New York Staff Report, No. 458, July, NY; revised February 2012.

Productivity Commission (PC, Australian Government), 2010, *Executive Remuneration in Australia*, Australian Government Printer, Canberra, www.pc.gov.au/projects/inquiry/executive-remuneration (accessed 6 March 2012).

Ramsay, I., 2001, *Independence of Australian Company Auditors: Review of Current Australian Requirements and Proposals for Reform*, Australian Government Printing Services Canberra, cclsr.law.unimelb.edu.au/research-papers/audit-ind-report/audit-ind.html (accessed 28 November 2012).

Ramsay, I. and Stapledon, G., 1998, *Corporate Groups in Australia*, University of Melbourne, Centre for Corporate Law and Securities Regulation, Melbourne.

——2001, 'Corporate Groups in Australia', *Australian Business Law Review*, Vol. 29, No. 1, pp.7–32.

Reich, R.B., 2012, *Beyond Outrage: What has Gone Wrong with Our Economy and Our Democracy, and How to Fix it*, Vintage Books, New York.

Rivlin, G., 2013, 'How Wall Street Defanged Dodd-Frank', *The Nation*, 30 April.

Rost, K. and Weibel, A., 2013, 'CEO Pay from a Social Norm Perspective: The Infringement and Reassessment of Fairness Norms', *Corporate Governance*, Vol. 21, No. 4, pp.351–72.

Ryan, F.J.O., 1967, 'A True and Fair View', *Abacus*, Vol. 32, No. 2, pp.95–108.

San, M.L.C. and Kuang, N.T., 1995, *The Report of the Inspectors Appointed by the Minister for Finance*, Barings Futures (Singapore) Pte Ltd, Investigation Pursuant to Section 31 of the Companies Act Chapter 50, Ministry of Finance, Singapore.

Sapienza, P. and Gonzales, L., 2012, 'A Trust Crisis', *International Review of Finance*, Vol. 12, No. 2, pp.123–31.

Schinasi, Garry J., 2006, *Safeguarding Financial Stability: Theory and Practice*, International Monetary Fund, Publication Services, Washington, DC.

SEC (United States of America Securities and Exchange Commission), 2003, *Study Pursuant to Section 108(d) of the Sarbanes-Oxley Act of 2002 on the Adoption by the United States Financial Reporting System of a Principles-based Accounting System*, SEC, Washington, DC, www.sec.gov/news/studies/principlesbasedstand.htm (accessed 28 November 2012).

Stigler, George J., 1971, 'The Theory of Economic Regulation', *The Bell Journal of Economics and Management Science*, Vol. 2, No. 1, Spring, pp.3–21.

Svanstroem, T., 2013, 'Non-audit Services and Audit Quality', *European Accounting Review*, Vol. 22, No. 2, pp.337–66.

Taibbi, M., 2011, 'Why isn't Wall Street in Jail?' *Rolling Stone*, May, pp.58–65.

Taleb, N.N., 2007, *The Black Swan: The Impact of the Highly Improbable*, Random House, New York.

——2012, *Antifragile*, Random House, New York.

Tett, G., 2009, *Fool's Gold: How the Bold Dream of a Small Tribe at J.P. Morgan was Corrupted by Wall Street Greed and Unleashed a Catastrophe*, Little Brown, London.

Tucker, P.M.W., 2010, *Shadow Banking: Financing Markets and Financial Stability*, Remarks by Paul Tucker, Deputy Governor, Financial Stability at the Bank of England, at BGG Partners Seminar, London, 21 January 2010, www.bankofengland.co.uk/publications/ Documents/speeches/2010/speech420.pdf (accessed 28 November 2012).

——2012, *Shadow Banking: Thoughts for a Possible Policy Agenda*, Speech by Paul Tucker, Deputy Governor, Financial Stability, Bank of England, at the European Commission High Level Conference, Brussels, 27 April 2012, www.bankofengland.co.uk/publicat ions/Pages/speeches/2012/566.aspx (accessed 28 November 2012).

Tuite, Lachlan, 2013, *International Accounting Standards and Financial Stability*, PhD thesis, University of Sydney (unpublished).

Turnbull, Nigel (chair.), 1999, *Internal Control: Guidance for Directors on the Combined Code*, Institute of Chartered Accountants, London.

Tweedie, D. and Whittington, G., 1984, *The Debate on Inflation Accounting*, Cambridge University Press, London.

Valukas, A.R. (Examiner in Bankruptcy), 2010, *In re Lehman Brothers Holdings Inc*, US Bankruptcy Court, Southern District, New York.

van der Laan, S. and Dean, G., 2010, 'Corporate Groups in Australia: State of Play', *Australian Accounting Review*, Vol. 20, No. 2, pp.121–33.

Walker, Sir David, 2009a, *A Review of Corporate Governance in UK Banks and Other Financial Industry Entities*, FRC, July, London.

——2009b, *A Review of Corporate Governance in UK Banks and Other Financial Industry Entities: Final Recommendations*, FRC, London, November.

Walker, R.G., 1976, 'An Evaluation of the Information Conveyed by Consolidated Statements', *Abacus*, Vol. 12, No. 2, pp.77–115.

——1978, *Consolidated Statements: A History and Analysis*, Arno Press, New York.

——2002, Submission 41 to JCPAA Inquiry, *Review of Independent Auditing by Registered Company Auditors*, www.aph.gov.au/Parliamentary_Business/Committees/House_of_Repres entatives_Committees?url=jcpaa/indepaudit/subs.htm (accessed 28 November 2012).

West, B.P., 2003, *Professionalism and Accounting Rules*, Routledge, London.

Whitehead, A.N., 1997 [1926], *Science and the Modern World*, Free Press, New York.

Wise, T.A., 1962, *Insiders: The Stockholders' Guide to Wall Street*, Doubleday, Garden City, NY.

Wolfe, J.T., 2011, *Crisis by Design. The Untold Story of the Global Financial Coup and What You Can Do About It*, Hugo House Publishers, Austin, TX.

Wolnizer, P.W., 1995, 'Are Audit Committees Red Herrings?' *Abacus*, Vol. 31, No. 1, pp.45–66.

Zecher, J.R. and Philips, S., 1981, *The SEC and the Public Interest*, MIT Press, Cambridge, MA.

Zeff, S.A., 2007, 'The Primacy of "Present Fairly" in the Auditor's Report', *Accounting Perspectives*, Vol. 6, No. 1, pp.1–20.

Court cases

Australian Administrative Tribunal Appeal hearing, *OPUS Capital Limited v. Australian Securities and Investments Commission*, 2010.

Dodge v. Ford Motor Company (170 N.W.668, 664. Mich. 1919).

Federal Court of Australia, *Wingecarribee Shire Council v Lehman Brothers Australia Ltd* (in liq) [2012] FCA 1028.

Federal Court of Australia, *Bathurst Regional Council v Local Government Financial Services Pty Ltd* (No. 5) [2012] FCA 1200.

High Court of Australia, *Australian Securities and Investments Commission v Meredith Hellicar and Ors* [2012] HCA 17, 7 May 2012.

NSW Court of Appeal, *Gillfillan & Ors v Australian Securities & Investments Commission* [2012] NSWCA 370.
NSW Supreme Court, *Australian Securities and Investments Commission v Rich* [2009] NSWSC 1229.
Santa Clara County v. Southern Pacific Railroad Company case in 1886 in the US Supreme Court.
US Supreme Court case, *Citizens United v. Federal Election Commission*, 588 U.S 310 (2010).
US Supreme Court case, *Liggett v Lee*, 288 U.S 517 (1933).
West Australian Supreme Court, *Williams v. Great Southern Finance & Ors* (S CI, 2011 03616) 29 October 2012.

Commissions of inquiry

1841   UK Gladstone Commission of Inquiry
1895   UK Davey Commission of Inquiry
1945   UK Cohen Committee Company Law Inquiry
1995   San, M.L.C. and Kuang, N.T., *The Report of the Inspectors Appointed by the Minister for Finance*, Barings Futures (Singapore) Pte Ltd, Investigation Pursuant to s. 31 of the Companies Act Chapter 50.

Acts of parliament

Australia

1961   Uniform Companies Act (Australia)

UK

1929   UK Companies Act
1948   UK Companies Act

USA

1999   Gramm-Leach-Bliley Act, also known as the Financial Services Modernization Act of 1999
2000   Commodity Futures Modernization Act
2010   US Dodd-Frank Wall Street Reform and Consumer Protection Act (Pub.L. 111–203, H.R. 4173)

INDEX

Printed in Great Britain
by Amazon